NOT IN GOD'S NAME

Making Sense of Religious Conflict

By Paula Fouce

©2015 by Paula Fouce

Published by Paradise Filmworks International

Ebook edition created 2015

ISBN 978-0-692-36473-4

Library of Congress Cataloging-in-Publication Data is on file at the Library of Congress, Washington DC.

Photo Credits:

Neal Brown
Paula Fouce
Joseph Stevens
Christopher Tufty
Jurg V. Walther

Cover Art by Jan Evans Bowman

"In this illuminating book Paula Fouce not only tells a compelling personal story, she also leads us through a deeply-layered understanding of the religious strife still present in our postmodern times, offering an optimistic view of the prospect of reconciliation and healing."

-**Michael Bernard Beckwith**,
author of *Spiritual Liberation*

"With the passion and authority of an eyewitness, Paula Fouce documents the origins of religious violence and the urgent threat it poses to the world. And with the insight of a long-time meditative practitioner, she demonstrates persuasively that this spiritual problem demands a spiritual solution."

-**Dean Sluyter**, author of *Natural Meditation*

"*Not In God's Name* resonates as a prayer and a plea to end our era of anachronistic, heartbreaking religious conflict. But its message is also practical. Paula Fouce recognizes that true compassion and respect for religious diversity arise from the experience of the spiritual essence that we share. The book is a welcome addition to the growing awareness of the Vedic precept, "Truth is One; the wise call it by many names.""

-**Philip Goldberg**, author of
*American Veda: From Emerson and
The Beatles to Yoga and Meditation,
How India Spirituality Changed the West*

For my parents Betty and Frank

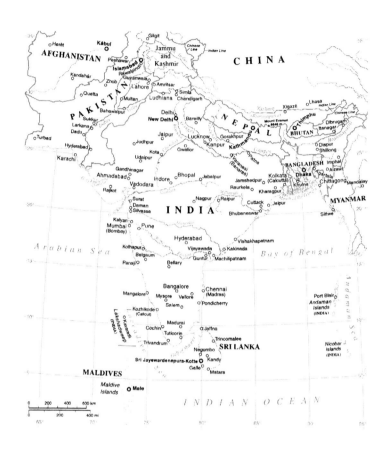

Table of Contents

Introduction

Acknowledgements

Thank you to my wonderful editors, Anita Rehker, Joan Liepman, and James Mitchell Miller for their guidance and work on this manuscript.

I feel blessed to have had the opportunity to work with great spiritual and faith leaders. It has been a privilege and I would like to express my deep gratitude for the solutions for peace they are teaching humanity.

I would like to thank my many inspiring friends and family members: Joseph Stevens, Herikhan Baba, Michael Bernard Beckwith, Inder Kaur Bhasin, Paul Bhasin, Traci Bonilla, Jonathan Brent, Chris Chapple, PhD., Michael Chaskes, Sri Amiya Roy Chodhury, Carolyn Conger, Ph.D., Amaury Cooper, Helene and Edwin Cooper, Susan Crutcher, Julie Deife, Rinchen Dharlo, His Holiness 16th Karmapa Rigpe Dorje, His Holiness 17th Karmapa Ugyen Trinley Dorje, Dr. James Doty, Raj Dutt, Buddy and Gertie Elias, Georg and Brenda Feuerstein, Maria Florio, Julian Fouce, Stephen Fouce, Joey Galon, Dr. Dr. Robert Hayward, Dr. Ruth Hayward Ph.D., John Hogue, Alice Howell, Catherine Jayne Ph.D., Linda and Alan Jayne, Catherine Josey, Mark Juergensmeyer, Ph.D, Henry Kang, Tim Kettle, His Holiness Tenzin Gyatso 14th Dalai Lama, Toni Ringo Law, LA Yoga, Lisa Leeman, Southern Asian Art Council; Los Angeles County Art Museum, Stephen Markel, Ph. D, Anandmayi Ma, James Mitchell Miller, Jackie Nalli, Syed Nazim, Ali Nazani, Dolly Oberoi, Daniel Otter, Danielle Otter, Victoria Fouce Otter, Jetsun Pema, Robert Perry, Annie Pignatelli, Pitzer College, Joseph Prabhu, Ph. D., Mohammed Rabani, Syed Badar Rabbani Qutbi, Mohammed Rabani, Steve Ross, Father John Ridyard, H. H. Gyaltsab Rinpoche, H.H. Jamgon Kongtrul Rinpoche, H.H. Tai Situpa Rinpoche, Dean Robinson, William Royere, Richard Seaman, Eva Schloss, Leslie Schwartz, Deepak Shimkada, Ph. D., Trilochan Nath Shrestha, Dr. Karan Singh, Maggie Smith, Bonnie Sorensen, Razia Sultan, Dr. Dorothy Taylor, Mother Teresa, Tibet Children's Village, Felicia Tomasko, Denise and Jim Tomecko,

Khen Rinpoche Lobzang Tsetan, Maya Rana Tufo, Christopher Tufty, Urgyen Tulku, Tenzin Thakla, Robert Thurman, Seppi and Uschi Weiner, and the YIVO Center for Jewish Research.

The most beautiful and profound emotion we can experience is the sensation of the mystical. He to whom this emotion is a stranger, who can no longer wonder and stand rapt in awe, is as good as dead. To know that what is impenetrable to us really exists, manifesting itself as the highest wisdom and the most radiant beauty, which our dull faculties can comprehend only in their primitive forms - this knowledge, this feeling, is at the center of true religion.

- Albert Einstein

Introduction

Like many Westerners of my generation, I was first introduced to Eastern religions and the magical land of India with the fabled Himalayas, as a curious teenager in the late 1960's. I was fascinated by the culture which seemed so drastically different from my own. I couldn't wait to travel there to experience it for myself. As it turned out that trip was the first of many. I would spend the next thirteen years living and working throughout India, Nepal, Tibet, Pakistan, Afghanistan, Kashmir, Sri Lanka, China, Bhutan and the neighboring countries. I not only learned about their ancient faith traditions, I experienced their practices first-hand. I was awed by the peaceful existence, the openness and kindness shown to me by total strangers who happily shared their paths to the Divine. My interest in them became the centerpiece of my life and continues to this day.

I had the good fortune to meet Mother Teresa. She spoke to me about how her spiritual convictions motivated her to work with the poorest of the poor. Her centers in Calcutta and many other cities help tens of thousands of destitute outcasts in need of shelter, medical attention, and the assurance that they are loved. For Mother Teresa, this was a religious calling.

With a great deal of luck and probably a little Divine intervention, I met the Dalai Lama on one of my first trips to India. I have had the honor of seeing him many times since. His wisdom and guidance have enriched my life immeasurably. When I set out to make *Not In God's Name*, a documentary film on religious tolerance, the Dalai Lama graciously agreed to meet with me for an interview and discuss the subject. He even suggested how best to approach it, the way he had personally explored the many paths to the Divine.

I lived with and accompanied Hindu yogis on pilgrimages through the storied Himalayas, meeting spiritual luminaries along the way. I also encountered countless "ordinary" people living extraordinary lives of spiritual devotion, doing their part to help make the world a better place. From the anonymous to the famous, I was welcomed, and humbly guided, beyond the words in the books I'd read, into a direct experience of their spiritual traditions. I saw compassion in action, and it filled me with hope and joy. The lifestyle I shared with devout villagers in India had a dreamlike serenity.

I was aware of the history of religious violence in the region, but it was far from the tranquil experiences I was enjoying at the holy sites of many faiths, which reflected the devotion and religious fervor for which India is known. But then something happened that shattered the bliss and shook me to the depths of my very being. I was trapped in the midst of a bloody religious riot that nearly cost me my life. Stunned by the level of rage I witnessed that day, and by the horror of the killing all around me, I was very lucky to get out alive.

I didn't feel safe until I was back home in Los Angeles. I may have been far from the mob violence, but I couldn't shake the awful memories of what I had experienced. It is still hard to fathom that such brutality occurs in the birthplace of so many great faiths. I had to rethink this paradox - and understand how it could happen. It is the hot button issue of our time.

Some of the very people who had kindly opened their hearts and homes to share their traditions with me, were suddenly maniacal killers. I was haunted by the contradiction between religious devotion and violence in the name of God, and how prevalent this issue has become in our world today. The peaceful regions where I worked, Afghanistan, Pakistan and Kashmir – were transformed into war zones due to religious conflict. I witnessed first hand the ferocity of aggression people have suffered, at the hands of their "brothers."

It is hard to realize that in this 21st Century, and that there is still so much religious intolerance and conflict in the world. It seems so archaic. Yet merely glancing around, one can find problems with Kurds in Iraq, Hindu Nationalists, Christians in China, Christians in Pakistan, the Orthodox in Russia, the animosity goes on and on. In the news we are constantly bombarded by barbaric reports of killing in the name of God.

The Taliban in Pakistan fired upon Malala Yousufzai, a fourteen- year old girl as she rode home from school in a van. Taking bullets in the neck, Malala was rushed to Great Britain for medical care. She was under guard in the hospital, her life threatened by extremists as she lay trying to heal.[1] Not long after there was a cartoon on the internet, depicting Malala as a "young girl terrifying the extreme Mullah leaders – and her only weapon is a book." The Taliban attacked Malala because of her promotion of "Western beliefs." [2] She went on to win the Nobel Peace Prize in 2014.

The number and frequency of such attacks due to religious bigotry has increased exponentially in the last few decades. Why? In this new millennium, we are capable of destroying each other now more than ever. We must find a way to live together in harmony.

Ever since I was trapped in the riot, I have been haunted by the question: why do people kill in the name of God? This horrifying experience sent me on a quest to find answers, to the ashrams, churches, synagogues, and even Himalayan caves of spiritual and faith leaders throughout South Asia. I wondered how we can make sense of the conflicts that explode between members of different faiths. Why is religious fanaticism growing? What lessons can we learn from the East, and what solutions might they have to help us deal with today's challenges? This book is an account of my journey.

Chapter 1
The Assassination and Riot

Men never do evil so completely and cheerfully as when they do it from religious conviction.
                                                            -Blaise Pascal

In the countryside outside Delhi, our car sped past endless miles of yellow mustard fields gently rippling in the warm breeze. It was 2002. My friend Arif was taking me to visit *madrassas,* Muslim religious schools, in the small agricultural villages. A Kashmiri Muslim, Arif was keen to help me comprehend the causes of religious bigotry. He too had witnessed strife between followers of different religions. I had met him years before in India, when we were both immersed in the peaceful lifestyle of the Himalayas. It was an idyllic time.

Turning off the main road onto a dirt path, we dodged ancient bullock carts lumbering past. The air was clean out here and I inhaled deeply. The village was peaceful and picturesque. Our car pulled up to a rambling clutch of cement buildings. One was quite elaborate, bearing a striking resemblance to a mini Taj Mahal.

As we climbed out, Arif said, "You don't know much about Islam, so here's your chance, to ask this guy whatever you want."

"True, I've been living with Hindu yogis, but this will be totally different."

Yogis eschewed society's distractions to seek the answers to the deepest questions of life. They allowed me to accompany them on the ancient footpaths to sacred shrines high up in the Himalayan Mountains. I had spent time photographing them for a book on yogis, *Shiva* that I wrote with my friend, Denise Tomecko. "The way the Hindus embraced me, their kindness was overwhelming! They invited me into their temples and homes, and offered me their only piece of bread."

"That's right, in India our favorite saying is, "Guest is God," he laughed.

"That's when I know the snacks and milk tea are coming. Even though they have so little."

It felt a little strange accepting the boundless offerings they showered on me. I had grown up privileged in Los Angeles with loving parents, and had been fortunate to attend the best private schools. "The yogis and lay people viewed me only as spirit, as an expression of God."

"That's India," Arif laughed.

"You're right, this is a good chance to talk to a Muslim holy man!" Walking across the powdery dirt clearing surrounded by yellow mustard flowers towards traditional buildings covered in intricate Islamic patterns, we were greeted by young Muslim boys attired in colorfully embroidered baggy trousers and long loose shirts, with skull caps, their huge smiles revealing perfect bright white teeth. A man with a long beard sitting on a hemp cot, greeted us with the traditional "*Salaam halekum*," and motioned me to sit. Hindu, Muslim and Sikh villagers were gathered at his feet in rapt attention as he sat relaxing outside.

Arif explained, "As the head of the *madrassa*, school they seek him out for prayers and healings, they scribble their problems and those of loved ones onto those small slips of paper". The faithful folded the scraps and dropped them on the cot where the holy man prayed over them.

He requested one of his young students to bring tea, as well as his massive, aged and dog-eared copy of the *Quran*. He stood and made a point of showing me passages in the holy book about Jesus and Mary.

He read in Urdu and Arif translated, "If somebody had leprosy, he would be healed. And he would go to the graveyard and tell the dead people, "get up," and they would rise. And he would tell the people what was in their house, and the house would be many miles, five hundred miles away. He knew all, this was a symbol of Jesus Christ."

I asked him, "What is Jesus called in the *Quran*?"

"Isa Massi. There are two stories about Christ in the *Quran*. This is another one." He turned the pages. Arif continued translating, "It's about Mary now. She was taking a bath in the jungle, cordoned off with cloth. Gabriel came. She was under a date tree, and she would just shake the tree and eat the dates during her pregnancy. And there was a spring right there, where she used to get the water, right there in that place. It's written in the *Quran.* And she came with the child, and people sort of looked down upon her wondering, how, where did she get this baby? And the child spoke at that time. He was ten days old. 'I am God's follower and I am sent by God, and I have come with the Bible, the book of God. And I will always listen to my Mother.'"

"He went to Israel, that is where he was crucified. From there he vanished. And he's alive up there," he pointed skyward. "And he'll come back again to us," the Muslim man smiled.

I was touched by how he sought to find common ground with me, pointing a bony finger at the Islamic script as if I could actually read every word; he enthusiastically recited the passages aloud in his gravelly voice.

The wizened holy man then led us into the *madrassa* where a row of boys sat on the floor huddled over a long, low wooden table supporting massively thick *Qurans.* Their haunting melodic voices recited from the holy book for hours as they tried to memorize its' words. "By the time they are eighteen," Arif explained, "they will know the entire *Quran* by heart. Considering how difficult this is to do, it's a major accomplishment. On several occasions I've tried to give toys and balls to the boys to play with during their free time so that they can run around and release some of the intensity that builds up, but such worldly distractions are not allowed." Arif's point was well made that such sports, commonly taken for granted by children in developed countries, would help tip the balance of these boys' lives in a healthy way. He came from a well off family and did not attend such a school.

We both spotted a young boy crouched outside at the water faucets washing his feet before the evening prayer. He shyly gazed up at us with his enormous dark eyes.

"He has such an innocent face," Arif remarked. But it was offset by a severe hair lip making it appear that he was barely able to eat food.

"*Salaam halekum,*" the boy uttered quietly. It was very difficult to understand his speech. A simple surgical procedure could have easily and inexpensively repaired the deep cleft.

"Oh, we could get him to the hospital in Delhi," Arif said.

"I was thinking the exact same thing." We leapt at the chance to offer the operation as a gift. Unfortunately, we found out later that the boy's parents were too frightened to allow their son to be taken from the village for surgery. I was disappointed, because such an act of kindness might contribute towards Muslim villagers cultivating a sense of trust towards Americans.

I was first drawn to studying religious tolerance by a shocking event years before in 1984. I was flying to New Delhi aboard an Indian Airlines 737 one October afternoon, and overheard a highly charged conversation between two Indian businessmen in the row behind me. "She was shot?" the gentleman seated on the right exclaimed to his companion.

"Yes, by her own Sikh bodyguards. They have taken her to Safardjung Hospital. It does not look good for Mrs. Gandhi."

We landed within minutes of their conversation. As we took our places in line to get off the plane the rising tension was palpable, though I was still unsure what was happening. Fear bordering on panic was etched on people's faces as I walked towards the bus that was to take us to the terminal. My heartbeat was keeping pace with my anxiety. At last I heard the dire news.

"Indira Gandhi's Sikh bodyguards pumped 16 bullets into her body as she walked in her garden," reported a newsman[3] on a TV in the terminal. It was October 31. "The shooting happened at precisely 9:20 AM."

Prime Minister Gandhi (no relation to Mahatma Gandhi) had made the fatal error of miscalculating the Sikhs' reaction to her having ordered the bombing and invasion of their Golden Temple in Amritsar. I knew the Sikh temple is the holy of holies of their religion. Of immeasurable spiritual importance to millions of worshippers, it is like attacking the Vatican, or Mecca.

Guru Nanak, who taught there is only one formless God, and all people are equal, founded Sikhism five hundred years ago. On the temple altar rests the Sikh holy book, the *Guru Granth Sahib*, a compilation of religious verses by Sikh, Muslim, and Hindu masters.

Radical Sikh separatists were attempting to force the state of Punjab to secede from India and form their own country, *Khalistan*, named after their brotherhood of soldier-saints. This area was the breadbasket of the nation, and produced 85% of the wheat that fed the country's population. The Indian Government wanted to divert part of its ample water supply to arid Rajasthan nearby, home to a desert so vast it can be seen from outer space.

After a long stand off, Indira Gandhi finally lost her patience and launched Operation Blue Star.[4] In June 1984, the Indian Army, equipped with mortars and automatic machine guns, stormed the Golden Temple. Their orders were to ferret out Bindranwale, the charismatic militant leader, along with his followers. They were holed up inside the sacred temple with a massive stockpile of weapons and ammunition. Bindranwale held some devotees hostage and the assault continued.[5] To Sikhs throughout the world, Indira Gandhi's attack was the ultimate sacrilege. Two of her bodyguards settled the score: they emptied all the rounds loaded in their Sten automatics into her abdomen.

The Golden Temple is considered the house of God, and every Sikh regards it important to visit the shrine at least once in their lifetime. I had been there, and crossed the narrow bridge sparkling Pool of Immortality surrounding the golden shrine. Since time immemorial, this temple in a grove of trees was a retreat for wandering mendicants. Sikhs there whispered to me, "Even Gautama the Buddha meditated here."

"It is so quiet!" I thought to myself, "This assassination shock wave has paralyzed New Delhi. There's no noise!" This was virtually unknown in this bustling city of millions. I jumped into the first motor rickshaw I saw and told the driver to take me to the Government Tourist Office to get updated information from a friend, KB Singh, a Minister of Tourism. KB, a Sikh who wore a turban, was in the back room when I burst in.

"It seems really dangerous out there," I informed him of the obvious.

"Oh, not to worry," he calmly assured me, "They won't do anything to foreigners."

"Are you sure? I don't have such a good feeling," I replied, "Its way too quiet."

"Yes. This is an act of revenge only upon Indira Gandhi, because she attacked the Golden Temple," he reassured me.

"Please don't be naive," I implored him. "You should go straight into hiding, please. The streets may not be safe for Sikhs for a while."

I raced back to my hotel. KB didn't feel this event was of any physical threat to him or me, but thanks to the kindness of a Hindu family who hid him in their home for several days, his life was saved. Countless other Sikhs, however, were not so fortunate.

I was standing with a few foreign tourists on the terrace of our hotel in Connaught Place, a clean, stately enclave in the center of New Delhi. We were looking down on the usually bustling street of shops that was now completely deserted, when one of the tourists exclaimed, "Look, so many buildings are on fire!" Structures in the surrounding blocks were blackened with smoke. Fiery embers curling skyward, rained down ashes on us. We could smell a putrid stench all around us.

"Isn't that the Sikh taxi stand in front of the Imperial Hotel?" asked an Australian. All of the taxis had been set on fire and columns of thick black smoke from burning gasoline filled our nostrils with an acrid odor. In an instant I knew I had to get out of the country fast.

A German alarmingly advised me, "Don't ride in any taxis driven by Sikhs." I rushed to the lobby, paid my hotel bill, returned to my room, hastily packing my few belongings while figuring out how I would get to the airport. I schlepped my luggage down the old marble staircase and hurried one block to the corner where the Indian Airlines shuttle bus stopped several times a day to take passengers to the airport. I waited with other anxious tourists, and twenty minutes later I was so happy to see a bus headed for us. "Thank God," I thought. The door creaked open, and we all breathed a collective sigh of relief as we hurriedly boarded the ramshackle bus.

Our bus driver checked to be certain that the doors were securely locked, with beads of perspiration moistening his forehead. We careened through the Delhi streets. "Oh, my God," exclaimed my seatmate. We were witnessing ravaged burned out buses and shells of torched trucks with extreme apprehension. Huge skeletal piles of twisted iron lay like ghosts of the prosperous Sikh transportation businesses. The stench of fire and death wafted through the smoky air of the capital, blocking out the sunlight.

Except for our bus the streets were eerily deserted. "Look, the patrols of police and soldiers are walking away from the crowds," I exclaimed.

"They're fanatics, and the cops aren't trying to control anything," she agreed. Wild-eyed young thugs brandishing crowbars, machetes, swords, and cricket bats in the air, manned roadblocks set up in the middle of each intersection, gunning for trouble. "Blood for blood," they repeatedly chanted. Anger and sheer hatred overwhelmed their contorted faces as a torrent of hatred had completely overtaken any remnants of clear thinking. They bashed clubs against our bus. Enraged Hindus were now clearly pitted against Sikhs.

Driving down the smoke-filled streets we nearly collided with roadblocks hastily constructed from iron drums and piles of wood. The bus driver swerved wildly to weave around them without having to stop. We watched breathlessly as he maneuvered the large squeaking bus, barely managing to keep it upright, every time I felt sure it would overturn. "Sikhs! Burn Sikhs alive," the crowd frantically chanted. They rushed our vehicle with hate filled eyes hungry for bloodletting, pounding on our windows menacingly. We cowered in the safety of the bus enclosure, praying they wouldn't get in.

We reached an intersection where smoking buses that had been halted and burned, barricaded the road. Our driver abruptly swerved to the left and then the right, trying to avoid getting stopped. Young thugs ambushed both sides of our bus, beating loudly on it with clubs, screaming wildly, while looking for people to massacre. Searching for Sikhs to butcher, they wielded swords, and machetes. This time, our driver was unable to get away from the angry mob, we were dead still, and the horde banged insistently on the door and wrenched it open. Two enraged hoodlums boarded our bus swinging iron crowbars wildly in the air. They marched down the aisle, stared intently into our faces one by one, and halted right in front of me. Their eyes glared deeply into mine, burning with curiosity and rage, surprised to encounter a blond-haired, blue-eyed passenger among their potential victims.

Suddenly, I remembered I was wearing a Sikh symbol around my neck; it was a gift from a friend. My heart was in my throat. I strained to maintain a neutral facial expression as they snickered at me. The pendant was hidden beneath my blouse, and I feared they would pull on the chain and see it. After what seemed like a heart wrenching eternity the hooligans finally turned and continued up the aisle. Searching with hate filled eyes, they became satisfied that there were no Sikhs among us. They disembarked, shouting at our bus driver to go. I exhaled in relief, feeling so thankful to be alive.

Police barricades set up at the airport entrance stopped anyone without an airline ticket and passport from entering. "They have to let us in," I hoped. We passengers were able to get by, our driver had successfully accomplished his mission of getting us there alive, and we thanked him profusely. We poured out of the bus and made our way into the terminal only to see that every inch of space was crammed with people, desperate for some way out of this country that was convulsing with violence.

Many flights were canceled because the airlines didn't want their crews and aircrafts landing in a country in bloody pandemonium. The airport had become a madhouse of desperation as they sought refuge from the killing. The rioting had evolved into an orgy of killing that continued unabated, and was beamed in news broadcasts worldwide. Passengers crouched on pieces of cloth stretched out on the floor while others squatted on their luggage. A tourist bumped me and smiled apologetically, "This place has run out of everything." The terminal had no more coffee, tea, or drinking water. The lines at the airline counters snaked for miles. "I've been standing here forever," he shook his head. Frantic passengers jockeyed for coveted plane tickets. When I finally stood before the Scandinavian Airlines clerk, it took a heated exchange before she relented and assigned me one of the last precious seats. After waiting six long hours, exhausted I gratefully boarded the plane in the wee hours of the morning.

"This was the first time that I have seen such terrifying devastation wrecked by religious hatred," I realized. "I feel so despondent." I later learned that some of my foreign friends were in far more dangerous circumstances then mine. In one popular tourist section of Delhi, my Austrian friends and their two children were staying in a guesthouse owned by Sikhs. Ironically they were in India studying non-violent religions when they had to crawl out of a burning second floor window and down a makeshift ladder to save their kids from the flames lit by anti-Sikh hoodlums who torched their hotel. And near the Golden Temple, at a flashpoint by the Pakistan border, another friend crossing into India witnessed a Sikh being beheaded right on the roadside.

Sikh temples in upscale Delhi neighborhoods were smoldering, burnt to the ground. Bloodthirsty men doused Sikhs with burning hot oil, randomly burning them alive on the streets. The sun's rays could not pierce through the smoke from fires and the stench of death permeated the air. Houses owned by Sikhs were branded with an ominous red "X" painted on their front doors, singling them out for annihilation by the marauding mobs. Approximately 3,000 Sikhs were slaughtered in Delhi alone.

Chapter 2
Disenchantment

Human society makes tolerance more than a virtue. It makes it a requirement for survival.

-Rene Dubois

Everyone suffered horribly during the riots - Sikhs and Hindus alike. One Sikh friend told me his terrifying story, "The day that the Prime Minister died, I arrived in Delhi and was near the hospital where Mrs. Gandhi's body had been taken. Many Congress Party gang members were hurling stones at the President's car. Sikhs were being beaten and killed all over. I saw a group of men slaughtered in their car. The whole atmosphere was menacing, death hung in the air."

"We were all very distressed about Mrs. Gandhi. I left for home, on the outskirts of town, but took a roundabout way to avoid the violence. By the time I got there, crowds of hoodlums were hanging burning tires around Sikhs' necks to immolate them. The gangs were made up of poor lower caste men who had been sent by political groups to terrorize us. They were slaughtering people, barging into homes, and looting. These people are marginalized, so they were easily caught up in the frenzy. They resent the rich. I saw four families slain with my own eyes. A gang grabbed a child, stripped her bare, raped her and torched her to death. It was sickening."

"For five days, local armed men guarded our neighborhood from gangs of roving killers and thieves. I could smell burning tires and hear screams as the lawlessness raged on, but dared not go outside."

The Sikh looked dejected as he fought back the hopelessness, "When it finally ended, I left for the US as soon as I could. I found out later that a mob of Untouchables doused my cousin with petrol and lit him on fire, so they could steal his scooter. He was only thirty-five years old. And in the next neighborhood, a young boy in a theater witnessed eighteen people from his clan being slaughtered. He has now lost his mind. He is completely insane."

My friend's mother, Inder Kaur, was also trapped in Delhi following the assassination. "At first, we didn't realize there was going to be trouble. We heard of strife in other neighborhoods, but we felt safe and went to sleep. In the morning, I heard the kids next-door shouting, 'Hurry! They're looting Sikh shops!'

"But mobs were also looting Hindu shops, using the assassination as an excuse. We had no idea how bad it was going to get. From the balcony I saw mobs raiding stores and heard shouting about killing Sikhs. They were throwing Molotov cocktails into houses."

"You must have been so frightened! Then what happened?" I wondered.

"In the morning three hundred people mobbed our house. They disrespected our holy book, and stole all our valuables. We locked ourselves up on the third floor. My husband shouted, 'if they are going to kill us, I'm not going to die like a rat.' He stood at the top of the stairs with our swords. I started praying. Some guy yelled, "Let's go." As they left, they grabbed the kitchen gas cylinder and lit a match so the whole place would go up. Thank God some neighborhood boys wet a rug, wrapped it and shut it off. We would have blown up.

Our home was stripped bare. Our next-door neighbors were spared because they were Hindus. We were friends and a ladder joined our houses; we crawled across it, and spent the night there. They took a huge risk hiding us. But our neighborhood must have been picked clean, because the hoodlums moved on to other areas."

"The next day, the police came and looked at the damage, but did nothing. Days later, the army intervened with orders to shoot on sight, things calmed down and people started venturing outside. Some believed the rioting was politically motivated, and that Gandhi's bodyguards were framed. The Sikhs used to love her. Some thought people in the government may have set up her assassination. On TV they were chanting, 'Kill Sikhs!' "But all the Sikhs we knew felt bad, and wondered why they killed Indira Gandhi?"

"Two days later, my cousin spotted two trucks on the road packed with the bodies of dead Sikhs bound for cremation."

I kept wondering why, so did she.

"What these people do is wrong, and I don't understand it, because we all have the same blood in our veins. There is only one God, and we all are human beings. This has nothing to do with religion! Like the Muslim terrorists who throw bombs - I don't think their violent actions have anything to do with faith; they act this way because their country has been hijacked, and their human rights usurped. They're angry. Very few fight in the name of religion, they do it for other reasons."

The plane finally lifted off from Delhi airport. I relaxed in my seat and welcomed the cool air conditioning, trying to relax after so many hours of tension. Gazing out the window, I could see countless fires blazing below. I was fortunate to be able to escape such a horrific situation, but in the pit of my stomach I ached for those left in the mayhem. As our aircraft rose high above the haze that was blanketing the city, it seemed like a separate reality.

I considered what I had witnessed. I knew there was a history of discord, but had to rethink everything after this horrible personal experience of religious hatred. I had met Mother Teresa, the Dalai Lama and so many others, and had witnessed how many similarities the faiths share. Religions stress that living side-by-side in peace is important. That people actually kill one another in the name of God is appalling. My rather naïve perspective on the issue of tolerance between faiths was now more wizened and realistic – unfortunately.

As soon as I landed in Hong Kong, I rushed to an airport newsstand to scan the headlines. They read, "CARNAGE IN INDIA." The *International Herald Tribune*, the *London Times*, and the *Herald Examiner* led the day's editions with the death and destruction that was wildly raging in the normally peaceful metropolises of India. The news worsened as the days wore on. In total, 3-6 days of murder and rampage went unabated, countless Sikh businesses were torched, and roving gangs set fire to Sikh homes with the families inside. Compassionate Hindus and Muslims risked their own lives hiding fortunate Sikhs.

Some say the appalling mass carnage that was allowed to occur on the streets of Delhi was a pogrom organized and executed by forces against the Sikh community.[6] There is still a great deal of controversy about what happened on the days following Gandhi's assassination. Rumors swirl of her murder being a conspiracy, and that the Sikhs were scapegoats. Some Sikhs regarded the killers of Indira Gandhi as heroes to be celebrated. The truth will hopefully be revealed someday. Inquiries are ongoing. A riot victim, Inderbal Singh Duggal wrote, "Can anyone imagine the amount of compensation we got from the government? It was 5,000 rupees!"[7]

I was shocked, realizing, "At the time that was the equivalent of $454!"

To witness this bloodletting was an experience that shook my very foundation. I had been in the Far East for years, and had experienced great peace and acceptance between faiths. Now I felt compelled to go on a personal quest to understand the reasons for religious intolerance.

Tolerance—"tol.er.ance,"—Webster's dictionary educates us, is "1. a fair and permissive attitude toward those whose race, religion, nationality, etc., differ from one's own; freedom from bigotry. 2. a fair and permissive attitude toward opinions and practices that differ from one's own."

It sounds simple enough, right? Why has humankind struggled for eons to live this definition? To begin with, as children we are exposed exclusively to the religion of our family; rarely do we have the liberty to choose our own. While through our friends we become aware that other religions exist, our knowledge is simply that they're out there somewhere. Our education system doesn't offer much in the way of exposing us to the world's faith traditions unless we are fortunate enough to take a high school or college class in world religion. Even then the information in the curriculum may be basic and generalized. For the most part, we're left to self-education either out of curiosity, or as an emerging spiritual seeker.

Taking my own view into consideration, I wondered, "How different might it be today without the earlier conditioning of childhood, society, religion and education?" Otherwise how might the global family interact if we genuinely believed and lived by the words of Gandhi that "our faith traditions are highways leading to the same destination?" Would conversions grind to a halt and conversations begin? Would we be less prone to view religions and their followers through the lens of discrimination or suspicion? The overall stability of our planet would be greatly furthered through respect for all religions, and lead to a safer, more economically, ecologically, spiritually and scientifically advanced civilization, resulting in a better life for world citizenry.

Since the tragedy of 9/11, the US has also experienced unbearable grief caused by religious fanaticism. Certainly such violence is not new to human history, but it is something we Americans used to learn about from classroom history books rather than newscasts of terrorist events happening on our own soil. Some historians claim that religious intolerance is the "new racism."

A few years before the murder of Indira Gandhi, I was flying into the city of Amritsar to visit the Golden Temple one morning, guiding a tour group of doctors and medical professionals. I was fortunate to have a window seat. "Look at that," I exclaimed. The plane banked, the clouds parted, and my eyes were taken captive by a stunning gold structure, glittering like a jewel in the landscape, surrounded by a tranquil pool of still blue water.

At the gates of the temple enclosure, water flowed from silver faucets where I joined hordes of devout pilgrims cleansing their feet before entering. A turbaned man smiled broadly and handed me a checked cotton cloth. "Here, cover your hair, it's a sign of respect," he explained.

"Of course, thank you."

I began the long walk across the gleaming marble surrounding the glistening pool at the Golden Temple of Sikhism, the most revered shrine in the Sikh world. Melodious harmonium playing, *tabla* drumming and Sikhs chanting prayers over loud speakers lulled me into a serene state. Twenty-four hours a day here, the atmosphere was charged with devotional music. Inside, priests with long flowing beards were sitting cross-legged at a shrine on which sat the Sikh's holy book, the *Guru Granth Sahib*, comprised of the writings of Hindu and Muslim masters, and confirms the two faiths' shared spiritual origin. It also includes the writings of the great Muslim poet, Kabir. I reveled in the matchless serenity.

500 years ago Guru Nanak, a social reformer advocated equality for all, including women. He denounced the Hindu hierarchical caste system and its' inherent prejudice and inequality. During his lifetime, there existed great strife between Hindus and Muslims. This went against Nanak's belief that all faiths should co-exist peacefully. He founded the Sikh philosophy to create a common ground between these faiths. His approach was a great stride forward in promoting religious harmony. Sikhs respect all images and paths to God.

Many Sikhs were part of the military caste, the fierce warriors who prevented India from fully succumbing to Muslim invasions. Sikhs traditionally practiced non-violence until one of their masters, Guru Tegh Bahadur, was beheaded for his refusal to convert to Islam. Once this happened they began to wear knives and swords, to use to protect anyone who is innocent and needs help. Sikhs do not cut their hair or beard, and wear turbans to distinguish themselves as members of the Sikh religion. Nanak transmitted his teachings through devotional songs, and taught his followers that there is only one formless, omnipresent God. Sikhs live as householders, remaining active in society as they seek to commune with the Divine.

Later, one memorable day my Sikh friend, Dolly Oberoi took me to meet Avtar Shah Singh, a Sikh master, just outside of Delhi. "You are going to love him," she giggled.

We walked in to meet Avtar, he was sitting in the main room and had beautiful soft eyes. When I began to discuss religious intolerance with him, he uttered, "All humanity is one religion."

"Yes," I agreed.

"When a child is born, can you tell which religion he is," he questioned me. I shrugged not sure of the answer.

"No one can!" His eyes twinkled merrily.

When I began my Eastern sojourn, my family was more concerned that my travels could result in the contraction of deadly cholera. Neither they nor I ever could have imagined that an assassination and unrest would cause me to flee a country to save my life. Back home in LA, I tried to understand what happened. I felt disillusioned by the terrible experience of the riot. It was heartbreaking. At least I was safe at home where I could think about it. I wanted to find out what really lay beneath the hatred. It had all started ten years earlier.

Chapter 3
Passage to India

*In religion, India is the only millionaire...the One land that
all men desire to see, and having seen once, by even a
glimpse, would not give that glimpse for all the shows
of all the rest of the globe combined.*
-Mark Twain

Driving through the hills of Los Angeles with my
brother, Thomas, a car careened around the corner straight
into us. Metal crashed and I catapulted from the backseat of
the car over the front seat and flew right through the glass
windshield. Airborne, I rocketed down the street a few
houses, conscious the entire time. I landed on the concrete
with a thud. Some kind neighbors covered me up with a
blanket, thinking I was dead.

"A drunk smashed into you," my Doctor explained in
the ER. This brush with death added to my teenage
discontentment. Just 17, I was faced with two months of long
boring days of recovery in a hospital bed, a leg hanging in
traction. Alone and disenchanted, one day I recalled a book
lying on my brother's coffee table a few years earlier. It was
Autobiography of a Yogi, the classic by Paramahansa
Yogananda in which he recounts his fantastic tales of the
Himalayas. I was mesmerized by his description of life in
India - a land of levitating yogis living in caves, Royal
Bengal tigers as tame as housecats cohabitating with *swamis*
sleeping on beds of nails in their ashrams, and ascetics in the
breathless state buried underground for weeks without
suffocating. These yogis who were forsaking the material
world, walked about clad only in ashes to represent their
renunciation.

I longed to go to India and find the same inner peace
and spirituality that Yogananda described in his book. Was
there really such a place where this painful physical world
did not matter so much? The fascinating culture he described
provided a great escape. His observations about life being
more then the worldly concerns and attachments we all clung

to seemed so true. It felt like I had a second chance that got me thinking about life. I could feel the intense pull of the Himalayas as I lay recovering from the accident.

A few months later, back in school, a boyfriend who'd just returned from Afghanistan regaled me with exotic tales of the Hindu Kush Mountains that traversed the area. I was riveted.

Serendipitously, a flyer arrived in my mailbox, titled - "There's a lot for you in Kathmandu." My imagination flooded with exotic visions of what such a place must be like. I went to my atlas discovering that Kathmandu is the capital of Nepal, over the northeast border from India. The possibilities grew even more seductive when comparing the photo of Kathmandu's majestic Himalayas to the sight of the smog-ridden air that clouded the mountains near my dorm at Pitzer College, one of the Claremont Colleges outside Los Angeles.

In a few weeks, seven adventurous students boarded Air India for the grueling 26-hour flight to New Delhi. From the moment we stepped off the plane onto the tarmac, we were plunged into a world where everything was utterly foreign. The unfamiliar sights, sounds, and smells overwhelmed my senses. The very air we breathed was tinged with aromatic incense and the fetid smell of bodies being burned on funeral pyres, immediately dispelling my romanticized notions about the country. A cacophony of lovely birdsong accented the atmosphere; it was different from anything I'd ever known.

Most of our ride was in silence, or more accurately, *in shock and awe*! Our old taxi careened wildly through crowded lanes, narrowly avoiding free-roaming cows, dogs, monkeys and wild boar. Out the window, in the bazaar barefoot peasants crouched at roadside fires cooking, smoke curling upward, warming themselves at the flames. Lining the streets were ramshackle storefronts with garish multi-armed gods painted on their doorways. Bicycle rickshaws clacked past us, bearing villagers clutching loads of clay and metal vessels. Fruit and vegetable sellers pushed antiquated carts piled high with colorful vegetables and strange fruit. I stared in wonder, the scene resembled a page ripped from National Geographic.

A poor family dressed in rags was eating on the ground, right next to a heap of trash. Their hollow faces watched our car pass; I could feel their eyes burn through mine. This first experience of India was not nearly as serene as I had imagined when I read about it back home. Clay sewer pipes were stacked awaiting installation. Families had taken up residence inside them! Their faded color *saris* hung out to dry were fluttering in the breeze. They were shooing away roaming monkeys and roving dogs begging for scraps of food. These villagers left the countryside fleeing famine and drought, their hearts filled with anticipation of the riches and better life that awaited them in this teeming metropolis.

Somehow, our driver maneuvered his way through the dense traffic, along streets with no lanes, horns blaring constantly, brakes screeching. Mounted on the dashboard was a veritable shrine to the Hindu god Shiva, the Lord of the Himalayas. Vermillion colored powder covered the deity, and there was a small golden crescent moon nestled in his long flowing hair. Incense burned before the plastic statue, and the pungent if fragrant smoke swirled up, filling the entire vehicle.

I hacked, coughing," It feels like only this deity's grace is gonna get us there alive." We fell out of the cab at Claridges, a stately old British hotel, excited about what further surprises awaited us.

"Come on, I can't wait to see this!" one of the students shouted.

An orange turbaned snake charmer perched cross-legged on the marble steps, coaxing a cobra from a woven basket with his hypnotic flute.

After checking in, we went nearby to a curio shop. The proprietor, a man with a glass eye, greeted us cheerfully, "Oh, American! Take one cup tea, looking is free!" We would hear these words from every shopkeeper we met in the months to come, but I was determined not to get "Delhi belly," dysentery.

"That's okay, thank you," I politely refused his offer. The jammed shop was permeated with a sweet smell.

"*Charas,* hashish," he offered.

We all tried to ignore him.

The curio dealer showed off his many intriguing artifacts, but he was proudest of his collection of erotic art. "Oh Americans, look…very sexy *tantric* art," he repeated hypnotically. The carvings of extremely well endowed bejeweled men and women were intertwined in consort with elephants and other animals in foursomes.

"Well," I thought, "*this* is different!"

"*Kama Sutra*, Madam. Very good, isn't it?" our proprietor inquired while winking his good eye.

"Oh, yes," I commented, squinting my eyes in an effort to make better sense of what I was viewing in the dingy room.

"Yes, Madam, he beamed proudly." "Hindu god, Ganesh the elephant... and Tibeti!"

He moved from representations of bestiality to spirituality without batting an eyelash. He smiled widely, revealing red teeth stained from chewing betel nuts. "Sixty-four positions!" He proudly turned the spotlight on a wall of paintings revealing couples in sexual positions only Cirque de Soleil contortionists could perform. *"Yab yum,"* he spoke in a reverential tone while pointing to two Buddhist deities with terrifying faces, engaged in a pretzel-like sexual stance. We made a hurried exit and headed to the hotel for a much needed night's sleep.

The next morning we flew north to Kathmandu, the capital of Nepal. Peering out the plane's windows I saw the craggy snow-covered peaks of the towering Himalayas, the tallest mountain range in the world, framing green rice terraces carved into the sides of the hills. These vertical wonders were so tall their peaks were next to our plane's windows, not below. I gasped in awe, pressing my camera against the windows, for I'd never seen such immense icy massifs.

They let us take turns going in the cockpit. "That's Mount Everest to your left," explained the handsome Nepalese pilot sporting Aviator sunglasses. There were so many massively tall peaks that it strained the imagination to realize that this range separating Nepal from India —the highest elevations in the world— was still rising inches each year as two tectonic plates squeezed together.

From the lofty to the mundane — the lovely stewardess passed out our meals. "Veg, non-veg?" she asked in a perky accented voice. This was my kind of place, or so I thought until I saw the "veg" meal, which featured a sticky green blob.

"What is this?" I tried not to sound like a rude American tourist.

"*Burfi*, milk sweet. Try it," she said. I took a taste and smiled at the stewardess. It would take time to appreciate the odd taste and texture of the food here.

I looked back out the window, just as the mountains ringing the Kathmandu Valley revealed a startling storybook view unlike anything I had ever imagined. Brass and copper pagoda rooftops gleamed far below us in the brilliant sunlight, nestled in a verdant green valley.

Coming in for the landing I could see colorfully dressed mountain people balancing heavy wicker baskets as they climbed up steep paths on terraced hillsides inhabited by water buffalo. Nepal's jewel-blue sky and massive puffy white clouds were captivating, no wonder it was called "the "rooftop of the world."

It was 1974 but Kathmandu seemed to be frozen in a bygone era centuries before. Traffic signals were just beginning to be installed, and Japan had gifted a fleet of Toyotas - immediately put to use as taxis, to honor the coronation of Nepal's King Birendra. The King looked like a nice man with lovely brown eyes, his portrait hung everywhere in Kathmandu. Every time you had a milkshake, changed money or stopped at a stall to buy toilet paper – a real luxury in the Himalayas, there he was, smiling down at you. Unlike New Delhi, Kathmandu was untouched by modernity save a few paved roads. Bicycle rickshaws pedaled by hearty villagers plied the lanes, where dividing lines had not yet been painted. I plunged head first into exploring it.

"Human sacrifice was still practiced here thirty years ago. Our shamans go deep into trance and heal people," I heard a singsong voice behind me. Startled, I turned to see a handsome Nepali man with dark hair and shining eyes grinning, puffing on a Yak cigarette, a popular Nepali brand.

"I better watch out," was all I could think of to remark back to him.

It was Trilochan, Trilo for short, who owned the Ying Yang restaurant, the landmark for overland travelers that was the place to be seen. International "freaks" perched on velvet cushions high atop platforms as rock music blared. This precious land, unblemished by modern life drew many embassy and consulate personnel, bohemians, art dealers, drug smugglers, and "dharma bums," the quintessential seekers of spiritual enlightenment. The 60's counter culture still dominated South Asia, and bands of roving international overland hipsters floated between Goa full moon parties and exotic Kathmandu, following the "Hippie Trail." The cost of living was so cheap in South Asia that foreigners could stay comfortably for a long time. Overland transport like the *Magic Bus* and the *Chapatti Express* plied the arteries from Istanbul to Kathmandu. Nepal was on a crash course, hurtling from the innocence of the sixteenth century into the twenty-first at breakneck speed. Locals were starting to refer to tourism as Nepal's "third religion," its' earnings were becoming so vital to this dirt-poor country.

In Kathmandu Trilo's family had a compound of modern houses near the 2,000-year-old Monkey Temple, Swayambounath, named for the wild animals that rampaged on its' hill. There was a guesthouse where I could live. The huge all–seeing eyes of the Buddha, painted above the gleaming golden dome of the temple, gazed down compassionately upon me all of the inhabitants of the Kathmandu Valley, including me. Paradoxically, right next to this holy site was the training ground of the Nepalese army, the Gurkha soldiers, reputed to be the fiercest in the world. At dawn each morning their piercing bugle call would awaken me.

Trilo was the eldest son of his family, and he instantly felt like an older brother. I met his father who was a former Board member of Royal Nepal Airlines. He had two wives, one a Buddhist, and the other a Hindu. When his Buddhist wife was in a coma for years, the community elders urged him to take another wife, to care for his young children. It was rare for a Hindu man to remarry while his wife was still alive, but his new wife, known as "Big Mommy," bore him

40

four more children.

When his first wife came out of her coma the two co-mothered their combined family happily and paid homage to each other's temples. This was my first example of religious harmony in the region, and these two faiths were the basis of my studies. The Buddhist wife, called "Little Mommy" remained in a meditative state from then on, praying every day.

The highest Himalayan peaks including Everest ringed the Kathmandu Valley. Southern Nepal was fortified by steaming jungles where we Westerners would ride atop elephants on safari to see tigers and leopards that inhabited the tall grasslands. Its' isolation from the rest of the world, had rendered Nepal centuries behind in development, but what had found fertile ground in this kingdom were two of the world's great faiths. Hinduism and Buddhism were intertwined in the countless temples, worship ceremonies and festivals that filled the mystical Kathmandu Valley. The fusion of two of the world's great religious traditions exists in Nepali culture like nowhere else on earth. Daily I observed Hindus and Buddhists venerating the Divine at each other's shrines, and they had both faiths represented in their homes. Spiritual seekers from all parts of the globe come here since Nepal is the Buddha's birthplace.

Stunning art and jewelry abounded; much of the treasure was smuggled out of Tibet by refugees escaping Red China's brutal occupation of their country. They carefully ferried their family heirlooms across the snowy Himalayan passes to be sold or traded for mountain gear. The Tibetans had long, shiny black braided hair, with facial features and bone structure reminiscent of Native Americans.

I got acquainted with many Tibetan refugees as I started exporting artifacts and jewelry to the States, always being careful not to deal in stolen art. One trader, Lobsang would meet me each chilly foggy morning at Pokhara Lake, spreading out his beautiful artifacts on a cloth on the ground. He clutched his rosary, uttering *mantras*, prayers all day in a deep resounding voice as tourists perused his offerings. The traders wore lockets stuffed with prayers and photos of their smiling revered spiritual leader, the Dalai Lama. Today the

Dalai Lama is known throughout the world, but in the early 70's he was not yet such a huge presence on the global stage.

A few thousand years ago, Buddhism spread from India to Tibet, where it flourished. But when the Chinese invaded Tibet, their Communist regime was intolerant of religion. When Chairman Mao told the Dalai Lama, "Religion is poison," His Holiness realized the grave danger facing his beloved country. The Red Army destroyed as many priceless Buddhist art pieces and texts as possible. They forced monks and nuns to break sacred objects, and use them as road pavers, ensuring they would be trampled upon. The People's Liberation Army consigned some of the clergy to prison, where many types of torture was employed against them. Part of the population was interned in labor camps with little food. The occupation has been brutal. This was the first time I encountered people who were undergoing cultural genocide, and endured great danger to escape and practice their faith in freedom. I longed to go to Tibet whose culture was based on compassion and see this country for myself.

Our international community in Kathmandu in the early 1970's was also populated by a multitude of adventurers, photographers, National Geographic writers, and foreigners working for a variety of Non-Governmental organizations, NGO's, including the United Nations Development Fund, World Bank, Save the Children, and the Peace Corps. We American ex-pats met at the US Marines bar where it was possible to drink imported liquor on Friday nights.

Trilo called one morning, "Let's go meet some yogis." I was exhilarated at the thought, not knowing what to expect. He was clad in his usual ensemble, a velvet jacket with Hindu and Buddhist rosaries piled around his neck. He took me on a cab ride, honking the entire way with the driver nearly running over a flock of chickens a villager chased across the road. I held my breath. We emerged at Nepal's holiest shrine of Lord Shiva, Pasupatinath, on a tributary of the Ganges River. Deep bells clanged as we walked along the steep wooded hillside that wound down to ancient cremation *ghats,* platforms, and an enormous Hindu temple behind walls, mostly hidden from view. Trilo explained, "It enshrines the sacred *lingam* of Lord Shiva."

"The what?"

"The phallic symbol, the creative principal. But only Hindus can go in."

"Oh, shoot," my spirits fell. Bands of roving monkeys jumped over our heads, squealing, they sprang along the rooftops, retreating to the treetops in the hills around the temple.

"Why would a phallic symbol be in a temple?" I was confused by this, remembering all the erotic art in Delhi.

"It symbolizes the creative principal of the universe," Trilo explained.

"That seems like a clinical answer," I mused.

"Come to Mother Teresa's," Trilo said. He led me through a stone enclosure into Mother Teresa's Home for the Dying, where her Missionaries of Charity nuns tended to the dying and suffering Nepalese who couldn't even afford the wood for their own funeral pyres. We entered the long stone building, it was perfectly clean, smelled strongly of antiseptic, and simple cots lined the walls where the infirmed laid. They called out to us. Trilo reached in his leather bag and pulled out his pile of money. Trilo offered some rupees to the nuns. "Here, to help with your work," he smiled. Trilo had a daily habit of doling out donations to all who were in need.

With a look of immense gratitude, the young South Indian nun declared, "Oh. We didn't have any money left, and no more rice and *dhal* to feed everyone, or medicine. But we knew someone would come help us!" Trilo and I were glad to be that someone. Thus started a tradition that carried on for several years. Whenever I flew from the United States back to Nepal, my Mom, Betty, would hand me a wad of bills to give to the Sisters of Charity, and thankfully US dollars went very far in the Himalayas.

As we admired the immaculately clean buildings, the Sister continued, "Many of these people are so poor their physical growth has been stunted. They couldn't develop without enough nutrition." Scratching out a life in a Nepali Himalayan village was tough. The average yearly income at the time was a measly $150. Although Nepal was one of the most economically impoverished countries in the entire world, this fact never registered in the sincere, broad smiles

43

gracing the faces of the Nepalese people.

"Come," said Trilo, "Let's see the yogis who are the most extreme, the *aghoris.*"

"How are they extreme?"

He leaned in and answered, "They live in the cremation grounds."

Trilo led me through a screen of acrid smoke billowing from the cremation *ghat* directly in front of Mother Teresa's home for the dying. Ash-smeared ascetics were sitting lotus style on the riverside next to the platform where dead human bodies wrapped in white muslin were laid atop stacks of straw. A few corpses were being consumed by crackling flames. The intense radiating heat propelled me backwards. "Take off your shoes. You can leave them there," he pointed to a crumbling brick wall where piles of cow dung paddies were stacked high to be used as fuel for the yogis' fires.

"Okay, we've got corpses, piles of shit, now what else?" I wondered.

We were about twelve feet from a platform where the eldest son of a family was freshly shaved, and wrapped in a white spun cotton cloth. Barefoot, he solemnly circumambulated the dead body stretched out on the pile of fresh straw three times. Finally overcome with emotion, he placed a lit flame on its' lips where a blob of camphor sparked and ignited the fire. I felt sorry for him, what an impossible task, to have to consign your loved one to the flames. The smell of searing human flesh made me feel like throwing up. "Why do these yogis sit by dead people they don't even know?" I asked, trying not to reveal my strong revulsion.

"They practice calming their minds by transcending feelings of pleasure and revulsion. To them, the smell of a burning body should be no different than smelling a lovely fragrant rose. They believe that this life is not real, it is just an illusion, and therefore it should not stir up strong emotions. Now bend down and the yogi will give you a mark on your third eye," Trilo explained. I bowed, and the yogi dipped his finger in the fire pit, and muttering holy *mantras* under his breath, he smeared sacred ash in the middle of my forehead, where the source of divine sight is said to be, and plopped a flower and sticky sugar sweets in my hand. I started to itch and tried to brush off the ants.

Many yogis live on the holy banks, they have renounced all worldly comforts, believing that by meditating here they will overcome suffering and realize the impermanent nature of human existence. When Trilo took me to sit with them, I could feel a deep abiding calm in their presence. They had no possessions except one change of cloth and a brass water pot, and they slept on the ground alongside a sacred fire. A trident representing Shiva's power and energy was driven into the ground at each yogi's holy fire.

Many Himalayan sages live in caves and practice yoga, a word derived from the Sanskrit root "yuj" meaning "to unite," one's soul with the divine. Mother India's saints and sages for millennia have sought to penetrate the illusory veil separating life and death, to attain spiritual liberation. And finally I was standing on this holy ground where seers through the ages had attained the mystical state of oneness.

This was decades before yoga became such a huge money making fad in the West. It now runs the gamut, and is being offered in such a variety of classes, as Georg Feurstein, the renowned author of yoga books remarked, "In every form, from Disco yoga to Elvis yoga."

Some of the yogis who lived cut off from conventional society went from antiquity to modernity overnight. One named Pagalananda, which means "crazy bliss," was the most accomplished at performing all 84 yoga postures; he lived off tips from tourists for twisting up pretzel like. Some became addicted to heroin, the freaks must have shared their bountiful stash of hard drugs with them.

Some yogis forgot their vows of celibacy, and sleeping with Western women was a real boon. I saw one well-known *naga baba* a few years later in the Delhi airport when Indira Gandhi was assassinated; a German lady had gotten pregnant by him and gave birth to his baby. Now he was going to be whisked away in the rarified comfort of a Swiss Air economy class cabin, to the "land of honey" in Europe. Not bad. He boarded the jumbo jet in his saffron robes, smeared with ashes, with his dreadlocks flowing down to the tarmac. "Hope he doesn't trip over his hair going up the stair," I thought to myself. "Hmm... if he does, is it *karma*?"

I had been staying high up in a cave in the Himalayan foothills a few years later, when a European girl shed her clothing so as to be dressed in the same fashion as the yogis who were sleeping around the enormous crackling fire. They were all clad only in loincloths, one strip of cotton. She must have craved attention; it was snowy and cold up at 16,000 feet.

This is not to say that there are not real yogis, those who truly embody the sacred teachings of Hinduism. There are, and I was fortunate to meet many. It is always up to the individual whether they will truly follow the heart of any spiritual teaching, or just pay lip service to it. Anyway it was not just Hindu yogis who longed for Western pleasures, one Buddhist Lama told me that many Tibetan lay people would ask him daily for blessings for their businesses. The *mantra* he taught them to chant was, "Money, money, more money, come quick, *swaha!"*

"I wonder if it works," I mused. Actually the international spiritual supermarket had some very funny aspects to it.

I would go to teachings where the students were supposed to be so spiritual and chill, sitting cross-legged on the floor to receive marvelous wisdom. One of them hissed at me with hate filled eyes like daggers, "Don't touch my meditation cushion or even get near it!"

"Uh oh, she must be Kali," I assumed. Kali was Lord Shiva's consort who wore a necklace of human skulls around her neck. She was a wrathful deity in the Hindu pantheon. And God – here she was living in the same leaking tent as me in the pouring rain up at Kopan Monastery on a slippery hillside on the outskirts of Kathmandu. In 1974, there were no buildings there yet. I was told that everything was your spiritual practice, and that I should show compassion to these awful rude people, they "may have been my Mother in another lifetime." I took a deep breath. "Okay, okay! Be nice, don't tell her where to get off! Don't tell her that she is an idiot!" It took a lot of compassion. Maybe more then I had?

This brilliant Buddhist teacher, Situ Rinpoche advised me, "People who would never listen to you - an American girl, about *dharma*, spiritual truth in a million years… will listen to me, because I am a Tibetan Lama. But other people will look at me and think, 'Hey, that is a shaved bald-headed guy wearing a dress (his robes) and he is weird! No way I will listen to him.' But they will listen to you, a blonde American girl, so we all have our place in communicating spiritual truth."

This was useful guidance put in cool manner, no wonder everyone called Situ Rinpoche, "the silver throated one." He had a gorgeous voice and spoke impeccable English.

In Kathmandu in those days, foreigners would walk to the main post office, dodging water buffalo and deep potholes filled with monsoon rain to pick up an aerogram, or make an international phone call. I would wait in a grindingly slow cue with jostling villagers, and then finally enter a wooden booth with a filthy glass window, securing the creaking door behind me. The contraption was supposed to provide privacy, but when the local operator finally put you through, you had to shout at the top of your lungs to be heard. By this time you were just grateful to be on a telephone. Any telephone.

"Los Angeles! Mr. Daddy, you have a trunk call from Mr. Polly," I could hear the Nepali operator authoritatively announce in her thick accent. When my parents answered the phone, I would shout at the top of my lungs into the grimy plastic handset, "Mom and Dad," commanding the full attention of the nation of Nepal. But at least it worked; I could hear my parents through our twelve-hour time zone difference, on the other side of planet Earth.

Many technological advances have occurred since that era, and now throughout the Himalayas and the vast Indian plains, multitudes of phone booths dot the landscape. Any enterprising person with infinite patience can finagle a phone in the Indian bureaucracy; hang out a shingle and post an "STD" sign. My friends and I started spotting them everywhere, and we wondered, "What is that? Venereal disease?" Such was the meaning "STD" had for us. 'Sexually transmitted disease.' But locally in India, it meant a long distance phone. Who knew?

We students were taken out to the foothills of the Kathmandu Valley, to study the Nepalese language. Our class trekked one day through the sun-kissed rice field paddies to a village home to partake in a traditional Nepali lunch.

The Nepali hosts smiled broadly, directing us to sit cross-legged on the ground. Our folded legs kept falling asleep in spite of our valiant efforts. The village family served exotic looking foods piled on banana leafs set on the ground before us, used as plates. As we ate with our right hands, they invariably would refill our plates, and it is considered rude to refuse food in a country where so many have little to eat. They also poured us the local beverage, *chang,* bubbly beer brewed from fermented barley, poured from a plastic gasoline container. Next came *chai,* the Nepali mother beamed while serving us pungent tea boiled with smoky flavored buffalo milk. A thin layer of fat floated on the top.

I exclaimed in Nepali, "*Meetocha,*" trying to tell her it was delicious.

What a mistake - she quickly refilled my glass to the rim. Just looking at the bubbles, my stomach started to revolt. After hurriedly walking back through the fields to our guesthouse, we students ran to the upper floor windows.

One of the female students screeched, "I am going to be sick!" We spent the evening hanging over the rails and retching our guts out. This was our first introduction to stomach dysentery, caused by ingesting amoebas and giardia, common in Nepal, where doe-eyed water buffaloes traipse through the gurgling mountain streams that flow down to the Kathmandu Valley. It was the first time we took Flagyl, an awful tasting antibiotic we had to ingest to kill the "sentient beings" as the local Buddhist Westerners laughingly called the hideous microorganisms that now wrecked havoc in our digestive tracks. I really learnt compassion toward all beings, by regarding these germs too, as my "brothers."

"Yuck," I thought, holding my stomach and running to our guesthouse outhouse. I had even seen a few villagers leaning way out over cliffs on the Himalayan hillsides; sanitation in Nepal was non-existent. And the choice of food in the early 1970's was very limited. The Swiss government had not yet set up a dairy; yak cheese would become popular later on, and the buffalo curds that passed for yogurt in clay cups smelled rancid.

Clean water was not available so we quickly got adept at carefully disinfecting every glass by boiling it, or plopping iodine tablets in to kill the amoebas. My personal study project involved Hindu and Buddhist art, photographing and sketching some of the intricate motifs that adorned the temples. Our semester flew by and the cultural, social, spiritual, and scholastic learning we students received was profound, so potent was Nepal's impact on the human psyche and spirit.

It was time to return to India for the trip home. Father John Ridyard, a Maryknoll priest I met there, suggested I look up Mother Teresa, who was a close friend of his in Calcutta. My friend Kathy and I decided to go. Calcutta was filled with old British colonial buildings with grand faded edifices. Despite their decay, they hinted at the past when life was genteel, rich and un-crowded. But now the city was teeming with millions of villagers who had come to escape drought and famine in the countryside. The bridge over the Hooghly, the main river was lined with beggars, and villagers who'd set up their households, inhabiting the city's pathways.

But Calcutta was still a bastion of culture; her classical music tradition and institutions of learning were unequaled on the Indian subcontinent. We checked out the Oberoi Hotel with its' disco, the Pink Elephant. Even though we managed to have fun on the town, we were existing on slim resources. We grabbed a bicycle rickshaw pulled by a painfully thin Bengali man, and piled out in front of the Salvation Army. We checked into the budget rest house, and went to our stark room with two wooden beds. Exhausted from our day exploring the city, we said good night and turned out the light. The minute it was dark, we heard loud scurrying on the floor.

"Oh God, I'm scared to put my feet down there!" Gingerly tiptoeing on the floor, and lunging quickly for the light switch, we were shocked to find gigantic rats racing in and out of our room, doing a giant loop around the Salvation Army, through a hole in the bottom of the wall. Complaining wouldn't do any good. The rat in India is considered to be Ganesh, the Elephant God's mount, so these rodents were considered sacred. Consequently we couldn't be expecting a fumigator anytime soon. But they were the size of feral cats, and sped around like Michael Schumacher in a Formula One race the entire night. We never slept a wink.

Everyone in Calcutta knew Mother Teresa, and early the next morning we headed out into the sticky climate, cautiously stepping onto the street crammed with a sea of humanity, honking dilapidated vehicles, sacred cows and pushcarts. People were camped out on broken patches of pavement, some wrapped in sheets. We treaded around them carefully and hopped onto a rickshaw pulled by a weathered bony man clad in cotton cloth cinched around his non-existent waist. Realizing how weak the rickshaw driver must be, we still knew that without us hiring him, he would not be able to provide a living for his family. We climbed up onto the cart, feeling sorry that we were so well fed and heavy, and he pulled us along, running in his split plastic sandals. His apparatus had no bicycle, as the rickshaws in Kathmandu did. He headed toward Mother Teresa's part of town, going up Bose Road to Mother House. We stopped at a plain grey four-story building accented with brown shutters. Mother Teresa had lived here since 1953, when she undertook her mission to provide for the "poorest of the poor." The inside of Mother Teresa's home was nearly empty and perfectly clean, with an alcove that held a candle and a crucifix. A smiling nun dressed in a plain white cotton habit looked up at us and uttered, "Mother is at prayer and will be back in a few minutes."

As we waited, I thought about my friend, Father John who knew Mother Teresa and had urged me to meet her. He had led a remarkable life in Africa and Mexico flying airplanes. For years, Father John had devoted himself solely to charitable grass root projects in Nepal, India, Burma and Sri Lanka, like buying sewing machines and rickshaws for villagers, to set them up in businesses. "Don't just give them fish, teach them how to fish for themselves," Father John would always tell me. He was an unsung hero to these people, building dwellings for families and clinics in third world undeveloped villages. He helped Mother Teresa when the King of Nepal refused to allow her to set up her Home for the Dying in Kathmandu. Nepal was a Hindu kingdom, and the King was considered a living incarnation of the god Vishnu, one of the Hindu trinity, so Christianity was not welcome in the country. But Father John was friendly with members of the Nepalese royal family, and he managed a very difficult feat, to get permission for Mother Teresa to set up her Sisters of Charity Kathmandu center.

Suddenly Mother Teresa was standing right before us. She grabbed my hands and held them tightly. "So, you are a friend of Father John's? How is he doing?" I was taken aback by her informality and her tiny stature; she barely came up to my mid-chest. But this pint-sized creature was a worldwide powerhouse who had once managed to walk away unscathed from a deadly plane accident in Tanzania that killed six when the aircraft crashed into a crowd of onlookers.[8] Her magnetic presence commanded rapt attention. She was clad in a white sari with three blue stripes, symbolizing the vows she had taken decades before: chastity, poverty and obedience.

"Father John is well, Mother. He sends you his regards," I replied. She spoke to us for a long time, very quietly with an interesting accent heavily spiced with years of living in India, and all the while she held my hands in her own. I felt guilty and embarrassed, thinking that she must be busy, and we were taking up her valuable time. Who were we, after all, to be showed so much kindness by Mother Teresa? I tried to leave, "Mother, please. Don't let us keep you. You must have so much to do." But she generously gestured for us to stay, and kept holding my hands. I thought, "I sure don't deserve to be treated like this."

"Where is your orphanage?" I asked her.
"Come, I will show you." She led us next door to another building in her compound. It was a long narrow cement structure. Inside it was simple, spotlessly clean and both walls were lined with cribs. Each bed had a child on it, some lying down, but most of them standing up and calling

to us from behind the safety bars surrounding their cribs. Their wistful eyes locked onto ours and followed our every move. The older children ran to us and clung to our legs with loneliness. They were so desperately poor, yet innocent and radiant, and so wanted someone to play with. We did and they yelled out happily. Their sheer numbers made it impossible for caretakers to give them enough physical affection. And Mother Teresa was managing orphanages in four large cities in India, each housing 100 children at a time, many of whom were infants, dropped off there by parents too poor to care for them. The problem was you wanted to take all the kids home, they were so darling.

This remarkable woman had dedicated her life to serving the wretched of society. Mother Teresa started her first Home for the Dying in Calcutta in 1952, in an abandoned Hindu temple, which she named Nrimal Hriday, meaning the Home of the Pure Heart.[9] She didn't ask about people's faiths when she picked them up from the gutters where they lay. The impoverished were Hindus, Christians, Muslims, Sikhs, it did not matter to Mother Teresa. When it was time for their last rites, the Hindus would be read to from the Bhagavad Gita, the Muslims from the Quran, and the Christians from the Bible. She believed that in their final hours, they deserved to die a beautiful death. As she put it, "They are all children of God."

Her unceasing passion to help the poor led to the founding of hundreds of centers throughout the world, including centers for lepers, when others were too frightened of contracting their disease, and for those suffering with AIDS.

As we were about to leave, we said our goodbyes, "Thank you so much, Mother." She leaned in close and quietly told us, "The most important thing is to love. Love until it hurts."

Kathy was going to travel back up to Nepal from India, by taking the train from Calcutta. Upon hearing this, Mother Teresa perked up. "Oh, can you do me a favor, please?"

Kathy was excited, "Of course, anything for you."

"Can you please take a box of sweets to my Sisters in Kathmandu? The Bengali milk sweets are so good and they love them."

Kathy agreed, "I'd be happy to, Mother." The next day, she braved the heaving train station platform and crammed into a bulging second-class tier car; Kathy squatted on a rusty upper berth on the Mithila Express as it pulled out of Calcutta. She peered out at the mass of humanity she was leaving behind as the train bleated its' farewell whistle. Her two-day train journey to the Nepal border began, and finally the crowds thinned out as they got further from the city. The local train stopped often in the sticky heat, taking a long time to start again. Kathy pried open the lid of the box of sweets and admired all the luscious pieces neatly nestled inside. She closed the box and put it away. The train journey droned on for hours of boredom, and finally she simply couldn't resist the sweets anymore, Kathy thought she would just sample a chocolate coconut milk sweet. She carefully broke off the edge of one piece. But by the time Kathy reached the India - Nepal border checkpoint at the steaming outpost in the jungle, she had devoured every last crumb of the delectable Bengali sweets. And man, was Kathy worried.

The train journey was followed by a two-day ride crammed onto a creaking Nepali bus for a terrifying drive along winding roads through the jungle, then climbing 4,200 feet straight up switchbacks carved into the Himalayan range. When Kathy finally reached Kathmandu, she raced out of the bus to the first sweet shop she could find on New Road, the modern upscale section of town near the King's palace. She carefully perused the glass cases smeared in fingerprints, and refilled the cardboard sweets box to deliver to the Sisters of Charity at the Home for the Dying on the bank of the sacred river. To this day I still wonder what kind of bad *karma* one would create by stealing from Mother Teresa?

Chapter 4
A Himalayan Home

A good traveler has no fixed plan, and is not intent on arriving.

-Lao Tzu

The music of the caravans runs strong in my ancestral blood, as my family had emigrated from Spain to the United States, and my grandparents and parents alike were enthusiastic travellers. My deep connection with the East had been confirmed, and the people, culture, rituals, spirituality, topography, textiles and art were all so exquisite I knew this was the place for me. After returning to the US and graduating from college that summer, I made plans to return to the Himalayas, and sold a graduation present to fund the trip.

I was settled into my humble Nepali home, happy to be part of the expat community with kindred spirits, fellow adventurers and spiritual seekers. Each morning, I'd go to the corner restaurant for papaya, being greeted by local women, smiling as they beat clothing clean against the rocks. Wild monkeys scampered around the neighborhood. The stunning snow-covered Himalayan range that encircled the Kathmandu Valley each sunrise and sunset provided a panoramic view of swirling colorful clouds, which crowned the majestic peaks, tinted pastel colors by the light. The intricately carved windows and balconies of the Valley's homes gave testimony to the intricate craftsmanship of the local artisans. The lovely Nepalese women wore vibrant hand-block printed clothing and strands of sparkling glass beads.

In those days there were still government-run hashish shops adorned with portraits of the King and Queen of Nepal benevolently smiling down upon patrons who selected from the various forms of hash - hash oil, Mandrex (Qualudes), Nepalese temple balls and Thai Buddha sticks, all elegantly displayed on tables.

Many expatriates who were known as "freaks" were

free-wheeling Westerners who made their way from Nepal down to Goa, in India, for full moon parties, often financing their jaunts by smuggling hashish from northern India, or Nepal. Another popular drug smuggling route was overland from Afghanistan, or "Hashganistan" as it was nicknamed, as it was the source of the coveted blonde hashish, which was sure to earn a boatload of *rupees.*

Since Nepal had remained isolated, it was essentially a sixteenth-century culture, with arranged marriages and other time-honored traditions, until it started to lose its in the late 1970's when international drug traders from the Golden Triangle, Burma, Thailand, and Laos began using Nepal as a transit point for their dangerous costly cargo. Sadly, some friends of mine, local street kids succumbed to heroin, ending up dead, face down in the dark dirty alleys of Freak Street. Kathmandu was transformed forever with the advent of heroin. I thought about going overland to India to meet some of the holy men and delve more deeply into the religions. With luck, perhaps I would even meet the Dalai Lama.

Chapter 5
The Dalai Lama

This is my simple religion. There is no need for temples; no need for complicated philosophy. Our own brain, our own heart is our temple; the philosophy is kindness.
                              -Tenzin Gyatso, Dalai Lama

Many years later in 2013, one sunny morning in Kathmandu at Bodhanath, a Buddhist shrine, a cripple crawled across the weathered cobblestones on all fours to the sacred monument. He set himself on fire. Karma Nyidun Gyaltso was 39 years old. The Nepali police discovered his wood crutch near his charred remains. The "Free Tibet" activist passed away after setting his body ablaze. He had purchased many butter lamps before the self- immolation.[10] He said prayers then crawled to a hidden corner to begin his sacrificial act of lighting himself on fire. This was the third time since 2011 that monks here in Nepal had burned themselves alive to protest the religious and political oppression their people had been forced to live under since the invasion of their country by the Chinese Communist regime. They were following the lead of their brethren living in Tibet. At least one hundred thirty-six Tibetans have lit themselves on fire in protest.

It was almost Christmas thirty-five years earlier when I left Bodhanath, the same Buddhist shrine. Its' white dome was sprinkled with saffron powder. The Kathmandu Valley was cold and blanketed with fog, and I traveled south to India with some Austrian friends to Bodhgaya, where the Buddha became enlightened sitting beneath the Bodhi Tree.

We took a horse drawn buggy to the bus depot. Bus stations in India are a world unto themselves where vendors sell a myriad of sweets, fruits, tobacco, and betel nuts, which are chewed for their digestive qualities. Hordes of people make their home in the stations, spreading out thin sheets on the cement floor for sleeping. The gray walls are splattered with red stains where bitter betel juice had been spat. When the bus finally arrived and we climbed on board, I was greeted by red-stained grins.

Personal space and privacy are virtually unknown in India's vast sea of endless people, a population of 1.3 billion. Many families share one room, while countless others are masters at adapting the roadside into a living space, even setting up pots for cooking. On the bus, I found tight accommodations, which seemed to affect no one else. I wondered if I would ever take on the relaxed air of the locals. Wherever you go in India you are frequently greeted with, "Englishman, what is the purpose of your visit?" or "Which is your mother country?" Everyone is eager to practice whatever little English they know. Their friendly open curiosity can be intense as they stare at you for ages. The sweetness in their faces prevents you from feeling invaded in any way.

My friend, Denise told me about one time when she had been intently stared at for three full hours by a local Indian man. She was travelling on a sweltering train across Northern India, and he watched her pensively for the entire journey, never averting his eyes even for a moment. Denise had no idea what he was looking at. He finally broke his long silence, leaning forward and seriously asking her, "Madam, what type of birth control you are using?" Shock had no time to register. Denise immediately blurted out with great hilarity, "The rhythm method!"

Reaching Bodhgaya, I contemplated the significance of this sacred place. Just a few more yards and I would step on holy ground— the Mecca of Buddhist pilgrimage— and stand before the Bodhi Tree under which Gautama Buddha reached enlightenment.

Strolling past the many Buddhist carved stone monuments surrounding the Bodhi Tree, a fragrant breeze caressed me. The tree overarched the area, mighty yet gentle, dominant yet humble. I approached the tree with reverence, marveling how its hundreds of branches reach out in the ten directions mentioned in Buddhist cosmology. Deities represent each direction of space, each full of awakened awareness. Colorful new as well as tattered prayer flags hanging on its' knotty arms waved in the gentle breeze. Buddha himself said, "Throughout the fields of awakening of the ten directions, there is only this single Path of Reality."[11]

The leaves of the Bodhi Tree were heart-shaped. It is still perhaps the most honored tree in the world. It stands nobly next to the gloriously tall, sculptured Maha Bodhi temple whose spire stretches so high it seems to pierce the heavens from where celestial beings cheered the young prince Siddhartha, as he escaped the trappings of royal life in his father's kingdom in search of ultimate reality.

I now felt these same beings caressing me, along with the rest of the seekers who arrived at this sacred spot so weary from the world, eager to discover the peace that is within. "If only I can just be mentally still and meditate," my mind wished. "Still enough to feel the bliss." I sat down, inwardly surrendering to being fully present to the moment. Buddhists from Sri Lanka, Cambodia, Japan, Laos, and every corner of the earth gathered in the quietude here. An Indian pilgrim in a state of deep devotion tied fresh prayer flags to a branch where flags of all colors gently fluttered, pale and worn.

Buddhism came into being 500 years before Christ, when a young Hindu prince named Siddhartha Gautama, who lived in the southern region of Nepal, felt a deep, gnawing dissatisfaction with his worldly life. Ever since a holy seer had foretold of Siddhartha's eventual renunciation, his father sheltered him from all suffering, especially old age, sickness, and death. But one day he unexpectedly came upon an old man who lay dying at the side of the road. This encounter with old age, pain, and the temporary nature of life shocked Siddhartha so acutely that he abruptly left the palace, leaving behind his wife, son, parents, and his luxurious life in the palace to discover how to go beyond human suffering.

Seeking out the most acclaimed Hindu mendicants of his time, he joined a group of ascetics who had attained a high degree of discipline of mind and body. However, the path of asceticism brought him close to his own death from neglecting the body's requirements. Not having achieved enlightenment, Siddhartha came to the realization that all of the physical needs he was renouncing did not lead to freeing oneself from ceaseless rounds on the wheel of birth and death. Siddhartha left the group of wandering monks. Traveling to Bodhgaya, he sat beneath the Bodhi Tree refusing to move until he reached realization and became the Buddha, or "Enlightened One." Out of his determination was birthed what is known as the Middle Path, which teaches that one need not practice asceticism of the body to reach *nirvana*, but that enlightenment is our natural state that can be discovered by turning within in meditation.

Buddha's path to enlightenment is based on the Four Noble Truths: Life is full of suffering, attachment is the origin of suffering, the cessation of suffering is attainable, and the path to the end of suffering is mindfulness. Buddhist philosophy had no icon to worship, since God was a metaphysical construct of man's mind. Buddhism, is non-theistic, and is not considered to be a religion but rather a philosophy for working with one's mind. Buddhism flourished and spread throughout India, even as far as the Persian Empire.

We friends took part in the same ritual practiced by millions of pilgrims who had come before us, reverently circumambulating the sacred tree in a clockwise direction. I chanted *"Om mani padme hum,"* meaning, *"Hail to the jewel in the lotus."* It refers to the enlightened consciousness that lies in each of us. Circumambulation is a common practice in Tibetan Buddhism, symbolizing turning the *Wheel of Dharma,* the Buddha's teachings of compassion and loving-kindness.

Loosely translated as "mind protector," a *mantra* is like a prayer that strengthens the connection between the practitioner and the deities that represent different qualities of our selves, when enlightened. One of the Buddhist teachers I've come to know, Khen Rinpoche Lobzang Tsetan, explained this *mantra* to me.

"Ohm mani padme hum, is especially powerful because it contains the essence of Buddha's teachings. Each syllable represents one of the *Six Perfections* that are cultivated by practitioners."

"Om helps us perfect our generosity."

"Ma strengthens the practice of ethics."
"Ni helps achieve tolerance and patience."
"Päd enhances the quality of perseverance."
"Me helps perfect concentration."
"Hum, the final syllable, helps us achieve the greatest perfection of all: wisdom."

I tried to stay mindful of this while walking around the Bodhi Tree. The Maha Bodhi temple was built to honor the place of Buddha's enlightenment in 531 BCE. I admired its' stone walls which were studded with shrines of carved *dakinis,* shapely female deities who were enlightened ones.

Overhead, burnt orange stained the Indian sky, and we all found it hard to leave the gentle tranquility beneath the Bodhi Tree. But there was a nearby cave where the Buddha had meditated, so I started walking on the deserted road with my Austrian friends. The brisk night air crackled with supernatural electricity, and with each step, my bare feet caressed the soft earth. I tried to practice "walking meditation" by mindfully placing one foot in front of the other, focusing on each movement, each breath, to stay in the present moment.

After an hour of ambling along, realizing that 2,000 years of pilgrims had traversed this terrain, we crossed the sloping hillside and picked our way through thorny brush illuminated by the moon. Stars twinkled overhead while wading knee-deep across a narrow river, emerging from the water to be greeted by a few viciously howling wild dogs. Managing to escape unharmed, save the stones that scraped our feet, the walking meditation was intruded on by an acute awareness of bodily discomfort.

I scrambled up a steep dirt path to where the dark cave entrance loomed before us. This was where Siddhartha had meditated for seven years at the beginning of his quest for enlightenment. It felt as though we were surrounded by the presence of innumerable invisible beings at this holy sanctuary. Switching on my flashlight, the stream of light illuminated interior walls of gleaming black rock. There was an altar of tall Buddhist deities. A wrathful stood guard on the left, and the peaceful guard on the right. The hands and fingers of the statues were in *mudras*, symbolic gestures conveying qualities of the Divine.

An acrid smell permeated the dank air. "Phew, this is intense, I hope it lightens up," I said.

Seppi started laughing, "It is to test your revulsion. *Tantric practice!*"

Uschi agreed, "Remember, all smells are just phenomena. No matter how disgusting, they are really no different then a rose." *Tantra* is a path to spiritual realization whereby one does not reject the body's feelings, such as revulsion and desire, but actually employs them, to realize that everything physical is illusory.

"Okay, got it," I agreed, trying to put their lofty goals into practice. Because the Buddha himself meditated in this cave, many pilgrims pay homage to him here, evidenced by the rancid yak butter lamps left as offerings. The cave radiated such peace it was tangible. "Tonight I will sleep alongside these Buddhas," I invoked the blessings of the Buddha: "May auspiciousness come to illuminate the world." Repeating *mantras*, I finally fell asleep on the hard cave floor.

Riding in bumper-to-bumper traffic along the dusty, congested Grand Trunk Road leaving Bodhgaya, we headed for Varanasi on the river Ganges, passing grazing water buffalos lazily wallowing in reflecting ponds. The pools were choked with a riot of pink lotus flowers. I thought about how the purity of the lotus was represented in many of the spiritual paths in India, and how I'd often seen Hindu, Buddhist and Jain deities sitting upon them. Suddenly I spotted a completely naked, bare-shaved man walking barefoot on the dirt footpath at the side of the road in the scorching sun. A single line of white-robed devotees followed closely behind him, heads bowed in devotion, dust swirling up from the ground each time their feet touched the path.

The juxtaposition of this nude man who had embraced the ancient hermit's tradition in the midst of the 21st century's stark modernity was startling. He trudged on, oblivious to the loud honking trucks and cars that were jammed in the frenzy of uncontrollable traffic. Lost in his inner world of utter stillness, he stepped along the Grand Trunk Road just as if it were centuries earlier. In a dimension of timelessness he passed the shimmering lotus ponds whose vibrant pink flowers peeked up at the sky. They, like all else on this earth, held no interest for him. His immersion was beyond all this physical realm had to offer, no matter how beautiful or seductive. This monk was of the Digambar sect, which means, "sky clad." His body was attired in nothing but space itself; the clouds were his clothing.

A few hundred miles from here, Jainism came into being 2,500 years ago when its founder, Mahavira, attained spiritual liberation, about. His practice of asceticism was to such a degree that he journeyed on foot for over thirty years until he finally fasted to death.[12]

The word "Jain" means the descendants of one who has broken the chain of rebirths. Jains venerate twenty-four *Mahaviras*, or prophets, and believe that to overcome negative *karma* one must lead a devout life so that the soul can attain liberation. Jains practice vegetarianism because *ahimsa*, non-violence, is of paramount importance. Some Jains are so non-violent they will not even step on an insect. Instead they use a small broom to gently brush them from their path as they walk. They wear a cloth tied across their mouth so that they will not inhale and kill any small creatures.

A few months after my visit to the Bodhi Tree, I was walking up a hill to meet the Dalai Lama at his exiled home in the Himalayan foothills with a group of health professionals. For the last several years, I'd wanted to meet him, and now because of my job, it was going to happen.

I had begun to escort tour groups throughout Asia, some were focused on health and spirituality, still others were for the world's top luxury travel company.

"Om mani padme hum, om mani padme hum, om mani padme hum" - a line of Tibetan pilgrims muttered mantras, meaning, "May the jewel in the lotus liberate us." They were snaking along the narrow dirt footpath to the Dalai Lama's residence in Dharamsala, north India. His name, Tenzin Gyatso means *"ocean of bliss."* Clad in traditional woolen garments, adorned with jewelry of coral and turquoise, the Tibetans snuck curious peeks at us Westerners.

We finally arrived at the gate of the Dalai Lama's residence, where the Indian Army security officers carefully scrutinized the guest list for our names. Even in the 1970's, years before he had won the Nobel Peace Prize, the Dalai Lama's importance as the temporal leader of Tibet meant that the Indian Government carefully guarded him. We were searched and stood in line expectantly, clutching our prayer scarves, folded in seven sections to represent the pure mind, the traditional offering to high teachers.

It was full moon day in October in upper McLeod Ganj, a quaint British hill station. At 7,000 feet, dense pine forests blanketed the hillsides and vast plains spread out below. Our group had been traveling all over the subcontinent - exploring Hindu, Buddhist, Sikh and Jain temples, a Christian church and a Jewish synagogue in Goa. We had met religious leaders and health experts in Sikkim, Darjeeling, Kashmir, Varanasi, and Amritsar including Hindu yogis, Tibetan Buddhist lamas and Mother Teresa's Sisters of Charity.

We were at the last stop on our itinerary, attending private seminars with the Dalai Lama's personal physician, Yeshe Dondon. Our group was comprised of mostly nurses and psychiatrists who received continuing education credit. We climbed up the steep hill to the residence of His Holiness, who is believed to be the incarnation of Chenrezig, the Buddha of Compassion.

Thousands of Tibetan refugees had come here, founding "Little Lhasa" around the Dalai Lama's home. The Chinese Communist regime occupied Tibet in 1959, killing and imprisoning thousands, as they began to decimate Tibet's culture. His Holiness was forced to flee for his life. Under cover of darkness, braving the dangerous journey across the treacherous snow-covered Himalayan passes, he fled to freedom in India.

In Dharamsala, what little was left of Tibetan culture was thriving in exile. Monasteries were built to keep alive threatened philosophical traditions that were thousands of years old. The Tibetan Government in exile was headquartered here, on the same hill as the Dalai Lama's residence. Countless refugees circumambulated it each day in prayer, shuffling along spinning prayer wheels, passing heaps of stones that had been carved with the sacred mantra.

We solemnly climbed our way up the hill to the entrance of the residence of His Holiness. I didn't know what to expect. My heart was beating fast. And there was the Dalai Lama, standing on the porch, the brilliant rays of the sun bathing him in light. I waited patiently in line behind my friends and at last it was my turn. His Holiness looked directly into my eyes, then down at my hands, then again into my eyes. His intense gaze pierced my being profoundly. I started to feel a surge of divine energy overwhelm me. I pressed my palms together in a *namaste* greeting, and he took my hands in his. Then unexpectedly he squeezed my hands very hard, so they hurt, and laughed heartily. I thought it was an unusual gesture. Then he let go. I continued down the line.

Afterwards, we had a discussion with him in his reception room. The kindness His Holiness maintained when speaking of the people who had invaded his country made a deep impression on me. He spotlighted non-violence as his government in exile's approach to engaging Beijing. There were similarities between the Tibetans' suffering under Chinese oppression and that of the Jewish people during the Nazi regime. There have been several symposiums when the two cultures have compared their Diasporas and shared what they have learned to keep their cultures alive in the face of such terrible repression.

As I walked back down the hill, a spontaneous feeling of pure bliss arose in me. The meeting with the Dalai Lama seemed like a capsule experience beyond time and space. I sunk down on a wall at the side of the dirt footpath to ponder this. The majestic Himalayan foothills framed the town and it was gorgeous, but I felt a huge void inside. Tears welled up in my eyes, the emptiness made me cry. Yet it was not out of sorrow, but from the emptiness itself. I realized that if one came from this place of joy, deep within, then every moment of life would be like an act of worship, filled with a glorious Presence. I was finally in touch with what I'd been searching for. This was what all the faiths were talking about…at least here was a taste of it.

Our China Airways plane sharply dropped 1,000 feet precipitously. I gulped, we passengers all shot each other frightened glances, it was a bumpy ride. It was 1981 and I was excitedly sitting on a flight to Lhasa, the capital of Tibet, going from Chengdu in China. The flight offered a panorama of stunning views over the highest Himalayan ranges. Gazing out from the aircraft for two hours, it seemed as if you could reach out your hand and touch the jagged peaks of ice comprising the perpetually snow-covered highest mountain range on earth. Enormous puffy white clouds perched like crowns on their pinnacles, and blanketed the piercing blue sky. It was 1981, and parts of Tibet had just been opened to foreign tourism. Living in the Himalayan region, I had gazed upon this Shangra-La with rapt curiosity for years, and jumped at the opportunity to journey there. It was a dream come true. With a couple of friends, I took a train from Hong Kong to begin the journey to Tibet. Nevertheless, wherever foreigners went in China, the Chinese Government Travel Agency governed our movements with an iron fist.

The crew of the Chinese airliner, like all flights here, only served sugary drinks, cheap candy and cookies. Due to cloud cover, the flight left at 6:00 AM, and my heart leapt with anticipation when I saw the stewardess coming down the aisle pushing a cart.

"Thank you so much, I am starving," I exclaimed. She handed me a syrupy glass of perfume tasting juice and a cheap plastic key chain, every flight in the People's Republic gave you one in lieu of food.

Gazing out the window, there was an enormous range of peaks as far as the eye could see. All of this, scientists maintain, was once covered with ocean, as evidenced by sediment and marine fossils millions of years old. The Indian tectonic plate was rising as it pressed against the Eurasian plate, causing the Himalayan range, along with the Tibetan plateau to rise over 10 mm annually.[13] Below us were the huge gorges of the Yangtze River.

I went down the stairs and stepped off the plane. When my feet hit the solid ground of the airstrip, it felt as though I had never disembarked from the flight. The elevation of Tibet is 12,500 feet. I felt I was still airborne. When I brought tour groups here, we dispensed oxygen pillows for them to suck on when they got altitude sickness. The air was so thin that a pain pierced through my skull. We were loaded onto a cold, dilapidated bus for the creaking four- hour drive from the military airfield to the legendary town of Lhasa.

"Pitu, pitu," my Chinese seatmate was sucking on sunflower seeds and he continuously spit the shells on my lap. The ride through the barren high desert felt even longer. I maintained polite ignorance, figuring you never knew who might be an undercover spy for the Chinese government.

We sped past villagers sprawled out face down on the ground, prostrating themselves along the road to Lhasa. They had donned kneepads of leather to cushion their skin from the constant up and down scraping motion, and had burlap strapped onto their palms that touched the ground in devotion as they rose up straight, then went flat down to the asphalt and stretched out, nose to the ground, repeatedly. The zeal glowed in their faces. Hills were carved with the sacred mantra, *"Ohm mani padme hum,"* meaning, *"hail to the jewel in the lotus."* Prayer flags draped from the rocks and trees fluttered in the wind. Ever since the Chinese invaded this land fifty years ago, the Tibetan people have struggled valiantly to keep their religion and culture alive. China attempted to eradicate their heritage, decimating most of the scared Buddhist places. Since then, a torrent of Han Chinese settlers has made the Tibetans a minority in their own land.

For the first time, I was witnessing with my own eyes the horrific devastation wreaked on Tibet by the Chinese occupation. I visited the monasteries around Lhasa, and in the towns of Gyantse and Xigatse. The institutions that once housed thousands of monks now were almost deserted. They were like living museums, with only a scattering of monks remaining. All that remained of Gandan monastery were fragments of walls looking as if the place had undergone scores of aerial bombing raids. We were followed by Chinese men clad in drab Chairman Mao suits as we walked through the few shell-shocked walls still standing. The local monks would whisper the meaning of the deities depicted in the cloth paintings that gazed down at us from the soot-stained temple walls. They could be imprisoned if discovered discussing religious iconography with tourists.

Tibetan culture was based on compassion and for centuries, all the country's resources were devoted to the quest for enlightenment. The population of this mystical land had turned centuries earlier from war to contemplation. Giving a son to the monastery to be a monk was a custom followed by many families. The culture was almost entirely devoted to Divine pursuits. The Dalai Lama was revered as its spiritual head. By example, he led the land.

At Lhasa's Jokhang temple, scores of Tibetans circumambulated the building in a clockwise direction, deep in prayer, *mantras* fluttering from their lips. Their fingers paused on each rosary bead, as they counted the repetitions. Devotees filled the courtyard, prostrating to the ground with each mantra. They would arise, advance a couple steps, and began again. Some had prostrated like this all the way from their villages, across the rugged Tibetan plateau, sometimes taking months to reach this holy spot. With every touch of their foreheads to the ground, their arduous practice was a purification. They dedicated the merit thus earned to the Three Jewels - the *Buddha*, the *dharma*, teachings, and the *sangha*, the community of believers. Finally inside, they would prostrate before the gold and silver statue of the Sakyamuni Buddha. Witnessing their society where living one's religion was so deeply imbedded made a strong impression on me.

A soot-covered Tibetan man standing in line gestured to me. He pulled out a picture of the Dalai Lama from his furry yak skin coat so that I could have a peek, careful that no one could see him. His eyes twinkled as he pushed the portrait back into the folds. I nodded to him aware of the risk he'd taken. Just having the photo in his possession was punishable by imprisonment, torture, and even execution by the brutal regime. Tenzin Gyatso is the only living link to a tradition of revered leaders stretching back to 1391, the birth of the first Dalai Lama.[14]

Inside the shrine, dozens of flickering yak butter lamps provided the sole lighting for the giant bronze Buddhas who had held court here for millennia. The odor that filled my nostrils was so putrid, I held my breath trying not to inhale it, afraid I might throw up. "What secrets did these Buddhas know," I wondered, looking at the endless line of pilgrims with semi-precious gemstones braided in their hair and sheepskins wrapped around their bodies, just as they had for centuries. In the semi-darkness I could see the devotion in their eyes; they gazed at me curiously. The sanctity that permeated the Jokhang was the hallmark of their civilization.

I strolled through the centuries old Jokhang bazaar, crammed with prayer wheels, turquoise and coral silver jewelry and artifacts. I did not realize just how lucky I was to be here. Years later in 2014, Robert Thurman, who was the first Western Tibetan Buddhist monk to take initiation from the Dalai Lama, wrote about the ongoing dismantling of the Jokhang Temple and its' surroundings in Lhasa,[15] the destruction of what Tibet House describes as "the very heart of Tibetan culture."

Thurman implores lovers of freedom, culture and faiths, to "...start an AVAAZ petition about, write congressman about – do something in whatever way – is the current communist government plan in Lhasa to destroy the Jokhang Cathedral neighborhood with its famous circumambulation streets in order to build shopping malls. It is truly a dagger plunged into the spiritual heart of Tibet. That cathedral and those old buildings have withstood 1,500 years of hard history, earthquakes, fire, flood, etc. and they represent the miraculous potential goodness in reality at the heart of the culture. They are a UNESCO World Cultural Heritage site. The already-under-way scheme to destroy them is truly culture-cidal, which you know is actually genocidal."[16]

Feeling the 13th centuries of Buddhism that had permeated this intensely spiritual place, I gazed up at the Potala Palace, where the Dalai Lama lived until he had to flee the country. With its' gilded towers and roofs, the 17th century Potala reigned over the entire valley, its' nine stories, 200,000 Buddha images, and 1,000 chambers that once housed thousands of monks. A steep climb up an ancient staircase and I reached the summit to view the Lhasa Valley stretching out below me. I explored prayer rooms and chambers of sacred statues and relics that echoed with emptiness. The ghosts of yesteryear seemed to inhabit the palace. A few devotional objects were all that remained. It had been turned into a museum. The Dalai Lama's apartment was hung with *thanka* paintings, and sacred frescos were painted on the walls, but he now lived far away from here, in exile.

Descending deep into the palace's damp basement, I ventured into the shrine room where enormous bronze statues of each of the Dalai Lama's fourteen incarnations stared at me; every one fashioned to look exactly like the leader it represented. They contained the relics of the entire lineage of the past temporal/spiritual leaders of this storied land of snows, Tibet. Here on the roof of the world had lived the Dalai Lama, who I had been so fortunate to meet in Dharamsala, Tenzin Gyatso, who embodied such a spiritual force for good in the world. The fact that the Tibetan people were not allowed to fully express their religion was not lost on me.

We had invited the handful of Western tourists who had made it up to this "forbidden Shangri-La" to come over for a Thanksgiving meal, compliments of whatever canned food we were able to buy in the slim picking of the Beijing Chinese Friendship store, which mostly stocked cheap candy. This was decades before China's modernization, and there was virtually no good food available. The morning was cold and dewy in downtown Lhasa's high elevation. That night we danced exuberantly in the faded Chinese Guest House for Communist party cadre, to Motown.

Our party was a great success, except for the over-exertion that caused us to have altitude sickness the next morning, debilitating headaches and fatigue. I grudgingly rose from bed, and stepped on the filthy carpet, pulling on clothes in the freezing cold. Peeking out of the window, I could see the usual morning scene. Daily at our Guest House was a line up of Tibetans, Chinese, and tourists clamoring with the tickets they had bought to take steaming hot showers in our outhouse. But today it was still dark as I pulled on my one-dollar Chinese canvas flats and shuffled out the door with friends. The walk to Vulture's Peak would take almost an hour. Only an occasional rooster broke the pre-dawn stillness, the lanes were deserted. Pungent smoke emanating from morning cooking fires curled above the low, flat roof houses. We had to walk to the outskirts of Lhasa to witness the Sky Burial.

One of the central themes of Buddhist philosophy is impermanence. The seeming opposites of birth and death are often meditated upon in Tibet. One Tantric, or unorthodox practice involves contemplating your own body as a skeleton, with its flesh hanging off. Definitely foreign to the Western mind is this "celestial burial," one of four methods for disposing of human bodies. Depending upon the family tradition, a corpse can be buried, cremated, or drowned in water. Some families engage in this animistic ritual of chopping up the dead and feeding them to the vultures. High in Tibet, the ground is so dry and rock-hard that burial can be problematic. My friends suggested that I go see this ritual. I didn't want to, but thought it might be an important experience. They explained, "It's another way of helping other sentient beings when a human body has served its purpose."

We padded along leaving Lhasa behind, making our way to a rocky dirt path that gradually wound up hill. As the morning light increased, a cock crowed and daily life began to stir. The sun rose, lessening the brisk chill in the air, as the aroma of cooking faintly reached us.

We passed a rock face that was carved with *mantras*. Then, rounding a bend in the path, we heard the chanting of singsong prayers. Faded prayer flags stuck to thorny bushes. A few Buddhist monks huddled together burning piles of pungent incense, reciting prayers from oblong books nestled on their laps. One old monk in a maroon cap sat hunched over on the ground, his bell and *dorje*, thunderbolt symbol spread out on tattered cloth before him. He beat a small two-sided drum and its "rat-a-tat-tat" punctuated the bracing morning air.

Just beyond the group loomed a gigantic, flat granite black rock. On top in a semicircle, the corpses of six human bodies were laid out, covered with weathered burlap. Each cadaver's head was tethered by rope to a wooden post driven into the rock's center. The boulder was pitted with deep pockmarks where human bones had been pulverized by mallets for hundreds of years.

A crackling fire flickered, where the waiting attendants warmed themselves as they knelt sharpening huge knives, loudly slurping yak butter tea from foggy glasses, and swapping stories. High above, on the crest of a steep cliff that rose sharply behind the rock, silhouettes of dozens of gigantic ravenous vultures perched, impatiently awaiting their impending feast. As the first rays of the rising sun hit the boulders, the men readied themselves, fastening aprons over their traditional Tibetan garb. Brandishing knives and mallets, they sauntered over to the dead to begin their grisly task. They stripped the cloth coverings from the naked bodies, revealing stiff corpses tinged grayish blue. They systematically began dissecting them, each man made an insert, and then grabbed the skin, stripping it off the skeleton, elastic-like. Next the corpses were dismembered as a Tibetan priest chanted supplications for the souls of the dead who were passing through the *bardo*, the dimension the soul transits for three days and nights when it is unsure of what comes next. The Tibetans believe this is when we all face our most frightening visions and ghosts, and the things that we did while alive on Earth.

The workers piled up the dismembered legs and arms, while the main torsos were kept separate with the entrails reserved for last. Some choice bits were tossed to the vultures that eyed them expectantly. The Tibetans sang, sucking on pungent Chinese cigarettes as they expertly hammered the bones with mallets into fine powder, ensuring that every morsel would be consumed, thus freeing the departed souls to take rebirth. It was also considered another way of helping sentient beings after a human body has served its purpose.

As a small crowd of tourists gathered to gawk at the gut -wrenching spectacle, I became sickened at the disgusting odor wafting from the rock, when an American next to me revealed he was a physician. He smiled, "This reminds me of medical school when I was assigned my cadaver." His words didn't make me feel any better.

The butchers continued to occasionally fling scraps of human flesh to the vultures, which swept down near the giant boulder to claim them. The muttering of prayers continued. The sweet fragrance of burning incense mixed with the odor of putrefying flesh, almost made me pass out cold.

The doctor informed me, "There are so many bodies today because it's Tuesday. Traditionally, the Sky Burial is not performed on certain days of the week, so they stack up."

"No wonder we hit the jackpot," I remarked. Suddenly one of the butchers hurled a human heart in the air to summon the waiting pack of vultures. As soon as the organ left his hand, the scavengers swarmed over the rock's surface. Each bird weighed; over 80 pounds due to such abundant food. As the Tibetans tossed the remaining flesh to the birds, they yelled at me to move out of danger. One of them smilingly approached me and shook my hand. I noticed that his apron was covered with clinging bits of human flesh; this was all in a normal days work.

I was reminded how my own human life was just temporary and illusory, and can be snatched away at any moment. The importance of trying to be ready for death at any time, by living the truth underpinning all religious philosophies, loving kindness, seemed so important. The piercing clang of the bell by the Tibetan monk suddenly cut right through my thoughts, transporting me beyond this time and space where I stood surrounded by a clutch of bystanders, and connecting me to the infinite. "Phew," I breathed deeply, grateful for the release of so many heavy emotions.

Facing one's own impermanence is at the core of spiritual practice. It underlines how our physical existence is short lived and cannot be taken for granted. So I thought to myself, as I watched the vultures hungrily scoop up human remains, "I best get on with it and do something meaningful with my life." In the West by contrast, we are shielded from death, we don't encounter cremation grounds when we are out walking around. Nor do we pass processions in public, bearing the departed on litters strewn with marigolds. We don't what to be morose, but it is healthy to be in touch with our vulnerability. We are in this human vehicle for such a short time, and it is up to the creator's divine plan when we may leave it.

Although Tibet was an inspiring place to visit, the people there were not free to express their true feelings, nor did they have the freedom to worship as they saw fit. This made me appreciate my own freedom even more and not take it for granted. A few years earlier in 1981, I had visited Burma, also ruled by a Communist regime, and witnessed a similar situation. Although Buddhist temples were everywhere, and lines of monks snaked through the streets carrying begging bowls, local people would surround me, desperately hungry for any outside stimulation, pleading to talk.

Today in the 21st century, the crackdown in Tibet continues. The Chinese government labels His Holiness "a splittist." While living in exile, he ceaselessly works for his country to be treated as an autonomous region of Tibet. People are still being tortured. Yet the world's highest railroad has been constructed to carry Chinese passengers to Lhasa, a policy of population transfer. So many Han Chinese have immigrated to Tibet, that the Tibetan identity and language is all but eradicated, and Tibetans have become a minority in their homeland. Tibetan language is not taught in schools, Chinese is. Carnival rides and brothels have been built directly in front of the Potala Palace, the Dalai Lama's residence.

Over 1,200,000 Tibetans have been killed during the Chinese occupation of their country, through torture, execution, murder, starvation, and suicide. The systematic dismantling of their culture continues unabated. However the faith of the Tibetans is hard to destroy though, no matter how difficult their situation is.

Such is life under a regime that is anti-religion. To experience such repression was a real wake up call.

Cho Oyu is the world's sixth highest peak. It is nestled near the Tibet-Nepal border, nineteen miles from Mt. Everest. On September 30, 2006, a group of Tibetans was crossing a nearby pass, trying to flee the country. Suddenly Chinese border guards brutally opened fire and shot a nun dead. She was Kelsen Natso, seventeen years old, and was en route to Dharamsala, seeking a new life in liberty as a refugee. This type of incident may happen often, but on this particular day, a group of mountain climbers witnessed and photographed the savage attack. They[17] reported it to the world.

Although Zhang Qingli, the Tibet Autonomous Region Party Chief recently categorized the Chinese Communist Party as a "parent" and a "living Buddha" to the Tibetan people,[18] demonstrations against their rule continue. In June 2013, at a teaching attended by 3,000 monks in Eastern Tibet, a nun, Wangcheng Dolma, set herself on fire. The Chinese police immediately intensified their crackdown in the region. She was one of 121 Tibetans who have self-immolated in protest[19] against the regime that won't allow them to practice their religion. Sadly, it is the only way that people who have been living under such tyranny for fifty-five years can fight back; rather then hurting others, they take extreme suffering upon themselves. The government closely monitors tourists so that images of Tibetans lighting themselves on fire are not snapped by phones and cameras, and dispersed around the world. Following such desperate actions, the Chinese government institutes a blanket ban on foreigners visiting Tibet.

There is still hope the situation will improve and Tibet will regain its freedom. The Dalai Lama and the Tibetan people remain steadfast in their commitment to non-violence and their attitude of compassion toward the Chinese people.

Robert Thurman explained to me, "Buddhism is primarily an educational system, rather than merely a religion, because in order to get away from one's egotistical sense of self - being the center of the universe, a re-education is required. That re-education is the equivalent of seeing through the illusory ways in which we think about and relate to ourselves." Robert's words aptly echoed those of his teacher's, the Dalai Lama, "The sense of genuine identification with other beings, automatically breeds the kind of compassion that feels the feelings of other beings."

His words reminded me of the Golden Rule of Christianity, and how its' message is so similar to the core values of other faiths. The concept of, "Treating others as we would like ourselves to be treated," was rooted in compassion, and in selflessness. This is the heart of tolerance and respect.

Instances of Buddhist practitioners being violent have flared up recently in peaceful countries like Thailand, Sri Lanka and Myanmar. In **Thailand,** several Buddhist monks have appealed for aggression. Since 2004, the Thai government has converted some Buddhist monasteries into militant outposts and commissioned military monks and vigilante squads.

Lately Myanmar has suffered a great deal of Buddhist violence. The Democratic Karen Buddhist Army is a militant organization active in the region since 1992. Monks and terrorists have engaged in ethnic terror attacks against the Rohingya and other Muslim factions. In 2012, over 200 people were killed and tens of thousands displaced. According to Human Rights Watch, the government and authorities displaced 125,000 Rohingya and other Muslims in the region. They promote a "just war ideology" and have organized an unofficial police squadron to monitor Christian missionaries and Muslim power. In 2013 a Buddhist horde attacked a mosque in Colombo.

In Japan, the Ikkō-shū Buddhist sect has also promoted violence.

One early morning in July 2013, at the Bodhi Tree where Buddha reached enlightenment, in Bodhgaya, India, bombs exploded shattering the tranquility. I never could have imagined that terrorists would detonate nine explosives at this sacred pilgrimage site. Two monks and three people sustained serious injuries. Suspects are the Indian *Mujahedeen* or Myanmar terrorists, who may have been targeting Buddhists in retaliation for committing violent acts against Muslims. [20] Inscriptions were scrawled on the cylinders filled with ammonium nitrate and RDX.

Chapter 6
Through the Khyber Pass

Let there be no compulsion in religion.

- Qur'an

"*Danger, he who enters here. Do not leave the main road.*" A signboard on the side of the road had an ominous warning, alluding to the Pass's violent history and reputation. I was relieved to be accompanied by five other foreigners. A young blonde American traveler like me gazing out the window of a funky overland Volkswagen van, felt extremely vulnerable.

"*Assalaam alaikum*", the bearded border guard brandished his weapon as he sized me up. I smiled back meekly, terrified inwardly. For centuries bandits had used these vertical cliffs to hide, as they exacted tolls on all who passed through the fabled Khyber Pass. Camel caravans had crisscrossed the Khyber, ferrying luxury goods like silk and aromatic spices from the Far East to Persia and lands far beyond.

The faiths had traversed it too, Buddhist monks walked the Khyber from Pakistan to Afghanistan, and it was through this Pass in 997 AD, that Muslim conquerors with their armies brought Islam to India. The Pass was used for millennia by military campaigns to invade the Asian continent.

Lined with the Hindu Kush's sheer cliffs and a few medieval forts, this pass gave rise to paralyzing fear deep in my heart. Even though it was 1976, everyone knew its' history. Seeing the local bearded tribesmen all carrying rifles and looking so fierce, I realized immediately the tribal people of the northwest frontier were not to be trifled with. In 326 BCE Alexander the Great found this out, as did the Aryans who took this route to India in 1,600 BCE.

I noticed a dramatic difference here, leaving India to traverse Pakistan and Afghanistan, I had now entered Islamic countries, and the cultures were markedly different. You could not miss the influence of Islam on the art, architecture and people.

Living in the East offered enticing adventures in all directions. Each year I would try to go to at least one new country, as well as other regions of India. The neighboring lands were romantic sounding locales like Burma, Darjeeling, Laos, Bali, Bhutan, and I would jump at any opportunity to visit them and investigate the faith traditions practiced in each. The overland travelers I'd speak with made Afghanistan sound so exotic, and the fact that one would drive along the Grand Trunk Road, one of Asia's longest arteries that links the east and west of the subcontinent, was too good to pass up. Over 2,000 years old, the highway begins at the Ganges, stretches through Bangladesh, and all the way through Pakistan. Once it was once dotted with caravanserai, and troops and goods plied along it as they made their way through the formidable Khyber Pass.

Rudyard Kipling had described this important artery in his novel, *Kim*, "The Grand Trunk Road is a wonderful spectacle. It runs straight, bearing as without crowding India's traffic for fifteen hundred miles – such a river of life exists as nowhere else in the world."

Now here at the Khyber Pass, I saw foreboding looking Pakistani and Afghani tribesmen in giant turbans balancing Kalashnikov rifles on their strong shoulders, fiercely standing guard. The town of Landikotal in Pakistan was the final stop before Afghanistan. Fruit stalls tantalized me from the sides of the road, stacked high with delectable apricots, pomegranates, and pistachios.

Driving through the treacherous Khyber, we soon reached the highest point of the infamous 28-mile long road. My ears popped, this gateway to Afghanistan led to Kabul, the capital city, with Chicken Street - the tourist mecca. Our alcohol had already been confiscated at the Pakistan border when we entered, it was not allowed in these Islamic countries. It was 1976, before the Russian invasion, and the Afghan culture, buildings, and lifestyle was still intact. Already the locals did not care for their northern neighbors, referring to them as "Ruskees." Here in the teashops, thick Bukhara carpets were stacked a few feet high and proud Pashtun tribesmen perched upon them drinking chai and devouring *Kabuli naans,* three foot long perforated crispy flat wheat breads pulled out of hot brick ovens, crusty and piping hot, by dexterous bakers wielding long wooden paddles. The bread would be topped with delicious fresh yogurt, tempting strawberries and drizzled with fragrant honey from towering glass jars lining the teashop counters. The men's chiseled faces featured high cheek -bones, handlebar mustaches and they sported thickly wrapped turbans. Most Afghani women were rarely seen, they had to stay at home. If you spotted them on the street, they were covered head to toe in *burkhas.*

One day I slipped one on over my head and strolled around the streets. It was stifling hot and uncomfortable. With a little mesh window slit in the fabric to look through, I was afforded very limited peripheral vision. Yet it was the perfect way to move about incognito. Travelling as a blonde foreigner attracted too much attention in these parts, and not all of it was good. The sexes were kept far apart once they reached puberty, so that a woman would be protected, and not defiled. As exotic as visiting these locales were, I was acutely aware that as a foreigner I did not have to adhere to the social mores of Hindu and Muslim societies. The *purdah,* head covering worn here, was also practiced in western India, where in bygone days, women lived in harems as concubines, and were given away in marriage with a dowry, often against their will. I'd hit the jackpot being born in the United States, where suffrage insured women's rights long ago.

The Islamic religion and culture in Pakistan and Afghanistan had produced beautiful intricate art and architecture. Shopping on Chicken Street, the stores were stacked with brocade vests, woolens, hats, silver and carnelian carved jewelry that was of particular interest to export to the States. No wonder Alexander the Great had stayed here so long, people were very hospitable. Men would come to the door of the shops, eyes twinkling and offer, "I will give your father all these carpets for you." They meant if I would be their wife.

I would playfully retort, "My father doesn't want your carpets." You couldn't help but peek inside the shops here, even the tiniest woven coin purse was a work of art, handmade with antique threads spun from real silver and gold, a lost art. A young merchant proudly showed me the amulet dangling around his neck.

"What is it?"

"*Tawiz!*" It was a carved silver tube, capped on both ends with lapis lazuli. "It contains a verse from the holy *Quran*".

"It reminds me of the *gau* boxes the Tibetan Buddhists wear that contain Buddhist prayers," I told him.

I wore a loose fitting long black dress covering my arms, with a black scarf tied around my hair so that it would not attract attention. This was a solidly Islamic country, and I'd been warned by many travelers to dress in this manner to be able to fly under the radar. Although I often heard the laughter and voices of women nearby, I could not peer over the tall mud walls that surrounded their tribal compounds. Actually these were fortresses, some boasted turrets and gun ports inhabited by fierce Pashtun tribesmen with glaring eyes; anyone who tried to look inside would have been shot dead immediately. The lifestyle here appeared unchanged for eons.

In those days, there were some modern women in Kabul wearing blue jeans, flashing an ankle and giggling in public. Educated females worked as lawyers, doctors, and teachers. All of this was to change radically in just a few years when the Taliban would come to power, enforce fundamentalist laws, and take away the rights of women. According to the Taliban, controlling females would ensure a "secure environment where the chasteness and dignity of women will again be sacrosanct."[21] Never mind that health care was no longer available and women might die of disease. Nor was education allowed, or even visiting a beauty parlor. Similar to social mores during the Middle Ages women must now live under gender apartheid and be systematically segregated and unable to express themselves or to seek freedom. Reports stated that executions and public punishment such as torture and beatings were to be employed by the Taliban's Religious Police to keep females "in their place." Very young girls were often forced into arranged marriages.

In 2013, the Taliban had severely impacted the female population here. Today, Sharia law allows a woman to be stoned to death, or disposed of in an honor killing. She often takes the blame for terrible atrocities committed against her, such as being raped. And although she is the victim of the sexual attack, she may be considered a prostitute. Female teachers who dare to go to work can be served "Taliban letters" that proclaim, "We will cut off the heads off your children and set fire to your daughter."

The twisting highway sliced right through the Hindu Kush mountain range in a series of switchbacks traversing northern Afghanistan and Pakistan. Headed to Bamiyan in a rickety bus, I had heard enticing tales of the colossal Buddha statues there, whose origins were quite mysterious. The crisp cold air was dry and arid as we drove through the remote terrain. It took seven hours to reach the Bamiyan Valley from Kabul. Along the way ancient fortresses and ruined townships stood now like ghosts of a flourishing time here before Genghis Khan invaded in the thirteenth century.[22] Colorfully painted trucks hung with dangling metal objects and mirrors, plied the highway, playing chicken with pushcarts and motor rickshaws, forcing them to the edge of the precipitous roads. Our driver barely managed to squeeze past.

We finally reached a wide-open space adjacent to a hillside dotted with small caves. This entire region was once Buddhist. Monks who lived as hermits inhabited the cave dwellings dotting the hillsides. It made me realize how violent the history of religious struggle was. Now Afghanistan was completely wiped clean of Buddhism. Only these remnants in the landscape remained - hollow reminders of a distant past. Without tolerance of the different paths to God, humans had killed, plundered, raped and invaded their way through this region leveling one religious culture and establishing another.

Suddenly the giant faces of the solemn Buddhas were staring directly at me. Carved deep into the cliff face opposite a snow-capped mountain range, their sheer size dominated the entire valley; they were "The two colossal images represented the potential of all beings to reach enlightenment

– no matter which faith we follow", I reminded myself. The taller Buddha, Vairochana was 175 feet high; he personified the clear light shining through the universe. In the 2nd century AD, he was the tallest statue in the world, and heralded a golden age of sculpting. Sakyamuni was somewhat smaller at 125 feet. A Chinese traveler reported in 630 AD, that the Buddhas were adorned with gold and precious jewels, their faces were overlaid with copper and their sumptuous robes were painted brilliant hues of red and blue. Even now, these colossal witnesses to history seemed to whisper intriguing tales of the glorious days when Bamiyan was a thriving oasis. At this junction, caravans plying the Silk Road would employ these caves as resting places, weary from their long excursions. I walked in solitude, retrieving shards of colored pottery wedged in the dirt, remnants of the merchants who passed this way so very long ago.

For centuries, scores of Buddhist pilgrims made the trek to Bamiyan. On the side of the deities an opening led to worn steps carved in the rock, which were climbed by multitudes striving to reach the summit and stand upon the Buddhas' heads. Up there, gazing out at the valley, I wondered, "How many monks lived here in retreat for eons, secluded from worldly distractions?" Ten monasteries with a thousand monks resided here until Muslim invaders prevailed. Now these Buddhas were the only remaining witnesses of the thriving spiritual community that once inhabited this land. I inhaled the fresh air and thought, "It is utterly silent in this place." I could never have imagined that it would be altered forever.

Today, the Buddhas no longer gaze upon Bamiyan with their beneficence. In 2001, Afghanistan's Supreme Taliban leader Mullah Mohammed Omar ignored the cries of the world community, and issued an edict against all non-Islamic imagery. Tanks, anti-aircraft missiles and explosives blew up the sandstone cliffs where the Buddhas were carved. The Buddhas would not leave quietly; it took weeks of continuous demolition to finally bring them down. They were victims of religious intolerance at the hands of a fundamental regime.

The world was deeply saddened at the destruction of these priceless archaeological treasures that had been designated a UNESCO World heritage site. It is an immeasurable loss to humanity. Even though the Buddhas did not represent God, but qualities of human beings if enlightened, they paradoxically were wrecked in a war of ideology. Some believe that the Buddhas were destroyed because foreign aid was requested by the government to feed Afghanistan's children and had not been provided. Yet funding was furnished to maintain and refurbish the Buddhas, which were sandstone statues.

Riding in a taxi in San Diego in 2014, the driver suddenly divulged, "My people, the Hazaras are from Bamiyan, and we have had problems for hundreds of years!"[23]

"What is happening to the Hazaras today?" I inquired.

The driver complained, "Recently 3,000 Hazaras lost their lives and over 5,000 were injured, a Sunni extremist group is suspected of being behind the attacks. Human Rights Watch has been critical of the local government for their incompetence in finding the perpetrators. He shook his head, "It still continues, ever since Genghis Khan."

In 1221 Genghis Khan invaded Bamiyan, then razed and murdered all of its' inhabitants because his grandson was slain in battle there. It became known as the "city of sorrows." Genghis Khan's soldiers remained there with slave women to guard the Valley. They are said to be the Hazaras' ancestors. The Hazaras are Shiite Muslims, the minority in Afghanistan, while Sunnis are the majority. They were declared infidels, and have suffered a long history of persecution.

"The men were beaten to death in full view of their families, who were then marched by the thousands to slave markets in Kabul," the driver explained.

In 1896 the Hazaras were ordered to attend Sunni prayers, and their worship centers were sold. They were forced to rent others, abandon their religious practices and follow Sunni customs.

The enmity between the Sunni and Shia branches of Islam is causing great strife in the world. The two branches of Islam have different beliefs as to who is the head of the Caliphate, the Islamic state. The Sunnis believe the people appoint him, while the Shias maintain Allah selects him. The drive to recreate a Caliphate is the battle cry of extremist groups today, a wish they have wanted to fulfill since the 7th century. Currently ISIS is conquering territory to unite in this mission. The resulting sovereign state would be ruled by a successor to Mohammed under Sharia law.

In Pakistan in the 1970's and early 80's, the narrow bazaars of Rawlapindi and Peshawar teemed with tribal people buying and selling gold, silver, tools, spices, fruit, and vegetables. Crumbling walls of massive forts leaned alongside colonial British buildings recalling days of glory past. Up north tribesman controlled the mountainous areas. The code of conduct they lived by was an eye for an eye, and a tooth for a tooth. The fierce tribesmen were fair-skinned descendants of Alexander the Great's soldiers. The Pashtuns inhabited the border regions of Pakistan and Afghanistan, and never accepted the boundaries drawn by the British decades before. Outlaws of all kinds could penetrate the porous demarcations.

When our tour groups flew into the country, all the liquor carried by the members was confiscated. Customs stated that it would be returned upon our departure. Strangely there never was anther mention of it when we left? Someone was enjoying Johnnie Walker.

Hunza was a few valleys north, surrounded by peaks over 20,000 feet that kept it isolated for centuries. We flew forty-five minutes on Pakistan International Airlines, PIA, fondly known as "Please Inform Allah" or "Perhaps It Will Arrive" - over treacherous passes including K-2, the world's second highest mountain. Passing over terraced rice paddies, the old Silk Road snaked below us, where lines of camels had shuttled treasures - ceramics, spices and cloth between China and India. In Hunza people lived to be 120 years old, and cancer, heart disease and bone decay were virtually unknown.

On the highway friendly young shepherds were driving their flocks up steep trails on the hillsides through dense pine forests and orchards. They queried, "Apricot," spilling the dried fruit in their shirts into my hands. Jagged snow-clad peaks came into view on a hairpin turn under the crystal clear sky. Finally reaching the rest house in Gilgit, I noticed a portrait of a pleasant smiling man beaming down from the wall in the lobby.

"Who is that?" I asked.

"He is Prince Karim Aga Khan IV, the head of our religion, we greatly honor him," the desk clerk beamed proudly.

"The Islam we practice here is the Ismaili sect, the second largest branch of Shiism," he explained. "The Aga Khan is its' present head, the 49th Ismaili Imam." In Islamic tradition, the leader interprets the faith, and helps raise their community's standard of living. The Aga Khan Foundation works with Asian and African countries promoting education, agriculture and economic development. It was dedicated to improving living conditions and opportunities for the poor, regardless of faith, origin or gender.[24] I could see the difference here, in Hunza the schools and roads were modern and in excellent repair. The status of women and girls was better, with a literacy rate over 90%.

Later I read that His Highness the Aga Khan said, "I firmly believe that peace will only be possible when the pluralistic nature of human society is recognized, seen as a source of strength, rather then weakness and used as a basis for the formulation of policies and structures at all levels of governance." His statement made a strong impression on me.

While Hunza was removed from the cares of the world, just a few hours away the highway snaked along the gorges of the Indus River through the Himalayas up to the Chinese border, where Red Army troops stood guard. At the time, Red China was still a sleeping giant. It was hard to imagine that in just a few decades, China would awaken from her long slumber and embrace a brand of crony capitalism, to become one of the preeminent financial powers of the world.

And just a few valleys over from tranquil Hunza, tribal drug lords would be processing a heroin crop worth billions.

The peaceful atmosphere of the Hunza region would soon be transformed.

At 26,658 feet, Nanga Parbat is the ninth tallest in the world. Elite climbers have dubbed it, "Killer Mountain" since so many have died in the ascent.

In 2013, climbers were making the dangerous ascent while several sick mountaineers and staff slept in in the camp below. Suddenly, cries of "Surrender! We are Taliban! Where are the Americans?" rang out. Pakistanis in camouflage gear descended on the camp brandishing AK 47's. [25] They gathered the team members, trussed them with rope and shot them in cold blood. A Taliban member proclaimed that the killing was in retaliation for an American drone strike that killed one of their leaders.

These days, *jihadi* slogans grace the local village walls.

Chapter 7
It's a Yogi's Life for Me!

When I read the Bhagavad Gita and reflect about how God created this universe everything else seems so superfluous.

-Albert Einstein

Thousands of stark naked, ash covered yogis led the massive charge into the holy river. This was the pinnacle of their religious devotion. It was 1976. The origins of these philosophers are so ancient, they are lost in the mists of time. Riding high, balanced atop elephants, brandishing swords, serpent-shaped trumpets and silver staffs, the eye-popping spectacle earned the adulation of the scores of surging pilgrims. The ocean of people pushed forward as yogis blowing conch shells plunged into the waters of immortality, ritually cleansing themselves and the sins of the pilgrims who had come here to the holy festival to seek salvation. The heartfelt devotion emanating from the throngs carried me into an ecstatic state of consciousness.

A few days earlier, I had jammed into a grubby Indian Railway sleeper coach among a pulsating sea of human bodies trying to board. I managed to get pushed through the door into the train to Allahabad. I knew it would be crowded, but this took my breath away. Every inch of space was occupied with pilgrims destined for the *Kumbha mela*, the holiest of all Hindu festivals. The Indian government added many additional trains to accommodate all the pilgrims who numbered in the millions. But still it was packed with excited villagers and yogis from the farthest reaches of India travelling to the most sacred event of a lifetime, the most auspicious of all bathing festivals, that assured the washing away of all the sins committed in their lives.

The anticipation in the coach was palpable. The devout donned their brightest colored *saris, and* turbans. A spontaneous devotional chant, like a jam session - with harmonium, cymbals, drums, vocals and hand clapping - created a celebratory atmosphere in the train, a turbaned man jumped up and danced in the aisle ecstatically. It was easy to get caught up in the fervor, and I felt welcome by all.

My fellow pilgrims offered me steaming *chai,* tea in a clay cup and milk sweets wrapped in beaten silver, as wheat fields tilled by farmers with buffalo swept by the windows in the diminishing golden light. Impoverished villagers who could not pay for a seat huddled together on the floor, bright light shining intensely from their dark eyes, passing between them the only sustenance they had, a few flat breads, which they offered to me. The spiritual zeal they shared created a sense of community I'd never experienced before.

About 6,000 years ago, when civilization first prospered in the Indus River Valley, the diverse cultures recognized that they could co-operate and survive; rather then do battle with each other, spending all their resources on war. And so, Hindu culture began with reverence for all living things and devotion to the sacred force that nurtures life - the River Ganges.

Our train stopped at every station, where hawkers proffered baskets of hot tea and snacks. My seatmate spoke perfect English and explained the importance of the *Kumbha* to me as I tried to straighten out the troublesome *sari* that kept slipping off my shoulder. There were still many aspects of life here I had not mastered. "India's sacred festivals are held on the banks of holy rivers. The most auspicious of these is the *Kumbha Mela.* Every twelve years there is a *Maha Kumbha Mela* (*maha* means great.) Now, it is such a month-long *Kumbha,* a tradition that dates back to the 7th century."

"Of course I had to come," I laughed. I remembered that Mark Twain in 1895 had made his way to this very festival in Allahabad to witness the *Kumbha,* and wrote in glowing terms about the Hindus' unparalleled devotion: *"It is wonderful, the power of a faith like that, that can make multitudes upon multitudes of the old and weak and the young and frail enter without hesitation or complaint upon such incredible journeys and endure the resultant miseries without repining. It is done in love, or it is done in fear; I do not know which it is."*

And now I would see it with my own eyes! These pilgrims lived such hard lives, yet totally existed for their love of the divine. Their belief in God was unshakable.

The majority of the Indian population practice Hinduism, over nine hundred million. It is considered to be about seven thousand years old. Its ancient philosophy evolved from adopting and synthesizing many sects of worship. Primarily based on the four *Vedic* scriptures, it teaches that there is one *atman*, or great soul, connecting us all. We are caught in this earthly cycle of existence due to our *karma*, actions that produce cause and effect. A person's position in his or her present life is believed to be the result of their behavior in previous ones. Karma causes us to reincarnate, to work out the lessons we have accrued. Enlightenment can be achieved through non-attachment and self-realization.

Hindus worship up to 300,000 gods, yet they are all seen as converging in the one Ultimate Reality, the spiritual force of the universe. The many colorful deities are expressions of the Absolute reality in which each person can have their own direct experience. Georg Feuerstein, author of many books on yoga, describes the Hindu path this way, "Yogis don't just want to believe or have faith in that ultimate being or state of existence, they want to *realize* it. This can be achieved by waking up from the dream-of-consensus reality. The path is meditation, the path is mindfulness."

Hinduism is saturated with spiritual expressions even in simple, everyday life. "The spirit in me respects the spirit in you," is the modern interpretation of the Sanskrit root of "*namaste*," which is the customary Indian greeting.

Nothing could have prepared me for what I saw when I got to Allahabad. No photographs I'd ever seen could convey the full impact of the *Kumbha Mela* with its endless parade of millions of people. It resembled the scenes I have seen of Mecca, when millions of Muslims go on the *hajj* pilgrimage and circle the sacred *Kaaba,* the black shrouded granite shrine.

I got my bearings as I started exploring the grounds of the mammoth *Kumbha Mela* festival. Cows, monkeys and pedal rickshaws shared space in the lanes with shops selling rosaries, statues, and fresh milk, which was patiently hand, stirred by the proprietors. Displays of colorful milk sweets and savory snacks towered over the passersby.

I made my way through huge camps of colorful tents set up by the yogis. The ascetics were engaged in many different forms of practice. One band of mendicants was draped in bright fresh marigolds, carrying coconut-shell begging bowls. A saffron-robed yogi adorned with sandalwood paste, his neck piled high with crystal rosaries, invited me to sit, gesturing to some burlap on the ground.

I plunked down, observing his deeply cracked and calloused feet. "That must hurt," I mimed in broken Hindi. Nonplussed, he shrugged. He had forsaken his worldly life of family, home, business, even his body.

Further along in the camp I saw ascetics who remained standing for 12 years. They even slept in an upright position, by resting their arms and heads on swings they had rigged to hang from tree branches. Their legs were swollen to a voluminous size, resembling elephantitis. Yogis who had taken vows of silence bestowed blessings upon me. Some were emaciated from their restricted intake of food and rigid discipline, and smiled blissfully as though in a trance. The *aghoris, Tantric* yogis who followed a left hand, unorthodox path, kept to themselves by the river meditating, and eating their meals from the human skullcaps, to remind them that life is temporary and illusory.

I wandered into massive camps of naked ash-smeared ascetics who resembled ghosts with long matted hair. They crouched around fires in a state of calm detachment, sporting tight metal rings around their penises to overcome sexual desire. They were celibate, and I couldn't help staring at others who wore gigantic iron chastity belts locked securely with huge padlocks around their waists, inaccessible. They avoid women, so they were not as welcoming to me; I hurried past their enclosure, but wondered, "Who keeps the key?"

Thousands of devotees ambled along the dusty lanes to present money, fruit, and sweets to the yogis and receive their blessings. The pilgrims longed for a glimpse of these holy men who during the sacred bath would cleanse them of their sins. I watched spellbound as pilgrims reverently approached the yogis, bowing low to touch their calloused feet. The pilgrims offered me food and coins, too.

It was my turn, I stood before a yogi with glowing eyes and a tower of hair wound high on the crown of his head. He grabbed ash from his sacred fire, his fingers tickled as he smeared it on my forehead, marking my third eye in blessing. I was about to move on, when he smiled, *"Ider aoo,"* meaning come here. He reached into his cloth bag and handed me a few crumpled *rupees* (money.) He viewed me as a yogi, albeit from the other side of the world. I was struck by the kindness of his gesture.

Allahabad was the confluence of two sacred rivers; one is the Ganges. It is the ultimate aspiration of all pious Hindus to take a dip here. But pollution, overpopulation, and poor sanitary conditions have taken their toll on the river. The water is pristine when it begins to flow down from the Himalayas, but when it finally reaches Allahabad, it is loaded with filthy sewage and dangerous bacteria. Add to that the fact that the Ganges is considered the holiest place to be cremated. Consequently the ash remains of millions have been swept off smoking funeral pyres into the rippling water.

Since the *Kumbha Mela* was like a city grown up instantly, I visited its' cremation *ghat* at midnight, walking down the narrow lanes, dodging cow dung paddies in the dark, to overlook the crackling pyres. The pungent odor of burning flesh reminded me of my own mortality.

Many smoky sacrificial fires dotted the landscape. As a Catholic, I had been taught it symbolized hell, and the sacred flame of the Holy Ghost. Devotional hymns wafted over loud speakers as I strolled past dozens of *ashrams*. I snuck into an enclosed area at the river's edge and discovered hundreds of young shaven men at fire pits solemnly being initiated as yogis, *sannyasis*. No outsiders were allowed to see this ceremony, but a yogi smiled, motioning me to give him my camera. He returned a few minutes later and had taken photos of the entire ritual for me.

They all were performing their own funeral rites. The yogi's heads were ritually shaved to mark the end of the worldly lives they were leaving behind. I felt so fortunate to witness them take their vows of renunciation. They received new Sanskrit names to signify their identities as ascetics. They then marched in a long line - hundreds of shaven yogis, back into the world to begin life anew.

I eagerly entered another camp. Ram yogis sat lotus style in circles of flaming cow dung paddies. Iron plates with burning fires were balanced on top of their heads! One long bearded yogi winked at me, in spite of the scorching heat. Other ascetics stretched out on beds of sharp nails as pilgrims piled up offerings before them.

Throughout the festival, I felt accepted by these people who lived immersed in their spiritual world, with total abandonment to God. They were so different from me, and yet we were kindred spirits.

There were not many female *yoginis*. Being a member of the fairer sex makes it harder for women to wander, sleep on the streets and live at the mercy of strangers. I met a few who were undaunted by these challenges and lived just like their male counterparts.

I joined the mass of pilgrims bathing in the shoulder-deep water, submerging in it felt enchanting. With floral garlands and coconuts swirled around me, it was enchanting. Finally emerging from the chilly water, I donned a clean *sari* then watched the pilgrims light candles, float flowers on the river's surface, utter prayers, and fill urns with blessed water. They meticulously painted markings of their deities with vermillion powder and sandalwood paste on their foreheads.

The festival had left me with a great appreciation for the Hindus, and what God represented to them. It was inspiring to witness such spiritual fervor. With heightened anticipation I wondered, "What other faiths might I experience in this magical land?"

Leaving the festival, I joined some yogis heading to the bus station. One spoke perfect English and explained, "We emulate Lord Shiva, the Destroyer of the Hindu trinity, who keeps the cycle of life turning. He demolishes the ego and all evil. Without him there can be no rebirth." The yogis, my Austrian friends and I headed to Kashmir, to hike up to Amarnath, a cave sacred to Lord Shiva. It houses a stalactite said to be his *lingam*, the fully erect phallic symbol, representing the cycle of birth and death. Since Shiva is the Lord of Death and is immortal, this storied pilgrimage draws thousands. Shiva's *lingam* waxes and wanes, and can only be seen during the August full moon when it is believed its' powers grant boons and bestow blessings. Nine months of the year, access to the holy cave is cut off by heavy snow blanketing the passes.

We hopped aboard a ramshackle bus decorated with stickers of a beautiful Hindu goddess enthroned on lotus flowers. "It must be safe," I reassured myself, "its Laxmi" (the goddess of wealth.) I crammed onto a dusty seat next to a village woman who was sporting gold nose rings and a multicolored headscarf. She balanced a restless drooling baby on her lap. Her goat bleated plaintively from underneath the seat. She would reach down to pet it reassuringly every few minutes. Her daughter's shiny eyes were kohl-smeared to ward off evil spirits. She burped continually for an hour necessitating non-stop patting on the back.

"*Engrezi*", she queried, meaning, "English?"

"*Acha,*" I answered, "Okay."

She decided I was trustworthy, handed her baby to me, and settled back, popping some beetle nut in her mouth, and chewing furiously. She grinned widely, her teeth bright red. We passed paddies with water buffalo similarly chewing their cud.

A few days later we reached Pahalgam, and the weather was rainy. I admired the forested mountain slopes in the fog with cascading waterfalls emitting such a delightful clean fragrance. In this valley of flowers, we gathered with thousands of pilgrims to acclimate ourselves to the thin air in preparation for the nearly13, 000 foot ascent. 600,000 people annually make this strenuous trek up the rocky footpath to the holy site. [26]

I joined my friends and other pilgrims. As we sat together an ash-smeared yogi authoritatively shouted, *"Engrezi, au!"* meaning, "English, come here." With his matted locks trailing behind him on the ground, he looked like Lord Shiva himself stepping out of a painting. I learned that his name was Shanker Giri, and that he was from Madras, South India. *"Baras to bodh hai,"* he said, meaning, "There is much rain." He handed me a sheet of plastic to cover myself. Shanker Giri's radiance pulled my consciousness inward to the center within. Speechless, I simply continued to meet his gaze, nodding in agreement. A *naga sadhu,* naked yogi, he had such yogic mastery, the shifting elements did not disturb him. I was shivering with cold and he gave me his only blanket. His sole shelter was the open sky and the occasional cave. Shanker Giri usually traveled on foot, never remaining longer than three days in any location. This was a common practice among the wandering ascetics to prevent attachment, which is believed to be the root cause of suffering. He owned a pair of carved wooden shoes, but going barefoot was his preference. Compared to these ascetics, I still had an umbilical cord to society – my US passport! Unlike some other Westerners hanging out with the ascetics, I hadn't thrown mine away... yet. It was very tempting. My legal identity intact, I dove into the yogi lifestyle headfirst. Rubbing ashes on one's skin and being regarded simply as a soul, the light of God, was an enticing romantic existence.

Shanker Giri set up his sacred fire amidst the other yogis who had gathered, waiting for the auspicious moment to begin the treacherous climb to the holy cave. Long ago the villagers here had dubbed this gathering, "The Fair of the Hermits." Over the fire pit, Shanker Giri handed me tea, and started cooking potatoes and *kichori,* rice and lentils liberally seasoned with chili.

The yogis were far from timid. One night I was abruptly awakened by the sounds of scuffling and shouts. *"Chor! Chor!"* the yogis were yelling, meaning, "Thief! Thief!" They were restraining a local villager and took justice into their own hands. In spite of the man's protests, they dragged him to Shanker Giri, stripped him naked and tied him to a tree where he remained overnight. It was extremely chilly at 7,200 feet, and the thief was miserable shivering in the cold. Shanker Giri checked on him early the next morning and was satisfied that he'd learned his lesson. The thief was genuinely remorseful, and he treated him with care as he untied him.

Finally it was time to begin our three-day trek up the mountain. We pilgrims headed to the ice cave, each on a very personal journey. All of us were lost in thoughts of the divine. We stopped at the tea tents that were set up along the route, where glucose biscuits and vegetable fritters were sold in the biting cold. Yogis' ritual fires lined the path up to the cave. The constant drizzle made the muddy path slippery. We skidded and slid as we made our way through the forest.

Muslims carried wealthy heavyset Hindus past us on wood chairs, groaning under their weight. Pilgrims rode on ponies hauling oversized bundles nearly knocking us off the steep mountainside into the stream rushing downhill. In the distance, eagles lazily circled snowy Himalayan peaks. "One day I will come to your home in America and sleep by your holy fire," Shanker Giri softly said. I held back a smile as I imagined my Los Angeles neighbors peeking over the wall at a naked, ash smeared yogi sitting cross-legged at a fire pit in my backyard!

The cold wind blew fiercely at the dizzying altitude of 12,700 feet. We gingerly picked our way across a small glacier to finally reach our holy destination, Amarnath Cave. Hundreds of pilgrims clamored to enter, some nearly falling off the cliff as police endeavored to maintain an orderly line.

Finally inside, we could observe Hindu priests singing Sanskrit chants. Yogis were shouting salutations to Shiva in between inhalations from hashish pipes. It resembled a spiritual carnival. We reached the front where the sacred stalactite stood, the phallus of ice.

The intense heat from so many fires had practically melted the ice-shaped Shiva *lingam*, but that didn't dampen our heightened spirits at having reached the pilgrimage's pinnacle. Now that I was finally here, I watched the pilgrims prepare themselves to receive Shiva's blessings. They included me in singing sacred *mantras* and offering candles, money, and giving thanks. Shanker Giri assured me, "Shiva will protect you, just keep him in your heart." My thoughts turned to God.

My friend, Denise Tomecko, and I wrote a book, *Shiva,* about the yogis in the mid 1980's, so in the coming months, I accompanied these holy men on sacred pilgrimages through the Himalayas, traversing the same footpaths their forbearers had followed for thousands of years. They gave me a homespun blanket to carry, and with them I stayed in caves, nestling down on the leaves blanketing the ground. They taught me to practice austerities such as fasting and taking vows of silence. Not speaking for a month built up a storehouse of energy within.

No matter how primitive such conditions were, they paled compared to the wealth of spiritual knowledge and joy that was transmitted by these teachers. I felt humbled and privileged to know them. It would turn out that I would make two documentary films about the yogis, *Naked in Ashes* and *Origins of Yoga: Quest for the Spiritual.* This was lucky, because their traditions too, are under threat. Nowadays many of them have cell phones.

While Hinduism is profound and one of the most ancient faiths in the world, it has developed a social order that promoted prejudice, a hierarchy known as the caste system. It forces human beings to live and work within a social strata based on heredity, which is to say a person's status and livelihood was prescribed at birth. From the highest caste, the Brahmins, to the lowest, the Untouchables, every aspect of a person's existence is governed by their caste. Sadly, those on the lowest rungs have endured terrible suffering with little or no opportunity to improve their lives. Mahatma Gandhi fought against the caste system to free the lowest castes.

Today prejudice based on one's caste is illegal in India and many government programs provide Untouchables education, jobs and opportunities. Yet inequality still exists, especially in some urban areas. Years later, in 2009, I co-directed the documentary film, *Song of the Dunes* in Rajasthan. I was shocked to discover that even today in some Hindu temples, Untouchables are not allowed to set foot inside. They must perform their prayers outside the temple. To escape the horrific limitations upon their lives and to fulfill their human potential, many low caste Hindus convert to Christianity, Buddhism, or Islam. People born into a low caste often endure terrible treatment at the hands of the higher caste families in their villages. Even today, prejudice against Untouchables remains. In bygone days, having the shadow of a low caste person fall on you was considered polluting and extremely unlucky. A few years ago in a dusty village in Haryana, five lower caste men were torched and burned alive for skinning the carcass of a dead cow. Hindus traditionally regard cows as having higher status then low caste humans. Such violence is rarely reported to the authorities. This stark inequality does not even allow an Untouchable to draw water from the same well or tap as higher-class villagers. Today, legislation and affirmative action seeks to address these ills and create a more fair and just society for all.

When the Muslims invaded India, many Untouchables converted to Islam, some willingly and many others by force. One Muslim general, Timur completely leveled Delhi in 1398 because he felt the prior Sultan was too tolerant.[27] In fact, Timur ordered the massacre of Hindu *Kumbha Mela* pilgrims, who he considered to be infidels. The famed historian, Will Durant wrote, "The Mohammedan conquest of India was probably the bloodiest story in history The Islamic historians and scholars have recorded with utmost glee and pride, of the slaying of Hindus, forced conversions, abduction of Hindu women and children to slave-markets, and the destruction of temples carried out by the warriors of Islam from 800 to 1,700 AD."[28] The number of slaughtered Hindus is estimated at more then 80 million.

Chapter 8
A Clash of Civilizations

*You can safely assure that you've created God in your own
image, when it turns out God hates
all the same people you do.*

-Anonymous

With a drop of sweat rolling down his face, the burly security officer in the New Delhi airport swung his AK 47 in my face. Grunting, he spoke gruffly to me. *"Eder nai oau,"* meaning, "Stand back!"

"Tike ji, quo baht nai" I answered in Hindi in an effort to calm and assure him there was no problem as I shuffled through the antiquated security equipment, ducked behind a tattered curtain and got a very intrusive pat down. I thought to myself, "In most countries, this would be considered sexual harassment!" But I wasn't going to rock the boat with the Security staff, India had been dealing with terrorism for decades before the US and they had it down cold. Since 1975, I had easily crossed Kashmir's border 2 or 3 times a year. And I had traveled throughout most of the region with Shanker Giri. Kashmir had been dubbed, "paradise on earth" for a very good reason, it was truly that stunning.

While standing in an Islamic graveyard in Srinagar, a Kashmiri explained, "We were Untouchables in the Hindu caste system, so when the Mughal invaders swept in, we converted to Islam." I could understand why they would, considering the prejudice and lack of opportunity dealt to the lowest caste in the Hindu hierarchical system. I'd change religions too. And especially given that all they had to do to convert was merely to pronounce, "There is no God but Allah, and Mohammed is his prophet." The only jobs they were allowed to perform as Untouchables were lowly and dirty: skinning dead animals, cremating dead bodies, sweeping the streets. Even their shadow was considered filthy, and those in the higher castes avoided walking into an Untouchable, so as not to attract a curse upon themselves.

However, millions of Hindus were forced to convert to Islam by the sword, or be slaughtered, during the bloody waves of Mughal invasions that conquered northern India.

Islam has many followers in Kashmir, and their melodious call to prayer, the *adhan*, rang out five times a day from minarets throughout the villages and cities. I would witness many facing east to pray toward Mecca, the holiest place of Islam, and the birthplace of the prophet Mohammed. Now it was 1987, and in Kashmir the potential danger was so acute, that Western tourists were no longer allowed to enter. I was departing Srinagar for the last time. Crossing the tarmac to the plane, I inhaled the intoxicating smell of the chinar trees and heard melodious birds chirping. I looked up to admire the lovely doves that soared overhead.

Kashmir had become a battlefield; Hindu majority India sought to maintain the territory while Islamic Pakistan wanted it to secede, since its population was overwhelmingly Muslim. It was ripped apart by bloody attacks that were occurring more and more frequently, leaving many innocent people dead or wounded. Lal Chowk Street, the commercial center where we would go, was targeted once the militancy started; many of the traditional antique carved wood buildings were lit on fire and reduced to ashes. The Kashmiri population, whose sustenance depended upon their celebrated hand woven carpets and handicrafts being sold to tourists, began to suffer.

The intricately carved luxury houseboats where VIPs stayed, (the locals whispered about Mick Jagger), stood vacant, gently rocking as the tranquil waters of Dal Lake lapped against them. During the days of the Raj, the British had travelled up to Srinagar's cool 6,000-foot elevation to escape the sweltering plains of India. And the magnificent houseboats had been places for them to relax, as they were not allowed to purchase property. The boats had names like *Butterfly* and *Mona Lisa.* The handsome barefoot houseboys who worked on the boats, balancing pots of saffron tea, and bowls of delectable lotus root curry, were not serving anyone these days. The baskets of delicious macaroon cookies and warm sesame breads delivered by boats each morning by smiling bakers were nowhere to be seen. The tourist trade was decimated. The *shikaras* (water taxis) piloted by Kashmiri boatmen wielding heart-shaped paddles, normally ferried honeymooners and holidaymakers along picturesque water lanes choked with lotus flowers. Today they sit poignantly empty. No other locale as romantic as Srinagar has ever been created.

In 1988 the idyllic "paradise" that was Kashmir was shattered. Gunfire rang out and artillery shells rained down on Srinagar. Islamists wanted the territory to secede from India, some desiring an independent state, others aspiring to join Pakistan. Terrorism was perilously escalating. Airports around India instituted heavy security checks and constant surveillance. Passengers were frisked three times, then bused to the tarmac to identify each piece of baggage before it could be loaded on their aircraft. Hotels stationed armed guards and cement blocks at all entrances. With bomb sniffing dogs, they inspected every vehicle entering the premises for explosive devices, as well as checking the underside of each chassis with mirrors. Analysts and journalists estimate over 600,000 people have died in the Kashmir insurgency as of 2014.

The exquisite Shalimar Gardens were still incomparably beautiful, but now stood deserted. The thousands of Indian honeymooners and tourists could not hear the whispers of their fabled past. Jahangir, the Mughal Emperor had built the gardens, the height of horticulture, for his beloved wife, Nur Jahan in 1619. They loved the grounds so much, that they departed the splendor of their Imperial Court in Delhi for 13 summers, and crossed the difficult Pir Panjal Pass with their entire court entourage riding high atop elephants. The spectacular gardens contained a black pavilion where a famous line written by the Persian poet, Amir Kusrau was inscribed, *"If there is a paradise on earth, it is this, it is this, it is this."*

Such was the alluring beauty of Kashmir that India and Pakistan repeatedly skirmished over possession, each claiming the spectacular region as their own. It had already been split between the two countries.

I had visited the Muslim shrine of Roza Bal, in a

quarter of Srinagar, considered by 150,000 devout Kashmiris to be the final resting place of Jesus Christ, who they called Yuz Asaf. I gazed around at the area surrounding the tomb, it was silent and desolate, without a foreign tourist or local worshipper in sight. The Ahmadiyya sect of Islam believes that this shrine in a graveyard holds the body of a man buried in the Jewish directional tradition, not by Islamic custom, and that he bears marks of the crucifixion on his feet. In 1747, a Sufi writer, Mohammed Azam first mentioned this shrine that is said to be that of a foreign prince. It is believed that after Jesus's resurrection, he travelled to the East and eventually died of old age in Kashmir. [29]

Kashmir did not reopen to foreign tourists for 20 years.

In 1995, six hikers were kidnapped while trekking in Kashmir - two Americans, two Brits, a German and a Norwegian, who was found dead. His body was dumped in Seer, with "Al Faran" the name of an insurgent group carved into his chest, and his decapitated head laying forty yards away. In his pocket, the terrorists stuffed a handwritten note, in which they threatened to murder the remaining five hostages if their demands were not met. The kidnappers claimed that since Western countries are "anti-Islam", the men were fair game. One tourist escaped, but the other four have never been found and are presumed dead.

Sadly, today going to the Amarnath cave in Kashmir, where I first encountered Shanker Giri could be very dangerous. During the annual pilgrimage trek in August 2000, 48 Hindu pilgrims died at the hands of Muslim terrorists; following this incident, the pilgrimage was banned for several years. The "trek to a source of spiritual inspiration" became a magnet for extremists of both sides intent on slaughtering Hindus or Muslims. The cycle of attacks and retributions escalated dangerously. Hindus are again allowed to make the pilgrimage, but in 2007, 15,000 police and troops had to be employed to guard them from attacks.[30]

Many Kashmiris dispersed throughout India to peddle the handicrafts they could not sell in Kashmir anymore, due to lack of tourists. I saw some hawkers at the Qutab Minar, near the first mosque ever constructed in Delhi, spreading their tempting wares out on the broken asphalt that pulsated with waves of heat. Street urchins who preyed on foreigners surrounded me chanting, *"Baksheesh, mem saab"*, meaning, Madam, give me something."

"Tike, Okay!" I found some American chewing gum in my purse and offered it to them, they convulsed with laughter and delight.

I made my way to the ruins of the "The Might of Islam," a structure that had been built from the remains of 27 Hindu and Jain temples. When the Mughal, Muslim conquerors overran north India, they were short on time, so they had to use carvings from temples, even though by doing so they were blaspheming Islam. Muslims are never allowed to represent God, because they believe no representation of the Divine can be perfect enough. I admired the mosque's pillars, but then noticed a jumble of intricate carvings. The faces of the Hindu deities had been brutally smashed off. Near the mosque stands the Qutab Minar, a victory tower that juts high into the sky, Muslims often erect these at the sight of battles to commemorate triumph. This is what caused some in the US to decry the building of a mosque at Ground Zero near the World Trade Center in New York City. They view it in the light of this historical context as a victory marker. While it may not necessarily be true, it has been extremely controversial.[31]

The largest outbreak of religious violence in India was over the Partition, which resulted in India being split into two countries, the Islamic Republic of Pakistan, and secular India. Muslims and Hindus had been living together peacefully in every village in India for centuries, but communal hatred began to tear them apart. Religious enmity was whipped into a frenzy by two political factions, Hindu and Muslim. A division of the country along religious lines was seen as the only way to prevent the situation from exploding into civil war. Volunteer forces of each political party had expanded, and they were slaying the other factions - Hindu, Sikh, and Muslim - tit for tat, as each bloody attack orchestrated by their leaders set off yet another in retribution. The most inhuman and brutal communal violence the world had ever seen. Today, many authors and scholars refer to the prelude and aftermath of Partition as the "Holocaust" of India, due to so the occurrence of so much ethnic cleansing. 14 to 18 million people were displaced.

Mahatma Gandhi adamantly opposed the breaking up of India. Upon Independence, he was deeply saddened and stated, "My whole soul rebels against the idea that Hinduism and Islam represent two antagonistic cultures and doctrines. To assent to such a doctrine is for me a denial of God."

During this volatile time, a group of students at the University of Cambridge came up with the idea to divide India into two separate countries along religious lines. They dubbed this plan the "Two Nation Theory", and in 1933 printed a pamphlet espousing it entitled, "Now or Never. "They did not support the idea of a federation, and asserted that India was not one country. They reasoned the Northwest region should be named "Pakistan," which is comprised of the first letters of Punjab, Afghania, Kashmir, Iran, Sindh, Tukharistan, Afghanistan and Baluchistan. This idea was supported by the All Muslim League, while The Congress Party did not favor the division.

Even though it was entirely out of the question to relocate scores of people along religious lines, the unthinkable happened. The creation of two new nations, Pakistan, "Land of the Pure" for Muslims from the Muslim majority areas; and India, a Hindu majority secular democracy, from the widely populated Hindu areas. The dissection took place at midnight on the fateful date of August 15, 1947. When India was finally rewarded her freedom from Great Britain, Mohammed Ali Jinnah and the Muslim league pressed for a separate state, causing Hindus to flee en masse from the territory that was to become Pakistan. Likewise, Muslims took flight from India to the new Islamic state. It was the largest mass migration in human history.

In June 1947, Sir Cyril Radcliffe, a government official in Great Britain who had no knowledge of the Indian region and had never visited it, had the daunting task of dividing 175,000 square miles of territory that was inhabited by 88 million people. He drew the boundaries of the two newly minted countries, so-called the Radcliffe Line, while journeying to India for a few short weeks. On August 16, 1946 at 5:00 PM, the information about the new boundaries was released to the public.

Upon hearing of the newly drawn borders, millions of villagers and city dwellers were instantly uprooted. They were forced to join the mass of humanity forced to leave everything, by train, plane, lorry, and cart, but mostly by walking on foot into the unknown. The columns of millions of people with cattle and bullock carts raised huge dust clouds as they trudged, exhausted to their new nations. Total chaos ensued and a bloody civil war broke out, although it was never officially declared.

The resulting migration was one of the largest in human history, dislocating fifteen million people in a gigantic population exchange. Eight to ten million refugees crossed the newly drawn border. Tragically, as the two unending groups snaked past each other en route, brutal killing sprees erupted. They were viciously attacked and murdered by marauders from the other faiths while marching to their futures as destitute squatters in a new land. The slaughter was so horrific that many never reached their new homes alive.

Between one to two million people were butchered alive, when trains pulled into the stations of the new state, they were filled with the corpses of Hindus, Muslims and Sikhs, their blood dripping from the doors. The "trains of death" were attacked and derailed as the passengers were looted, killed and thrown off.[32] Untold suffering took place as religious tensions were inflamed beyond all imagination. Twelve million displaced people, both rich and poor, became utterly homeless. They lost every possession their families had worked for through generations - their entire way of life. Forced to walk away from all their entirety of their worldly belongings, they were now destitute, forced to carry on their backs only a few articles to set up housekeeping in a new country – if they could reach it, without being slaughtered.

The city of Rawalpindi in Pakistan was especially hard hit by the violence of the Partition. Inder Kaur was living there at the time. A Sikh, she had not seen any

107

religious strife in her community before this time, Muslims and Sikhs had been living together harmoniously. But when the rioting erupted, many Sikhs were assaulted and killed.

It is believed that 75,000 women were raped and abducted on both sides of the border. Women were the most victimized by the senseless killing in the name of religion; mobs would rape, torture, sell them as chattel, or execute them. Often the Army and police officials would collude in these acts against women, be they Hindu, Sikh or Muslim, they would pass the females around, gang rape them and force them to convert. There was mass ethnic cleansing in both countries. Brutality from one group triggered acts of retribution, and the violence continued escalating. Army and police officials sanctioned the murder of many minority groups. The Partition of Punjab forced an epic population exchange, the size of which the world has never seen.[33] The worse hit area was Rawalpindi.

Inder Kaur had told me she was trapped in the same riot in Delhi that I was in, following Indira Gandhi's assassination. Unbelievably she had been a victim of religious hatred twice. She was uprooted in the human calamity of the Partition decades earlier. Her family did not change their faith to ensure that they would be able to maintain their property and lives as they were.

Recounting her story, Inder said, "It was 1947, and we were living in Rawalpindi. I was nineteen, pregnant with my first child, and I went into labor during the political tension of the Partition. It was late, and angry mobs were roaming outside ignoring the curfew. My husband grabbed a sword for protection and we rushed through the streets to Holy Family Hospital. Just fifteen minutes later, my baby was born.

"The situation was very uncertain. The majority of Sikhs lived in that region of Pakistan, and a huge massacre was going on. Most Sikhs were escaping across the border to save their lives. But I had just given birth, and there were complications, so we stayed longer. We had to go to the hospital for the next two weeks. Then my husband made a plan to leave, he locked up the estate thinking we would return in a few days. We owned a big textile business, with shops and a large house. Time was passing, and all over the city, Muslims were slaughtering Sikhs and Hindus.

"We kept up with the news from our Muslim neighbors. They heard that a train heading to Punjab, the new border with India, had been attacked by Muslim mobs. Females were kidnapped, old ladies killed, and all the men were slaughtered onboard. Sikhs were targeted along with the Hindus, because we were infidels who did not believe in Islam.

"My sister had a son in the army, who sent word to us that the last train was about to leave, and it would have armed soldiers standing guard. He said 'you have to go right now' to what was to be the new India and safety.

"I started crying and said a prayer for our family. All eight of us rushed to get ready. My husband went out to get two horse buggies, but the people who were taking them to the station were being savagely murdered, so the drivers were refusing to go. We tried to bribe them, but they would not accept, it was too dangerous. Finally my husband spotted a truck parked on the road. He asked the driver where he was from.

"Morida."

"Morida? That is where I am from."

"It turned out to be very synchronistic - they had friends in common, and one was a Muslim who had exchanged turbans with my husband. It was the highest honor that could be bestowed by Sikh men, and that forged a bond between them. So he agreed to give us a ride.

"Two petrified Hindu families were hiding in the bushes near by. They overheard the conversation and hopped into our truck. About twelve people took shelter in it, and the driver asked us all to lie flat so that the mob could not see us.

"Several large groups of Muslims were killing people on the streets. We could see pools of blood everywhere and I was petrified. But luckily they did not halt the truck. They thought that it was empty.

"There was one group who stopped a terrified fleeing family and demanded their money and jewelry. They tried to take the wife, but the husband refused, saying that you can have the valuables, but not my woman. The enraged mob took all the riches, murdered the man and seized his wife anyway. We saw an old lady crying in despair, but we could not stop because the crowd would get us, too. It was terrible. It took an hour to reach the station. We were so relieved to see Sikh army guards protecting the trains.

"The train departed at 6:00 PM sharp. On the way out of town I saw body parts strewn all over the ground. We were so terrified that at any moment the mob was going to come and massacre us. The gangs had shut off Lahore's water supply and almost all the infants who were onboard died from dehydration before we got to India. Thank God, my little son survived. It seemed like divine intervention.

"All the doors and windows of the trains were locked, so we could not see out. But we could hear a few trains passing in the other direction. My baby was sick with diarrhea; due to the curfew I could not get proper food during my pregnancy. In our coach, people kept shouting, 'throw the baby out! It's as good as dead, get rid of it!'

"When we reached Lahore, the train engineer wanted to stay, because he knew that a huge throng was planning to attack the train further down the tracks. He was a Muslim. But a Sikh officer went to the locomotive, held a gun to his head, and ordered, "If you don't drive this train out of here now, I will shoot you." So the engineer got moving. The train was jammed; everyone was sobbing, telling stories, chanting and praying desperately. Almost every family had lost members. I realized our family was very lucky, thank God.

"The locomotive of each evacuee train was posted with the designation, 'Indian Special' or "Pakistan Special," so the attackers knew who was aboard, so they could wipe out scores of refugees. As soon as a "ghost train" arrived on one side of the border, another train of immigrants headed to their new country would be massacred; the entire train full of corpses would be dispatched in retribution.

"We brought no clothes or money, we left everything behind, except our self-respect. From Lahore, it took 4 hours to get to across the Attari border, where hundreds of relief workers brought us food and tea, and welcomed us with shouts of, 'He who cries God is Truth!'

"It was pitch black, so we could not see the masses of people crossing the border in the other direction, to the new Pakistan. Relief workers guided us to temporary camps and fed us; we finally got to rest. A day later, we took the train to

Dhuri, where my sister lived. But the station was deserted because there had been so much violence. We asked someone to find our relatives; they took us home. Grandmother had a bit of jewelry and my father had some money, so we could pay rent. After five months we were invited to live in a huge house in Delhi that Sikhs had taken over. The original occupants were Muslims that had fled to Pakistan.

"My husband bought a bicycle and rode to the British Mills to look for work. He had wholesaled cloth for Iran and Pakistan, so they gave him credit and some fabric. He started carrying bolts of cloth on his bike to sell. Soon the government gave shops to all the refugees in Old Delhi, near the Red Fort. He started his business in the bazaar and grew it slowly."

I asked Inder, "How do you feel about religious intolerance?"

She thought this was not truly a religiously motivated incident. "It was the British who had divided the area into Pakistan and India," she explained, "Some people misused religion for political means. In the past, we'd always loved our Muslim friends, even today I think of my young friends I grew up with and how we were so close." She shook her head dejected, "Unbelievably, I went through this horrifying situation twice!"

Acute resentment and mutual distrust resulted from these horrific actions. It still alive today in Pakistan - India relations. The division of Kashmir between the two nations during Partition is a constant thorn in the side of peaceful relations, spurring terrorist attacks and even dangerous nuclear confrontation. This enmity in the name of religion has resulted in the region being one of the two most dangerous global hot spots. Since Partition, keeping the balance among the disparate religious groups in India has been a challenge. Relations between Muslims and Hindus have been the most difficult to balance, but altercations involving Christians and Sikhs also tragically occur.

India has controlled Kashmir since its Hindu *Maharaja* Hari Singh joined the Republic in 1947, the year of independence from Great Britain. Like the Israel / Palestine dispute, this territorial struggle remains a flash point of contention today. Many have perished in Kashmir, mostly innocent civilians caught in the crossfire. Some claim that *mujahedeen* fighters are trained in Pakistan to support the insurgency.

After 25 violent years in the once serene valley of Kashmir, finally a tenuous peace appeared to be on the horizon. Little did I suspect the extent to which religious conflict such as this would soon spread across the globe.

In 1999, a regional terrorist network in South Asia continued to worry authorities there. On a warm sunny day, an Indian Airlines Airbus A300 took off from Kathmandu's International airport, flying near the snow covered Himalayan range. While en-route to New Delhi, five Pakistanis hijacked the plane in Indian airspace. The terrorists forced the Indian pilot to fly to Kandahar, Afghanistan. The aircraft had limited fuel and had to land in Amritsar, Lahore and Dubai before reaching Afghanistan, where they were met by Taliban militia on the tarmac. One passenger was bludgeoned to death and several others were injured.

After seven days of negotiations, the insurgents finally succeeded in their goal of getting some of their associates - militant prisoners released from jail. One of them would later be arrested in 2003, for the beheading of Wall Street journalist Daniel Pearl in Karachi, Pakistan. The 9/11 Commission would dub him as, "the principal architect of the 9/11 attacks," the most deadly carried out against the United States – Khalid Sheikh Mohammed.

A wave of unimaginable violence committed in the name of religion was about to hit the United States. On the morning of September 11, 2001, Dr. Bob Hayward, a radiologist was downtown near the World Trade Center.

Bob explained, *"My wife Ruth and I were living in New York. She was working for UNICEF on ending violence again women, and women's rights in South Asia. We had an apartment on the East side, right by Bellevue Hospital, so she was close to the headquarters. I could go across the street to the Medical Center; I wasn't practicing at the time. At their neurological science area, I had gone to one of the meetings and it was 10:00 AM. There was a bookstore a couple blocks away and I thought I'd go browse around. I walked in, it was just like any other day, the TV was on and I heard, 'A plane just flew into the Twin Towers of the World Trade Center!' I thought, 'What the hell is this?' I've been in the World Trade Center and it's giant.*

"You could see on TV that the plane had hit the top section of the tower. It must be a huge mess down there, near the subway station. I thought, 'I'm a physician, maybe I should go down to see if I can help.' So I jumped on the subway thinking I could transfer to the one that went right into the World Trade Center. But as I was riding they kept stopping and starting. All along the route I thought, 'This is crazy,' I had some premonition I could be walking faster. At City Hall I got off and there were police and emergency vehicles cordoning off the area.

"I thought, this is a really a big mess. There are a lot of people and I probably wouldn't be able to do much, but I'll find out more. So I walked over, I hadn't seen the building itself. Then I saw the two towers, both of them were on fire. People yelled, 'A plane just hit the other one!' Then someone screamed, 'Oh no, a plane just flew into the Pentagon!' It was horrible and they announced there was a fourth plane in another state. People were streaming out of the building and fleeing. I looked up, and the building slowly started to crumble and fall down and I thought, 'Oh Christ, this is awful!' Because as a kid, my Dad took us to see an old smelt plant blown up. It all came crashing down, and within minutes, giant clouds of dust enveloped everything. I thought, 'I've seen this before.'

"So I got off the street. I looked across the way and there was a Starbucks. I ran in because it was a public place, and they were starting to help people. There was so much debris in the street it was blowing in all directions. I thought,

'Am I glad I'm in here.' So I took the door, reached out and pulled people in, saying, 'Come on we'll take you and clean you.' So the Starbucks workers and I were cleaning and wiping their faces and eyes. After about a dozen people, I thought, 'I have to find out what's going on with my wife, Ruth.' When the air was a lighter color, I could figure out where I was. Starbucks gave me a damp towel and I headed out, not knowing what was going on. Then the second tower collapsed right as I was watching it.

"I went across the Brooklyn Bridge. I was so glad I got over there. The air was clean. I crossed over it and met a few people along the way. One guy asked me, 'Where are you from?'

I answered, and when I asked him back, he replied, 'Muslim.'

I suggested, 'You should probably shave that beard off, and don't grow it back for a really long time.' There had already been terrorist attacks in Europe, in India, and all. 'You'll be better off, don't let anybody see it.'"

Chapter 9
Guidance on the Quest

I looked in temples, churches and mosques. But I found the Divine within my heart.

-Rumi

The more I discovered about the heartbreak and calamity wrecked by humans in the name of religion, the worse I felt. It was so sad to realize that time and again such positive and constructive spiritual traditions were targeted and misused as weapons of hate.

The idea of making a film about religious tolerance to examine this appalling conundrum seemed vital to me. Although there would be several answers, it seemed urgent that the subject be explored. Right now capabilities of massive destruction are in the hands of zealots. With the help of friends I managed to get an appointment to interview His Holiness the Dalai Lama in Dharamsala, to explore religious tolerance. A film crew accompanied me, and we set out to produce the documentary, *Not in God's Name*.

The sky was a brilliant blue, crowning the pine covered hilltop upon which His Holiness lives with its' backdrop of snow capped Himalayan peaks at his residence in Dharamsala, 6,000 feet high in the Himalayan foothills. The Dalai Lama refers to India as his adopted home, since he has dwelled here in exile for over fifty years.

We approached the Dalai Lama's residence in Dharamsala, India at 6,000 feet. He has been in exile in India for over fifty years and considers it his adopted home. Now having passed through a very stringent security check, we felt a quickening of excitement. A true example of non-attachment, His Holiness is someone who had lost so much, even the country he ruled. Yet, with the ideology of non-violence, he has fought back against the Communist regime that invaded his land. The Dalai Lama's strong moral authority continues to inspire Tibetans to follow his nonviolent example, and for the most part they have not taken up weapons. Serendipitously I discovered in the interview, that one of His Holiness's three main commitments in life was to promote religious tolerance. Years earlier, when I sat in this very meeting room, I never realized I would one day make a film on this subject, or that I would be trapped in a life - threatening riot.

An assistant in monk's robes led the Dalai Lama into the room. He had a big smile on his face, which lit up the surroundings. He blessed us, then sat in his chair, motioning not to indulge in the usual Tibetan formalities. He expertly put on the microphone and was exceedingly friendly. I began by asking, "What should people do to learn tolerance for other faiths?"

"The main thing is to have closer relations with other religions. According to my own experience and also that of my fellow spiritual brothers and sisters, we should have more interaction with people of other traditions. With these other traditions, meet with their scholars on an academic level and inquire, 'What are the differences between our faiths?' What are the similarities?' And on another level, we have meetings with spiritual leaders, who are the practitioners of different paths, and with them exchange everyone's deeper spiritual experiences, according to their own traditions.

"I think that it's exceptionally useful to understand the value of other traditions, or their potential. But the first step is for us to meet on an intellectual level. The second step is meeting from the heart...about each one's real spiritual experiences.

"Then the third step, without the use of any human communication, we can go to different sacred places with a group of people, to visit places of different traditions. Then if possible, do some prayer there; if not, do silent meditation as a group – with a combination of people from different faiths, and different beliefs. Sit together, and experience some vibrations in that place.

"So, with this belief, I have had many experiences in India. I started practicing this, which year I can't remember, but from sun-up in one day. I first visited one Christian church, then one Hindu temple, one Jain temple, one Muslim mosque, and one Sikh *gurdwara*. "So, that's very useful, and then in Europe, in Barcelona - Montserrat Monastery. In Portugal, Fatima, and in France, Lourdes, it's these places.

When I visited them, it was not as a tourist, not just as a mere visitor, but with a deep admiration for Christianity, and respect. Go to such places on pilgrimages, it is very useful. There are some very powerful vibrations or feelings.

"One time, I visited a Christian community in England, where I gave a lecture on the Gospel. In return, some of their members came to Bodhgaya, and we had a few days seminar, with some synthesis and dialogue between Buddhism and Christianity. Each morning, we spent half an hour at the Bodhi Tree in Bodhgaya, the most sacred Buddhist site. Christian brothers and sisters, and Buddhists sat together under the tree in silent meditation. So this is on another level, making closer relations with each other. And like our meeting in Assisi, the heads of different traditions can come together, speaking the same language, and share the message of peace.

"Today, technology and communication make it very easy to reach different parts of the world. In ancient times, we were isolated but now, that situation is over. It is readily available and much easier to contact one another. Under these circumstances, we have to make every effort to develop closer relations between different traditions. It is very useful to develop genuine harmony on the basis of our mutual respect and mutual learning."

I queried, "Your Holiness, what can people do to overcome religious intolerance?"

"I think historically where there are closer relations between different traditions, there's genuine harmony. India is one clear example. In this country before Buddhism came into being, there were already different Hindu traditions. Then Christianity arrived, then Islam. Zoroastrianism, the Persians' religion also came to India from Iran, eventually the followers found shelter here, mainly in Bombay, though they were a very small community. But they carry their tradition, among the millions of Hindus, Muslims and Christians. So, this is a very clear example.

"In India, there are so many varieties of religions, so many different traditions. But on the grass root level, family to family: one Christian family, one Hindu family, one Muslim family - they live together. They take for granted that there are many different traditions, whether they accept that all the paths have the same potential or not. People here all live closely together from childhood and experience that there are different traditions. So, why not remain together peacefully? In today's world because of technology, the barriers have broken down. And due to nuclear proliferation, the weapons available today are much more dangerous. So eventually, this kind of attitude can build and develop. We need some effort to send a message of harmony - that all religions have the same potential, and humanity needs different traditions. One tradition simply cannot satisfy the variety of people with so many different dispositions."

"What about the cycles of retribution that cause ongoing conflicts to continue," I asked.

The Dalai Lama commented, "In some cases, unfortunately, one party has a feeling of revenge, it is really counterproductive. Whatever happened in the past, now today, think that there are new circumstances. We must look forward, don't talk about the past. Forget it!" I took the Dalai Lama's wise words to heart as I embarked on my quest to find the reasons for religious intolerance.

Recently while visiting San Francisco, the Dalai Lama took part in a Conference entitled, "Gathering of Hearts Illuminating Compassion,"[34] and worked to change the mistaken impression many Americans have of mainstream Muslims, he is attempting to shed light on Islam's role as a religion of peace. It would be helpful if moderates of the Islamic faith and their views would be more publicized.

The Dalai Lama also seeks to spread the message that all faiths are similar at their core. The Conference attendees discussed fundamentalism's rise, and how faiths can be manipulated politically to foment trouble. Huston Smith, the well-known religious author commented, "It is a high-jacked religion that causes violence."

Machupuchare, "Fishtail" peak, Nepal.

*A beggar dressed as Shiva works the
highway in Kulu Manali, northern India.*

Village children in the Himalayan foothills of Nepal.

Tibetan men circumambulate the Jokhang temple in Lhasa.

Chapter 10
The Smiling Buddha

"If we can't love the person who we see, how can we love God, who we cannot see?"

-Mother Teresa

"This is my favorite Muslim holy place in Delhi," Arif explained, while driving and barely dodging a skinny camel in the road. "It's the shrine of a famous Sufi saint, of the mystical branch of Islam, Hazrat Nizamuddin Awlia. Look at that," he beamed as we crossed the potholed freeway overpass. Nizammudin was situated directly next to a multicolored Hindu temple that resembled a decorated birthday cake, though constructed of cement. "Tensions may simmer below the surface between Hindus and Muslims, but even during times of violent killings, this holy place, Nizammudin is always peaceful," Arif commented.

There was an air of great sanctity. "Even at the time of Partition, during the greatest carnage between Hindus, Muslims and Sikhs, this place always remained a safe haven." India has 250 million Muslims, the second largest Muslim population in the world, and through Arif, I was lucky to be exposed to their beliefs.

We jumped out of the SUV, and ambled through a narrow dusty passageway to the shrine of the great saint Nizammudin Auliya, careful not to trip on the uneven stones. Beggars clamored for alms, sitting on burlap stretched out on the ground in front of dilapidated wood stalls. The chilly air was biting, and the vagrants were draped in fragments of old ripped cloth to withstand the foggy climate. I stooped and gave a beggar the bananas I was clutching. Hawkers sold devotional rosaries, hewn from semi-precious gemstones and wood, and cloth skullcaps.

We reached the interior of the courtyard, where many holy tombs surrounded a resplendent mosque. The soft music drifting through the air coaxed me into a timeless state.

The musicians wore embroidered skullcaps, and sat on the ground playing *qawwali*, mystical music, on the harmonium and drum, bobbing their heads to the rhythm, entranced. The head *nizam*, Syed Fida Mohammed Nizami, sat atop the marble step of Nizamuddin's mausoleum. He invited us for tea, and we joined him. He was handsome and dapperly attired in a long jacket down to the ankles with tight-legged trousers and a skullcap. He poured sweet cardamom tea and served salty snacks, spilling them onto a sheet of newspaper. Then he guided me to see the many tombs in the surrounding grounds. Some were covered in mounds of fragrant flower petals sprinkled in devotion by visiting pilgrims. A tall man with a close-cropped beard, his love for Nizammudin was evident. His weekly practice was to feed all the people who came here once a week, exactly as the Saint had done. Plates woven from leaves overflowing with aromatic food were distributed to pilgrims seated in long rows on the ground.

"The essence of Sufism is the way of mystical love. The Saint entombed here, Hazrat Nizammudin Awlia, taught that love is the way to transform our baser human qualities into higher ones. Although he lived in poverty, his heart was rich with generosity and he selflessly served others with joy." The *nizam* explained, "Nizammudin reached spiritual illumination when he was twenty. He lived then under a pile of straw in the desert near Delhi. His physical body emitted a lovely fragrance, the cause of which was said to be his highly realized soul, one who knew and loved Allah." Syed told me, "Nizammudin loved *qawwali* so much, even the animals near his retreat stopped and listened whenever the music was played."

For seven hundred years the pious of all faiths have flocked to this tomb for inspiration and blessings, and the atmosphere here was magical. Walking around I joined a group of believers tying red threads on a white marble pearlescent screen as they made wishes, I felt one with all who came here in devotion, to lay green cloth and sprinkle petals on the holy tombs, where men sang prayers from the *Quran.*

The shrine was jammed with diverse people. A Sikh in a turban and several Hindus were paying their respects to this great Saint of the Chishti order, who sought to find God in this life through serving others and renouncing the world.

Love for God meant love of all fellow men without prejudice or division, and kindness was paramount. This Islamic sect welcomed all, including Westerners. Nizammudin believed in the role of devotional music to unite different communities, such as Hindu and Muslim, even though this was considered un-Islamic.

I joined rows of devotees sitting on the ground as the musicians swayed in devotional fervor. Dervishes, Muslim mendicants attired in shiny green satin, danced with rosaries dangling from their fingers, lost in divine bliss. They had renounced the world to reach ecstasy with Allah.

At other mosques, I had to stand with the women behind a screen during prayers, but here there was no separation. It was evident in the way people sat praying together on the mosque's marble floor that there clearly was no caste system like in Hinduism operating here. All had equal status as they knelt towards the east, touching their foreheads to the frayed carpet. I wondered how many people with similar worries and dreams as mine had come here to get in touch with their inner spirit? People were very kind; I got shy smiles from the veiled women and curious glances from the men in skullcaps.

The *nizam* explained, "Sufis believe in peace for all. "We practice meditation and go into ecstasy," he elaborated, "to realize direct experience of the divine."

I responded, "That sounds much like the Buddhist, Hindu, Jain and Sikh philosophies I've been studying in India. And the Catholicism I grew up in."

The *nizam* nodded in acknowledgment and continued, "Wherever a Sufi saint dies, it becomes a *dargah*, a sacred place which Muslims visit for spiritual inspiration." I was reminded of my Catholic tradition of saints and pilgrimages to the holy shrines of Saint James – Santiago de Compostela, Lourdes, the Virgin de Guadalupe, and the Holy Land where Jesus was born and lived. It brought into focus the similarities of the world's wisdom traditions.

Nazim Nazami continued, "Kings rule by fear of the sword, but the Muslim
Sufi saints rule by love of the heart." He led us upstairs to the roof where a loud speaker broadcasted the call to prayer several times a day. My visit to Nizammudin was inspiring,

so much so that I returned there several times to sit quietly by the tombs and reflect.

The shining innocent eyes of the young boys in the *madrassas* reminded me of what author Mark A. Gabriel wrote in his book, "Islam and Terrorism." He notes that one of the 114 chapters of the Quran has the title, "The Spoils of War." He explains that in Islam, you are not guaranteed entrance into heaven upon death, even if you spend your entire life performing good works. The decision of whether you go to paradise or not, is entirely up to Allah. The only certain route to paradise for a Muslim man is to die while fighting for Islam. This route does not even necessitate one's going to the grave and awaiting final judgment. Paradise is achieved directly. Gabriel explains that this is the reasoning behind many *jihadists* leaving their own countries to go fight in other lands.

The *Quran* contains contradictory passages. Some are peaceful and compassionate, while others promote warfare, for example:

"Fight and slay the pagans wherever you find them, seize them, surround them and lie in wait for them." - Quran 9:5

Likewise, in both Hebrew and Christian Scriptures violent passages may also be found:

"And he that blasphemeth the name of the Lord shall surely be put to death, and all the congregation shall certainly stone them." - Bible – Leviticus 24:16

And similarly in Hebrew scripture we read:

"Do not leave alive anything that breathes... completely destroy them —the Hittites, Amorites, Canaanites, Perizzites, Hivites and Jebusites—as the Lord your God has commanded you."
-Bible - Deuteronomy 20:16-18

Most of us do not take scripture that was written for societies long ago literally. Today the issues in the struggle for the heart of Islam are: should political violence be permissible, the place of women in society, and how religious law should be applied. I have read that some fundamental Muslims do not accept Sufism because it preaches non-violence and permits music, which they don't. Some of the Sufi saints had even been put to death.

I asked Dr. Joseph Prabhu about Islam in India. He is a Trustee of the Parliament of the World's Religions, studied at Cambridge University and is a Professor of Philosophy. Joseph was Mother Teresa's first altar boy during his childhood in India. He works diligently to further peaceful relations between faiths. He explained, "The early period of Mughal, Muslim rule was in fact a very tolerant and harmonious period, unlike the representations that are given in the modern press. The Hindu and Muslim claim that there was inherent conflict between these two religions is in fact complete nonsense. The Muslims in India are an oppressed group, so they look to institutions like *madrassas* to give them a sense of identity and a sense of belonging, which largely explains their popularity. India today sees itself as being surrounded by Muslim states. It's easy to get a sense of being besieged. Unscrupulous political leaders are very easily able to exploit these wounds that even sixty years after Partition are very deep in the Indian psyche. One hopes that nuclear confrontation doesn't happen."

Joseph described Kabir, the great poet who lived in India from 1440 – 1518. He was both a mystic and a simple householder' who closely fused the two religions, Hinduism and Islam. Kabir was revered by Muslims, Hindus and Sikhs alike. "Kabir is on record as saying, "Look, my religious identity is a matter of complete unimportance to me. I don't know if I'm Hindu or Muslim. One day I'm Hindu, one day I'm Muslim, it doesn't really matter to me in my search for God."

Joseph reminded me that the goal of all spiritual paths is the same: to the Sufis, *baqa* is the ultimate state of consciousness, just as *moksha* is for the Hindus, *nirvana* for the Buddhists, and salvation for Christians.

As years have gone by, enmity between some Hindus and Muslims has driven a deep divide between the great countries of this region. It has also created a nuclear race. As of 2014, it is estimated that Pakistan currently has upwards of 100 nuclear warheads in its' arsenal. It is currently spending billions of dollars building a fourth reactor to produce plutonium. Fission materials are enriched near Islamabad as well as in the Punjab province. The nuclear weapons sites of Pakistan are located in the North, far from their mortal enemy India, but dangerously close to Afghanistan with its' Taliban extremists. *Jihadis* have waged three attacks on them. Shaun Gregory, Director of Pakistan Security Research confirmed that the primary infrastructure of Pakistan's nuclear program is located in areas under Taliban rule, who are known Al Qaeda sympathizers.

Approximately 9,000 Pakistanis are employed in nuclear work. "Securing the Bomb 2010," a report by the Belfer Center for Sciences and International Affairs, states that: "Pakistan's nuclear weapons face a greater threat from radical Islamists seeking nuclear weapons than any other nuclear stockpile on earth." Bashir Mahmood, the former head of Pakistan's plutonium reactor facility, was arrested for having ties to Osama Bin Laden.

The rebel scientist dubbed the "Father of the Islamic Bomb," Abdul Qadeer Kahn, head of the Pakistani Weapons Program was clandestinely supplying nuclear secrets to Libya, North Korea, Iran, and nine other countries, and running an international black market. He is currently under house arrest. The atomic weapons program is a source of tremendous Pakistani national pride, much as it is in India, and Khan is considered a great hero.

The Atomic Energy Agency, overseer of Pakistan's arsenal, indicated that their weapons and cache of enriched uranium have not been formally tallied. It is estimated to possess sufficient plutonium for 90 nuclear weapons, 60 warheads, and 10 reactors, according to the US Congressional Research Center.[35]

Learning that a program has been instituted by the Agency to teach the public how to recognize fissure materials as a national safeguard gave me some measure of comfort.

Because the wounds of Partition, when Pakistan was created as a separate country from India, remain fresh, both nations are heavily armed and engaged in a breakneck nuclear rivalry. They have already fought three wars over Kashmir.

India's nuclear arms program was born in 1974 when they created a device code-named the "Smiling Buddha." Upon its startling success, Pakistan's Prime Minister Zulifiqar Ali Bhutto proclaimed, "If India builds the bomb, we will eat grass and leaves for a thousand years, even go hungry, but we will get one of our own. The Christians have the bomb, the Jews have the bomb, and now the Hindus have the bomb. Why not the Muslims, too, have the bomb?"[36]

India has also amassed a gigantic arsenal of weapons of mass destruction every bit as dangerous as Pakistan's. Several have Hindu names including *Agni,* (the Lord of Fire) and *Prithiviraj,* after a Hindu ruler. Its' nuclear program is a source of great pride for the nation. Villagers danced in the bazaar celebrating successful tests in Pokhran near the Pakistan border, only a few miles from where I spent time with the original gypsies, tribal musicians, shooting the film, *Song of the Dunes.*

A confrontation between India and Pakistan would be more devastating than anything the world has ever seen, given the fact that both territories are some of the most heavily populated regions in the entire world. It is horrifying to realize the fallout from any nuclear explosion would result in millions of deaths and poison the region for millinea. India has made a pledge against first use of nuclear weapons and claims that its' arsenal is to insure stabilization of peace in the region. It has up to 110 nuclear weapons.

In 2001, immediately after the World Trade Center attacks, the animosity between Islamic Pakistan and Hindu majority India escalated so dangerously that they brought the world to the brink of the unthinkable – nuclear war. I held my breath, recognizing that millions could be annihilated, but thankfully both nations backed down.

A few years ago however, right after completing a round of peace talks, Pakistan test fired a nuclear capable missile. Three days later, India fired theirs.

Chapter 11
Please Join the Caravan of Martyrs

*Not one of you is a believer until he loves for his brother
what he loves for himself.*
-Fourth Hadith of Nawawi 13

Outside Delhi, Arif drove us along a tree-lined road
to a *madrassa*, a retreat center set in a grove of tall trees. We
strolled past green cloth-draped tombs and kicked off our
shoes to go inside and see where boys stayed in isolation to
pray and meditate on Allah far from the problems of the
world. Much like the early Catholic cloisters, the young men
sat on the floor wearing skull caps, one per room in dimly lit
corners praying out loud in singsong voices, their hands
upturned in a gesture of surrender to the Divine. They gazed
at me with mild curiosity, because normally Western women
do not enter their private prayer areas. The post 9/11 world
felt quite tenuous in this region. Yet I needn't have worried.
The young men were immersed in prayer. And Arif was at
my side.

At another *madrassa, a* few brothers between ten and
seventeen years old were sharing tea with us. Suddenly the
youngest one adamantly insisted, "I hate America!"

"But why?" we asked.

"Osama Bin Laden was not involved in the
September 11 attacks on the World Trade Center."

"But he admitted he had done the attacks. Don't you
know that? It was in the press everywhere."

"No."

It turned out the local newspaper did not report the
fact that Bin Laden had admitted his part in the 9/11 attacks.
It was their opinion that the US had not been provoked and
therefore was at war in Afghanistan for no reason, other than
killing their Muslim brethren.

I showed him my arms. "Don't you know that we all
have the same blood flowing in our veins? Look at your
blood, and look at mine. Aren't we just the same?"
The little boy shrugged, but did not look very convinced.

We drove back through the dark night towards Delhi, past orange fires flickering at the roadside restaurants, *dhabas* frequented by truck drivers. I was thinking about those young boys already learning to hate, and the sad schism between us.

The US had not yet begun the second Iraq War. The countless deaths and destruction that resulted from it, plus the War in Afghanistan was to be beyond tragic. These conflicts have caused mounting hatred toward the United States, and our allies, and have added to the ghastly cycle of violence which war perpetuates. Today I would not feel as safe venturing into the Muslim *madrassas* I visited, considering that so many individuals have died in wars with my country.

The most powerful enemies we are dealing with are religious fanaticism, lack of education and economic opportunity, and inaccurate information filtered down from government leaders. Adding to these are the media, and the great misunderstanding that war solves problems, and that "peace keeping" weapons when used often become anything but.

When it comes to education and accurate information, how many individuals know the real meaning of the word *jihad*? In Arabic it translates as a noun meaning "struggle," and appears 41 times in the *Quran* to indicate a struggle for the sake of the goal. It does not mean "holy war" and it is incorrect to limit the meaning of the word to warfare. In Islam, the spiritual significance of *jihad* and its wide application to nearly every aspect of human life comes from understanding that Islam bases itself upon the idea of establishing equilibrium within man's being as well as in human society, where he fulfills the goals of his earthly life. The term, *jihad* is often misused by Islamic radicals to promote a modern day "holy war," whereas *jihad* literally means the dignified effort of improving one's self, family, nation, and the entire world. The "war" it points to is the battle against the lesser thoughts and habits we adopt, which is universal. In all faiths followers are mandated to rise above their base nature.

Following the attack on the World Trade Center, Osama Bin Laden delivered a message saying, "...It remains for us to do our part, so I tell every young man among the youth of Islam: It is your duty to join the caravan of martyrs until the sufficiency is complete." Such an agenda of radicalism requires a steady stream of young people to carry it out, so he praises all those who have died by stating that they have "fulfilled their promises to God."

Bin Laden concluded by proclaiming, "As for our own fortune, it is not in this world." Young men are convinced with the promise of a paradise on the other side, complete with 64 virgins to do their bidding. The logic for the Crusades and other religious wars was no different, only the promised 'rewards of paradise' varied.

When Pakistan was founded, it was not as an Islamic state, but simply as a safe haven for Muslims. The young democracy was guided by Mohammed Ali Jinnah, and a group of intellectuals. They intended Islam to have a cultural role in the new state, rather then a political one. They believed in Pakistan, Islam could blend with democracy and be a modern player on the world stage. However, leaders such as General Muhammed Zia-ul-Haq pushed for the Islamization of the country. Today many citizens are moderate, wanting peace to prevail rather then an extremist ideology. Fundamentalism is becoming more widespread, and the balance of power in South Asia could tilt dangerously.

Right next door, the two most populous countries in the world, India and China, watch with great interest. The lack of a wider Worldview, education and opportunity is what could recruit young boys studying in fundamentalist *madrassas* ripe for an extremist ideology that sanctifies suicide, (therefore making them choice recruits.) Some schools in Pakistan today teach a pro-Taliban agenda, with an eye toward transforming Pakistan into an Islamic state. The boys here are given three meals a day and a roof over their heads for free. Libraries near the schools have most probably had all non-Islamic texts removed from the premises..

WikiLeaks released a secret US diplomatic cable suggesting that some *madrassas* are used as recruiting stations for the Taliban, and that some even have military training after school. The indoctrination into *jihadism* is multi-faceted, and is reported to be non-flexible. Perhaps the best defense for such youth in underdeveloped countries is education with a more moderate curriculum. One that prepares them for a future where boundaries are breaking down as technology informs the world that we are all interconnected global citizens. Education is sorely needed to ensure a peaceful world where it is understood that diversity is not a threat, or a detriment to one's own good. Diversity is to be celebrated.

A college student from Pakistan attending a *Not in God's Name* film screening at UCLA, remarked, "I grew up in Pakistan in the 1990's, and was taught that our number one enemy is India, with the runner up being Israel. Bosnia and Chechnya were also viewed as being against Muslims. *Madrassas* must administer a great deal of charity. 85% of these facilities are directed by the Pakistani government, and must provide a well-rounded curriculum for students."

I asked, "How did you feel about the emotions expressed by some when the planes hit the World Trade Center?"

"Why was there a celebration after 9/11 by some Muslims? The 'shock and awe' bombing by US Forces in Iraq was construed in the same way." Then he added, "One month after the attack on the World Trade Center, my opinion about it changed, when I understood that the victims were 3,000 innocent civilians, including many Muslims who worked in the towers."

Terrorists in Pakistan have slain Christian relief workers and international aid organizations staff members in retaliatory raids.[37] One attack was against the Institute for Peace and Harmony, a Catholic organization that promotes accord between faiths in Karachi. It opposed the harsh blasphemy laws condemning Christians to death for offending Islam. The terrorists found guilty of the killings received death sentences, but they remain incarcerated.

In 2006, following a huge terrorist train attack in Mumbai that resulted in the death of over 200 people, relations between India and Pakistan deteriorated so much that train service between the two nations was halted. The Samjhauta Express, whose name means, "understanding", used to link the two countries. In 2007, as the train chugged towards Pakistan, a bomb explosion incinerated two coaches and sixty-seven passengers. Many of the charred bodies pulled from the wreckage were children. The attack was suspected to be sabotage aimed at derailing the peace talks between the two nations.

Today Pakistan is in a struggle between moderate Islam and hard line religious militancy. If fundamentalism gains the upper hand, an extremist religious coalition could be in power ruling the country within 12 years. Many Pakistanis feel hopeless about the loss of tolerance in their homeland. They have to be careful about voicing their support for minorities and women's rights.

I used to stay with our adventure tour groups at Islamabad's Pearl Continental Hotel. We spent the hot dusty days roaming through Peshawar's exotic bazaars. They would enjoy taking a break, to sip cold drinks in the pristine marble lobby, or float lazily in the sparkling pool. More recently there was a sign posted in the lobby declaring, "Personal guards or gunmen are required to deposit their weapons with Hotel Security."

Three militants stormed the hotel in 2009.[38] The security guards were shot dead then the terrorists exploded a massive car bomb killing 17 and injuring 50. The Pearl was reduced to chunks of rubble, its parking lot a gaping crater of rising smoke. Ikram, the Hotel's accountant ran, taking shelter in the mosque on the grounds. It saved his life.

Immediately following this brutal attack the United Nations evacuated its entire staff in Peshawar. This further endangered the lives of two million Pakistani refugees displaced by fighting against Taliban insurgents in the formerly serene Swat Valley.

This beautiful valley was next to Hunza, where we adventure travellers would relish a nice picnic laid out on the grass by a bubbling stream in utmost tranquility.

On December 15, 2014, a horrific tragedy took place when seven Taliban militants attacked a school in Peshawar, Pakistan. They massacred 145 people. 132 of the victims were children. It is reported that the school was targeted because the students were the children of the army officers who had recently undertaken a military offensive against terrorists in Waziristany.

Chapter 12
Three Reasons for Intolerance

*Those who praise their own doctrines and disparage the
doctrines of others do not solve any problem.*
                                            –Jainism Sukritanga 1.1.50

In the fall of 2001, having slept soundly in New
Delhi's Park Royal Hotel. The next morning, awoken by the
sun streaming through the window, I noticed a paper had
been slid under my door. Picking it up, I saw that it was
signed by the British Ambassador and issued by his
Embassy. It advised all American and British citizens not to
travel to Pushkar, Rajasthan where a colorful camel festival
was taking place. The warning declared that serious threats
had been made on our lives in the region. Pushkar happened
to be exactly where we were headed. I went down to the
lobby to meet our cinematographer, Jurg Walther, who
ironically blew out a breath, "Great. We're in India making a
film on religious tolerance. Now we ourselves are being
targeted."

Just glance at today's headlines - religion is often the
cause of genocide, crimes against humanity, rage, and
intolerance. But what is behind this hatred? Is it really the
faiths themselves, or people who misuse them? It is not the
belief systems themselves that are at fault, religions are
manipulated by cunning people to control the followers, they
seek to create division and exploit the faithful for monetary
or political gain. Sadly, the ruse is usually successful - as
world history shows us.

While working on *Not in God's Name* we collected
reams of information about altercations being fought all over
the world in the name of religion. Even though our research
turned up disputes in the most far-flung corners of the globe,
all of them had one or more of three underlying reasons for
killing in the name of God.

The first cause of religious intolerance is political
manipulation. This is when a politician or social group tries
to pit one segment of the population against another for

political gain. There are many examples of this. Some politicians purposely wreak havoc by spreading hatred and discrimination between members of different faiths communities to create divisions between them, while they fulfill their own worldly ambitions. This is the old "divide and separate" method of governing, and the real problem is that once the bottle of religious hatred is opened up, they can't easily just screw the lid back on, trapping the negative force again. [39] The mob mentality that stirs people up is too hard to control. A tempest of hatred, once unleashed, will swirl unabated as it grows, wrecking untold destruction in its path. Once begun, strife between religious groups has a tendency to continue on unabated. And as more violence occurs, more people are hurt and killed; there are then more reasons for people to seek revenge.

Political leaders, or unscrupulous religious leaders for political reasons use religion to scare and manipulate people, to stir them towards anger towards others or to a narrow view. Beneath this also lies motivation for power, money, or spreading the faith.

Many of the conflicts troubling our world today have strong religious dimensions. On all continents there are circumstances in which politicians sway believers to channel their hatred at certain religious groups perceived to be the enemy, thereby amassing huge followings. This hate dispenses a vast flow of emotional energy to enrage the crowds, and such a mob mentality channeled into hating a specific group can be an extremely strong force with which to fight a war against the perceived "others", and makes it possible to carry out political plans.

The most well-known and horrific example of this is Adolph Hitler's Nazi regime that attempted a mass extermination of the Jewish and Roma people, homosexuals and the disabled. They systematically annihilated over six million human beings. Prejudice against the Jews and a belief in the "mastery" of the Aryan race were employed to manipulate the German people, reawakening of age-old prejudices. The Nazis committed untold atrocities and plunged the world into the abyss of World War II, which ultimately killed seventy million.

The historian and Pulitzer Prize winning author, Saul Friedlander writes that the human spirit has not yet even been able to digest or understand this terrible era of history. The acts committed by the Third Reich were beyond heinous. In his book, *The Years of Extermination*, Friedlander dispassionately details the Third Reich's campaign of terror.

In 2001, when the Taliban was in power in Afghanistan, they issued an edict ordering all Hindus to wear a badge distinguishing their religion. This action was reminiscent of the Third Reich forcing Jews to wear a yellow star.

It is of grave concern that once the forces of hatred have been unleashed toward a particular religious group, it is virtually impossible to control the mad crowd. Reconciliation becomes almost unattainable because feuds escalate into retaliatory strikes. Also extreme elements seek to ruin peace efforts by spawning incidents of violence.

Territorial disputes are the second most common excuse for religious bigotry. When two groups claim a particular area of land, they often struggle over it believing it belongs to their faith. There are two well-known examples of this:

1. Israel, the Holy Land - the struggle between Jews and Palestinians
2. The battle over Kashmir - between Hindus and Muslims

These two disputes are immense, and have caused so much hostility in our world for decades, that our civilization is precipitously balanced between peace and nuclear annihilation.

The holy places of different faiths are supposed to unite and inspire us with their peacefulness, but oftentimes they have the opposite effect. There are many incidences of this, for example, Ayodhya, in Northwest India is a disputed site. Hindus claim it is the birthplace of their Lord Ram, yet Muslims centuries ago knocked down their Hindu temple there and built a mosque in its place. Then in the 1990's Hindu extremists destroyed the Babri mosque "liberating" the site at last. They plan to erect a new Hindu temple on the land. Riots and mass killings from this incident have resulted in thousands of deaths. There is a cycle of retribution in full swing, as two other mosques built on ancient Hindu sites have already been earmarked for destruction by Hindu radicals. In order to end this cycle, all parties must choose not to retaliate. The lives of the entire population of India, over 1.2 billion people are at risk.

A similar scenario is taking place in Jerusalem at the Temple Mount, which is considered Judaism's most sacred site. Here the holiest temples stood. First they were destroyed by Babylonians, and then by Romans.

To Muslims, the area is known as the Noble Sanctuary and is their third holiest site. It is said to be the place where Mohammed ascended into heaven. A mosque was erected here, in 692 AD. Claimed by both religions, the Temple Mount is one the globe's most hotly contested religious sites, and remains a focus of the Israeli - Arab conflict.

In 2002, the Alexandria Declaration was signed by Muslim clerics, Jewish Rabbis and Christian Bishops to promote peace and to keep the holy sites open for all. Peace might be reached at last if the religious leaders would add their voices to those speaking out against Palestinian suicide bombers and Israeli rockets, to find a peaceful solution.

Jews are not allowed to pray at the site, which some feel may lead to further violence. On November 17, 2014, two men armed with a gun and meat cleavers ran into the synagogue and killed four worshippers.

One million people were exterminated in World War II in the Balkans by the Utasa regime of Croatia. Under the Nazis, they sought to establish a Roman Catholic majority. This annihilation set the stage for another religious conflict, this time in Kosovo in the former Yugoslavia, between Catholic Croats, Muslim Bosnians and orthodox Christian Serbs. An ethnic cleansing took place when the Serbs attempted to exterminate the entire Muslim population. The vast number of killings, rapes and persecutions that happened there have been designated as crimes against humanity.

The so - called Holy War initiated on America by Osama bin Laden was waged to evict the United States from Saudi Arabia. Bin Laden saw the presence of foreign powers in the holy land of Mecca as an affront to his religious beliefs. He believed no outside power should be allowed in the land. This age old need to maintain territorial integrity has been the reason for endless struggles in the name of religion. It is tragic that holy sites, intended to be inspirational to humankind, are often horrifyingly miscast as sources of appalling conflict.

And these struggles over holy sites are more widespread then we realize. Even in Thailand and Cambodia, their armies have been sparring over an eleventh century temple, Preah Vihear, resulting in many deaths. Such altercations over holy sites have occurred here before. Much violence could be avoided if our civilization could move past the ancient beliefs that identify any piece of land as being more "possessed of Godliness then another." Untold wars and carnage have been caused by this this thinking. Perhaps these centers should be signified as "universal holy places."

One day in New Delhi I was fortunate to interview Dr. Karan Singh, a religious scholar and Member of Parliament with a storied background. His father, Hari Singh, was the Maharaja of Kashmir. At the time of the Partition he had to decide whether his princely state would go with India or Pakistan. Though three-quarters of the citizens were Muslim, Hari Singh decided Kashmir should remain with India.

Dr. Singh works for religious harmony. On the subject of holy places, he commented, "Who are we, tiny little creatures on this speck of dust in the universe to say that the illimitable Divine can only be worshipped in this place and only in this way? We cannot expect the Divine to be bound by *our* prejudices and our limitations."

Back in Dharamsala, the Dalai Lama had explained how the cycle of revenge keeps these territorial disputes alive, and creates more violence. I asked him, "Can you speak about forgiveness?"

"Forgiveness is important - whatever happened in the past, now today, there are new circumstances. We must look forward, not talking about the past. Forget it! We should look with a common interest at our future," he said.

The third and most dangerous reason for killing in the name of God is the exclusive claim to truth. It is an extremely perilous attitude when followers of one creed insist their path is the only true way to God. All others are invalid. Those who do not accept this must be killed. History is littered with countless innocents, who were murdered for this very reason.

A main cause of religious intolerance is ignorance, pure and simple. From uninformed people, who often lack education, come many stereotypes and assumptions about the "other."

The Abrahamic religions, including Judaism, Christianity and Islam have had terrible conflicts with each other, even though they share a common heritage. Interestingly, "Abraham" is originally a Sanskrit word. It comes from "Brahma." In 1,800 BCE, Abraham, the founder of the Hebrews, Abraham could not have a son with his wife due to her age. A maid, Hagar bore him one son, Ishmael, and Issac was born to his wife, Sarah. All are mentioned in the Old Testament. Issac became the forefather of the Twelve Tribes of Israel, and the descendants of Ishmael became the Semitic tribes and followed Arabic traditions. Moses and Jesus descended from Abraham, while Mohammed was through Ishmael. There are disagreements as to who is the Chosen One. Christianity was an offspring of Judaism. It makes sense that the various tribes naturally share the same gene pool.

An example of one such conflict between these three faiths is the Spanish Inquisition at the end of the 14th century. Jews, Protestants and Muslims were brutally mistreated. Mass conversions and forced baptisms were ordered. Many Jews were murdered in pogroms. Some, known as "Crypto - Jews," were driven to practice their faith in secret. Muslims were stripped of all their possessions and expelled from the country.

The holy books and scripture of many faiths contain allegories and fables written to illustrate teachings of morals or correct behavior. Some fundamentalists take these writings so literally, they consider them as directives to take action against other faiths. Passages written centuries ago as social directives may no longer be valid in today's cultures. In the Old Testament for example, stoning is mentioned as a punishment. Yet today in the West, we do not stone adulterers to death.

In some instances in the United States, abortion clinics have been bombed and doctors who perform abortions have been murdered by self-proclaimed fundamentalist Christian churches and organizations. Again the extremist views of a few have painted many church going Christians as hardcore avengers, when in truth it is only a small minority who act so extremely. Militant evangelical Christian groups in Great Britain have voiced similar opposition to abortions. They also oppose homosexuality.

Opposing something does not give anyone the right to take violent action against others with diverse beliefs. The problem is often fundamentalism itself, if it does not allow thoughtful reasoning to be the overriding guide, but rather relies on literal interpretations of scripture, such as in the Bible or the Quran.

Fundamentalism in some Islamic sects promotes living under *sharia* law, which treats women as second-class citizens, in some cases as possessions, and does not promote education. Practices such as this, including child marriage, do not respect the rights of the individual and do not allow the population to evolve. Indonesia and Malaysia are examples of countries where more moderate Islam is practiced with more moderate social mores.

Presently the schism in Islam between Shias and Sunnis threatens to cause untold bloodshed. Volunteers and funding for religious skirmishes are pouring in from countries where young people are dissatisfied with a lack of jobs and opportunities, and can be easily swayed.

In today's world, the simmering conflicts that could explode: India/ Pakistan, and Israel/ Iran, may well become full-blown religious wars. The news often features stories that are a mix of politics and religion: rigid fundamentalists vs. the tolerant. Animosity in the name of religion is the very antithesis of what our ideologies teach. Yet age-old hatreds still fester today, and this is a critical juncture for humankind. It begs us to ask the question, will we keep repeating history, or learn from our mistakes? The world's political stability and economic progress must insure that terrorism carried out in the name of God does not grow stronger. Reaching out to our brothers and expanding prosperity in developing nations is perhaps our best insurance policy for a peaceful future.

A friend suggested I interview his Professor, Mark Juergensmeyer who works in a large wooden house set on a cliff overlooking the crashing waves of the Pacific Ocean. He is a Professor of Religion at University of California Santa Barbara. Mark is a highly regarded religious and social studies scholar. He has written such books as, *Terror in the Mind of God: The Global Rise of Religious Violence (2003)* which contain interviews he conducted with religious activists around the world, including members of Hamas.

Mark was very cordial. The bookshelves in his study held a collection of writings on international relations that was so comprehensive, I wanted to dive in at once. We began the meeting, discussing terror and religious intolerance.

"There has been a worldwide loosening of social control," Mark explained. "This is the most important security issue we face since the Cold War." He outlined the causes and implementation of religious violence as described in his book. Violence he stressed is used to elicit political intimidation, and that it was timed carefully with certain events, and maximized to hit the highest number of targets possible.

Mark dubbed the current use of such attacks as "performance violence," meaning a kind of "spectacular theater." This fits with the latest beheadings that are disseminated worldwide as propaganda to entice disenchanted young men to join their ranks. He commented that young men who suffer with acute anxiety over jobs, sex and other matters could be attracted to such ideology.

"Our Western culture is beamed around the world today," Mark reasoned. "So terrorism is used to reclaim the center of public opinion for the "defenders of the faith." He pointed out that since global religious war is fought by the usual means, it really does no good. The tit for tat attacks only instigate more retaliatory assaults. The teachings of Islam are ambiguous about violence. While specific lines in the Quran read, "Slay not the life that God has made sacred," others justify the use of violence.[40] Mark also noted that the warriors who engage in such acts then have a sense of earned pride and identify themselves for having defended the faith. This is the current global climate of "strident religious visions" that we are facing.

Chapter 13
The Tapestry of Faiths

Our faith traditions are highways leading to the same destination.

-Mahatma Gandhi

Taking to heart the Dalai Lama's advice, I kept visiting the shrines and leaders of different faiths. It seemed clear that those who create strife in the name of religion would benefit from realizing the obvious - that using God to justify killing goes against the very tenets of their own religious beliefs. Wise words from the interview with His Holiness echoed in my mind: "I think we need to make some effort to send a message of religious harmony, that all religions have the same potential. Humanity needs different traditions. One tradition simply cannot satisfy the variety of people. Since there are so many people with varying different dispositions, we *need* different traditions."

Living in India, I was confronted by the dizzying array of religious sects that permeate every sector of society. Dr. Karan Singh is extremely dedicated to the interfaith movement. I spoke with him.

"Now," he began, not wasting a second in getting to the main point, "four of the world's great religions have been born here: Hinduism, Jainism, Buddhism, and Sikhism. Hinduism was the first and then came the rest. Christianity arrived in India with St. Thomas the Apostle, a thousand years before it reached Europe and fifteen hundred years before it reached America. We also have Judaism, which is prevalent in a small but vibrant community in South India. Then there is Zoroastrianism, also a small but significant religion that came to India when she welcomed Iranian refugees. And India has interacted with Islam for a thousand years, some of which was disastrous, some of which was creative."

I asked the obvious, "Would you say that India is a very tolerant country?"

He responded, "Yes. Hinduism by its very nature is tolerant or should be tolerant, because there's a pluralism built into Hinduism. You can worship a non-dual, formless aspect of the Divine, or you can worship the Divine with form as Vishnu, Shakti, or Shiva. There is an openness about all spiritual paths.

"Hindu culture," he continued, " has not taken the line that there is only one path of salvation. If I may say with all due respect, the Semitic theologies, although there are individual exceptions, believe that theirs is the only path to salvation. They may be very good at interfaith conferences, remaining seemingly open, but in their heart of hearts, they *know* that theirs is the correct way and there is no other way. This is not true for Hindus. We genuinely believe that all these paths ultimately lead to the Divine."

His words persuaded me to delve further into all the paths in India. It happened that a few days later, I discovered an Interfaith Conference would be taking place the very next afternoon.

The following morning found me edging through Delhi's jumble of traffic with its' cacophony of noise. This lovely capital city of British colonnade buildings was now bursting at the seams, since each drought that caused crop failures sent waves of villagers flooding to relocate in her urban center. New arrivals would find a space on her crowded footpaths and go about seeking jobs, food, shelter, and everything a bustling metropolis has to offer. Delhi's population has quadrupled since I first visited it as a young college student 40 years earlier.

Dilapidated cars and trucks played chicken on the dusty streets as our fearless driver, Munsi Rana dodged monkeys, cows, rickshaws, holy men, beggars, and even a painted elephant being lead through the vehicles by its' barefoot mahout. Little children touting boxes of tissue and magazines begged for rupees at each stop. A leper bearing a portrait of Kali, the terrifying goddess with her necklace of severed limbs, was propped up on a tray with incense smoke curling skyward. He tried to catch my eye each time our vehicle slowed down. Finally at a stop, he gave me a *rupee,* and I handed him a flower.

We missed several near collisions on the streets, which had been constructed years earlier for twenty times fewer vehicles than now choked them. I held my breath, praying for safe passage until we finally reached the serene flower gardens at the meeting center.

I took a moment to collect myself after the hair-raising trip across town, gazing into the lotus pond in front of the building that reflected the morning sunlight, unaware that I was about to meet a most remarkable woman.

When I strolled in through the massive iron gate, a striking lady with thick silver hair and beautiful eyes greeted me. Her garments of raw silk and homespun cotton were sumptuous. I wasted no time in asking her what the gathering was all about, and discovered a beautifully expressed human being.

Smilingly she informed me, "This meeting is a dialogue organized as part of the International Day for Tolerance. Then with a wry little smile, she added, "People might be very cynical about a day like this. I mean, why have one day for tolerance and the rest of the year for intolerance?

This charming lady was Razya Suthan, who continued, "This is the second time we have organized a dialogue like this. We try to bring together people from different disciplines, not only different communities. We are beginning to 'understand' that if we really dissect "tolerance" as a concept, what we find is *respect*. Otherwise, it's tolerance on whose terms: the tolerator's terms? Or the terms of the tolerated? If you aim for respect, then maybe the question of tolerance actually disappears. And that would be ideal. There are people who would say respect is not good enough, that you should look for reverence. If you revere life, if you revere difference, you're capable of celebrating that difference.

"Some of our group belong to the Mosaic Charter, which is an idea based on the concept that diversity is not an accident. If we believe in Divine Will, diversity is probably God's will. If we believe in evolution, diversity is probably the natural order of things. So why do we try to correct it all the time? We should celebrate it! And if we celebrate it in every respect, then respect for other living things, respect for other ideologies, respect for other kinds of people, respect for the fact that we are Technicolor and multi-faceted becomes a cause for satisfaction, rather than dissatisfaction.

"People like us have a problem with the word "global," she emphasized. "Because it sounds too uniform as in, everybody's blue, or everybody's green, or everybody's round. No. Using the mosaic, what we believe is that the pieces do fit together as a whole, but also of each distinct part having its own place, its own character, a wholeness that celebrates diversity."

She was 'preaching to the choir,' of course, but I was relieved and delighted.

"So, you believe that with diverse religions, cohabitation is critical?"

Razya mused, "How else do you survive? Of course, it's vital. Life depends on other things also being alive. Ecology depends on that, on a cycle of things that depend on one another. It depends on co-existence, and not on uniform existence. So yes, you can't just exist by yourself. And we seem to fit together. We have commonality; we all belong to the human race. If we were all meant to be Chinese, we would be. We're not. We're different in appearance, in the way we express ourselves, in the way we perceive the world..."

"And religion," I added.

Razya nodded, "And religion, in our beliefs and our convictions. But most of the world's faiths talk about there being many mansions, many doorways. The *Quran* says, 'God opens many doors.' Why would He open more than one door if there were not a reason for it? Why would there not just be one tunnel? Maybe all of them are the true path. So, why should the true path not have many facets? These are questions for us. I'm not saying we're proposing all the answers. But if we begin to explore them, we're on a better track. And then we will be able to respect other 'isms,' not just of faith. To feel that anybody has an exclusive title to the truth, or an exclusive insight, or has been specially chosen…this business of, 'I am a child of God, but you might be a child of somebody else,' is ridiculous."

"What message would you give people about respect for each other?" I asked.

"I think we're moving toward a very homogenized melting pot view of what the world should be like, that everybody should become similar. But I think that's a mistaken direction. We must learn to co-exist. We must learn to co-exist politically. I'm a very good example of what I say. I come from four faith communities: Islam, Sikhism, Christianity, and Hinduism. They're all part of my heritage, and I think that's very good! So, if somebody asks me, 'What are you?' I have to think...I'm a nice mosaic myself.

"My name is Razya Suthan, which is my given name. My family name is Ismael, and my married name is Abasi. So, I carry all four. It's a nice Muslim name, but it raises questions in Indian society. 'Oh, you must be a Muslim,' they say. 'No, I'm not,' I respond. 'But you sound like one. You look like one. You're named like one,' they retort. 'Well, that's in the eye of the beholder,' is the thought I leave with them."

I next visited a synagogue in New Delhi, and met Rabbi Ezekial Issac Malekar, the representative of the Jewish community in India. An open and friendly man, he enjoys opportunities to network with religious leaders. He began, "When Indira Gandhi was assassinated, I sang the Jewish prayers at her cremation. And it so happens that the Dalai Lama telephones me when interfaith gatherings involving Jews and Buddhists are taking place."

"How wonderful," I thought.

In addition to their respective faiths both having historical Diasporas, the two religious groups have suffered enormous numbers of deaths, the Jews at the hands of the Nazis in the Holocaust who annihilated six million, and the Tibetan Buddhists, under the Communist Chinese, who killed 1.5 million. Often Tibetan Buddhist and Jewish leaders compare tactics of how to keep their civilizations alive in the face of cultural genocide.

"Jews have been in India since 587 BCE, when we left Palestine to seek asylum in India," the Rabbi continued, "we comprise a very small minority here." Although just a few thousand; they have always been able to practice their faith in peace. India is distinctive in including the Jews.[41] In

149

many parts of the world the Jewish people have suffered prejudice and persecution.

Jews believe in one God, and we are created in His image with an equal opportunity to do good things in this world. The essence of Judaism is to be concerned about humanity. Their scripture, the *Torah*, contains the Ten Commandments, but also 163 others, known as *mitzvoth*. Jews believe a Messiah will come, who will bring great peace to the world.

Having grown up Catholic, I decided to visit a few churches in India. I had heard about mass conversions of Untouchable Hindus to Christianity and Buddhism. It was interesting to find out that Christianity has been in India since the time of Christ. St. Thomas the Apostle traveled to India from Galilee and preached the Gospel. He was so successful at converting Hindus that the Brahmin priests had him pierced with a lance and stoned to death.

St. Francis [42]Xavier also journeyed to India to preach. Much like the wandering Hindu yogis, he never stayed more then twenty days in any place, and traveled to convert souls. Walking barefoot and dressed in old, ripped clothing, he ate only rice, fish, and yogurt. Many pilgrims visit Goa to view St. Francis's incorruptible body. I saw his remains years ago, but they became quite worn, having been touched for years. Now his body is only displayed on holy occasions.

Christians believe that Jesus Christ is both the Son of God and the Messiah prophesied in the Old Testament. Accepting Him as humanity's savior they teach, assures freedom from the torments of eternal damnation. Christianity is a monotheistic faith based on the teachings of Jesus Christ. The concepts of sin, confession, charity and sacrifice are important to Christians.

Pope John Paul II worked to spread tolerance among faiths. On a journey to India, he spoke about freedom of religion as a right. Meeting with leaders of other faiths, he read a quote from Mahatma Gandhi on the non-exclusivity of religion.

Pope Benedict XVI, in one of his books, wrote that the Jews were not responsible for the death of Jesus, which does contribute to some degree of peace and reconciliation between the two faiths.

Standing on Malabar Hill in Bombay, I could see the Towers of Silence. It felt spooky, considering that I'd heard that Zoroastrians placed their dead in these structures so vultures could swoop down and eat them. Behind this practice was the belief that even in death, nourishing the life of animals was a final act of charity. Had it not been that our crew needed to film the vultures for *Not in God's Name*, I might have passed on this one.

Back in our hotel dining room, we grabbed meat from the buffet. Driving through the jammed streets towards the city's outskirts to an area where the scavengers are known to congregate, we tossed the meat onto the ground. We were on the hunt, despite the fact that we were told the vulture population had decreased 99%, due to pollution and extreme overcrowding in the urban centers. After a long time, we resigned ourselves to the truth of that statistic. The population boom of modern India and China was decimating Asia's birds.

Zoroastrianism was one of the first religions to teach God is invisible and omnipotent; it is traced back to Bronze Age. In 1,500 BCE, Zarathustra, the prophet, taught religious accountability is the inner work of every individual. He revealed the teachings of God to the nomads of Persia, emphasizing that they should choose good over evil. Zoroastrians believe in the existence of heaven and hell, and that even in hell we can improve ourselves. Millennia ago, threatened with persecution by Muslims in Persia, they fled by boat and landed on India's welcoming shores.

"Nowadays some Zoroastrians are trying to breed vultures, so few are left," the head priest of the Zoroastrian temple in Delhi explained. He donned a long white garment and performed the sacred fire ceremony for us to film, which is *never* seen by outsiders. He revealed this ritual for the sake of *Not in God's Name's* intention of promoting peace between faiths. He too, was upset by the escalating violence caused by religious hatred.

Fire is the Zoroastrians' symbol of God, and he chanted and made offerings to the flames. The priest explained, "Our religion teaches us purity, also that we do not harm anyone. I perform my ceremonies five times a day, and wear a cloth over my mouth so germs don't touch the sacred flames. I performed two ceremonies for you—the first whilst sitting down, for the invocation of a new home or premises. The second, standing, is for departed souls. We worship fire, in all religions it plays an important role. It's not a God, but a symbol of God. We worship the five elements of nature: fire, earth, water, air, and trees."

I asked, "What do you think about strife among faiths?"

He responded with a heavy heart. "In the name of religion, when people fight, it's not right. In Ayodhya they are having a problem over who will build the temple there. Build one huge complex, in which small temples of every religion should be erected! The Hindus and the Muslims must have theirs *next* to each other, with the floor of both temples made of *one* piece of marble, where they will never fight again! India is a country of religions, why can't we stay united? Why can't a Muslim take part in a Hindu Festival? Or a Hindu in a Christian Festival?"

"Here in my place," he continued, "I've got staff working from all religions, and I go to prayer meetings with followers of all faiths. Our ceremonies are five times a day. Muslims pray five times a day, and in Hinduism, they worship five elements. So, there is no difference between these religions. All faiths have taken ideas from one another. They are one."

Today, Zoroastrians are becoming extinct since they only marry within their own community. UNESCO has declared the distinctive culture of Zoroastrianism a world treasure.[43]

At a beautiful lotus shaped temple in Delhi, considered to be the Indian symbol of religious harmony, I was introduced to the Bahai faith. It was founded in 1863 by Mirza Husayn ali Nuri, known as *Bahaullah*, to promote communal harmony in Persia. Drawing from Islam and Christianity, Bahaism is based on the teaching that all religions are one, as are all people. Developing the spiritual nature that lies at humanity's core is considered to be the purpose for which we were created. Bahais believe in one united race, for the betterment of humanity.

Bahais accept there is only one God, who is unknowable and has many manifestations. Messengers teach, and when it becomes necessary, God is revealed to humankind. Each era requires a new messenger. After death, the soul is said to continue to evolve through levels that are an extension of this universe, to reach God. Gandhi called Bahaism, "a solace to mankind." There are 2.2 million Bahai in India, the largest community in the world. In Iran today, they are persecuted.

The Dalai Lama's comments had inspired me to study what lies at the core of each faith, and to discover their similarities. Such an education at an early age is of great importance. In our quest for world peace, teaching respect for the world's faiths to our youth may go a long way in eliminating or at least reducing acts of bigotry and hate, from bullying to killing. Ignorance about faiths other than one's own, contributes to unnecessary fear and superstition, which keeps us separate from the realization and experience of our interconnectedness with each other. It is tragic when individuals are silenced because of fearing religious fanatics who would harm them and their families just for having a different view.

At the root of all religions is the innate human desire to answer the perennial questions: Who am I? Where did I come from? What is the purpose of my life? What happens when I die? The world's wisdom traditions have emerged to answer them. And while their rituals, tenets, social customs, food, clothing, and mores differ, their purpose doesn't. Every being longs to be happy, to find his and her place in the universal scheme of existence. Every prayer is directed to the One, to our Source, no matter by which name the Great Mystery is called. Our collective religious beliefs are threads that weave together the rich tapestry of humankind and its common search for answers to the big questions of existence.

Georg Feuerstein, author of many books on Yoga and Hinduism, had elaborated on this theme. [44] At his ranch near Mount Shasta, California, he expressed to me that, "All spiritual traditions in the world aim at a state of existence that exceeds or transcends the human condition. In the great religions, this extraordinary state of existence is taken into account in daily life, in the form of prayer, meditation and moral conduct." This commonality offers the greatest impetus for not only overriding our differences but also appreciating them."

My journey convinced me that an exploration of the many roads leading to God contributes greatly to realizing our oneness. This understanding tears aside the veil of ignorance, fear, and confusion and reveals that hatred for those of a different religion is the antithesis of faith. It is not the religions themselves that are in conflict, but the people who misinterpret and misuse them by perpetrating terrible acts of violence against their fellow man. Promoting understanding by focusing on the similarities in our faiths breaks down the prejudice and cultural barriers that separate us. As we embrace one other as one universal family emanating from one Source, we promote peace on the planet.

In 2010, the University of California convened a panel named, "Secular Ethics." The Dalai Lama participated, making a rich contribution declaring, "I am a Buddhist, but I should not develop attachment to my faith, because then I could become biased." I have heard him caution that if we are too attached to our own religion we may develop a conscious or unconscious tendency to disrespect other faiths. His potent message rings especially true now.

When was the dawn of faith? The June 2011 issue of *National Geographic* featured an article on a recently excavated archaeological site that sheds light on the origins of religion. Archaeologists, high atop a remote hill in southern Turkey, discovered Gobekli Tepe, a massive stone structure far older then Stonehenge. There is evidence that 12,000 years ago, people erected what appears to be a temple which may be mankind's first site of worship. This structure is composed of a set of concentric stone rings, which appear to have been constructed at the dawn of the Neolithic Revolution, when hunter-gatherers began practicing agriculture. It is set in an area known as the Fertile Crescent, which is today's Gaza, Turkey and Iraq. It is posited that religion arose from agriculturalists who formed beliefs in a celestial order that helped to promote peace and co-operation among different tribes.

Predating the pyramids of Egypt by at least 6,000 years, the limestone was fashioned with astonishing craftsmanship into pillars covered with animals including boars, scorpions and gazelles, which were considered to be guardians of the spirit world. This site is considered to be the largest structure in the world up to that time. Archeologists are currently trying to determine why and how each 16-ton pillar was constructed. Their most recent hypothesis is that they were used to hang offerings.

I consider myself fortunate to have been exposed on many continents to faiths practiced by indigenous peoples including Guatemalans, Tibetans, Brazilians, Balinese, and others, who share several similar traditions. The main theme they share is their profound connection to Mother Earth, *Gaia*, and her natural elements. They have an innate love, respect, and enjoyment of the cosmos, and are content with their place in it. Although these belief systems have adopted some aspects of the religions brought to them by various conquerors, they have maintained their own traditions by infusing new religious concepts with their original beliefs.

In 1983, the Hindu teacher, Swami Vivekananda travelled to the US to attend the Parliament of the World's Religions in Chicago. He spoke to the audience about religious pluralism. Quoting the *Bhagavad Gita,* Vivekananda proclaimed, "As the different streams having their sources in different places all mingle their water in the sea, so, O Lord, the different paths which men take through different tendencies, various though they appear, crooked or straight, all lead to thee." His talk made a great contribution towards the conception of the Inter faith movement in the United States.

Reverend Michael Beckwith is a minister in Los Angeles, who had a vision of a trans-denominational spiritual community. Coretta Scott King wrote to him in a personal letter, " I greatly admire what you are doing to bring about the Beloved Community, which is certainly what my dear husband worked for and ultimately gave his life." Michael is the Co-Chair of the Season for Nonviolence with Arun Gandh, Mahatma Gandhi's grandson. [45]

Michael grew up in a tough neighborhood in Los Angeles, and felt although he had heard the word of Jesus, many were not following his actions. He overcame numerous obstacles to become a faith leader for thousands. Michael began the Agape Spiritual Center as an interdenominational community.

At the UN for World Interfaith Harmony Week, as reported by Rev. Michele K. Synegal, "The speakers appealed to our sensibilities and sensitivities regarding the need for interfaith solidarity in eradicating violence through peaceful interactions and dialog and an increase in religious 'tolerance.'" She relates, "We were encouraged to take action by participating in efforts that advance the goal of world peace."

At the conference, Reverend Michael asked all the participants to, " Go deep within to that place that only knows peace." He is an American New Thought Minister who founded Agape International Spiritual Center in Los Angeles, he works for interfaith harmony. When I asked Michael about violence in the name of faith, he explained, "This radical element is in every religion. In Islam, in Christianity, you'll find individuals that are very zealous in their faith. These extreme elements are not the majority, but they get all the press. They have a tendency to be the loudest. And they do the most zany, crazy, destructive things. You find them in all faiths. Here in America, particularly in our media, whenever there is some kind of negativity going on and the person is a Muslim, we'll say, "Muslim terrorist."

Yet they don't necessarily say "Christian terrorist" whenever a Christian bombs something, it's our perception here. It's just, "Jack Smith blew up a building." They don't say "Jack Smith, Christian terrorist" blew up a building, even if they're bombing an abortion clinic. So there's a bias there. But this fundamentalism in every religion has a loud voice, even though it does not have a majority following. And if one is not careful, you can begin to perceive the whole religion that way. You'll hear the word, "Islam" and you'll suddenly think of a radical who wants to bomb something rather then most of the Muslims who love and take care of their family, pray a number of times a day, and have a powerful and wonderful relationship with the presence of God."

I recalled the Dalai Lama summing up his comments about religious intolerance during our interview in Dharamsala: "Whether due to a political reason, an economic reason, or a religious reason, some people can make a distinction, and create distance between us—from one another. And that's unrealistic. Reality is not that way, particularly in the name of religion. In faiths yes, there are differences that occur, such as different concepts. But the real message of love, compassion, forgiveness, self discipline... all major religious traditions talk the same language. We need different traditions."

Recently at a teaching in New York, the Dalai Lama remarked that it is equally important to respect those who have no belief in God, as it is to honor other faiths. There are often lawsuits by atheists in order to remove the symbols of faiths from our government buildings, classrooms and currency. Perhaps if we included an atheist symbol too, the people who object to religious symbols would be more content. Upon googling "atheist symbol," I found out that the Darwin fish is used most often, but there are several other symbols that denote atheist beliefs.

In 1963, the American Atheist Association or Society designed an atomic symbol to denote human beings can best progress through scientific and logical inquiry theory. Atheist symbols could be as widely used as the crescent moon of Islam, the Jewish star, the Christian crucifix, and others.

In his latest book, *Beyond Religion: Ethics for a Whole World*, the Dalai Lama suggests the values universal to all faiths should be taught in a secular fashion in order to avoid skirmishes and misunderstandings which can arise in the name of religion. These human values will help to ensure a good society, and that the universal values of kindness and compassion are taught and practiced. With this simple solution, we can all believe as we see fit, without forcing our belief systems on one another. Surely this will result in a more peaceful world.

There is a consensus among Agnostics, Atheists, Theists, Polytheists, and Henotheists that God exists as a concept. There are many thousands of faith groups in the world who believe that they know without qualification that God exists; further they "know" "his" attributes. Unfortunately they cannot agree on what the attributes are. If they had been able to agree, tens of millions would have been spared wars and holocausts.

At a talk in Los Angeles, the Dalai Lama remarked, "What is the use or benefit of religion? Is it just a custom?" He described religious beliefs in the past when, "Everyone thought good was done by the deities, and bad was done by the ghosts. 2,000 years passed like this, then people did research into reality. In this 21st century with scientific advancements, many things are cured. So people began to lose faith in belief, and saw it as custom."

The 17th Karmapa, Ugyen Trinley Dorje, is only twenty-nine years old and wise well beyond his years. In the interview "Young People Meet the Karmapa,' filmed during a recent visit he made to Germany, he explained, "When belief started, it was real spiritualism, not just custom. Spirituality is more effective then just belief in a faith. It is within us and all the forms. Gurus, belief systems, etc. are all just tools."[46]

The Pew Research Center reports that in 2010, 84% of the world's 5.8 billion population had some kind of religious affiliation. Of the 1.1 billion remaining, many believe in a higher power. [47]

Earlier when I met Dr. Karan Singh, he remarked about the current situation in India, "India has been a very tolerant country. Of late, I must admit that there have been some rather disturbing indications that this tolerant attitude is beginning to change. Partially, I must say, and perhaps predominantly, it is a reaction to Islamic fundamentalists, because Islamic fundamentalism has become so strong and so aggressive that, in some ways, some sections of Hindu society are beginning to try and develop a sort of defense mechanism. Yet I still feel that the basic Indian ethos is one of tolerance, and not only tolerance. Tolerance can be a little negative: 'I know I'm the best. You are there, so I have to tolerate you.' We go beyond that. It's an acceptance of multiple paths to the Divine. There's an important difference between tolerance and acceptance, tolerance being a negative virtue and acceptance being a more positive attitude."

"Will you please speak about your personal views on religious tolerance?" I inquired.

"Yes, well, let me also say something about the Interfaith Movement. It could be said it began in 1893, with the first Parliament of the World's Religions in Chicago. Swami Vivekananda turned up unexpectedly and made an impact. Then, in the 20th Century, half-a-dozen major interfaith organizations were founded and there were a series of interfaith meetings. And in 2000, for the first time, the United Nations took cognizance of religion and called a Peace Summit of the religious leaders, which was held in the United Nations Building. So, it is ongoing and, personally, I have been active in the Interfaith Movement for the last quarter of a century. Obviously, my view is that all these religions are so many different paths to the divine."

"You see," he shrugged philosophically, "all religions have positive and negative features. Take how, in Christianity for example, you have Jesus Christ who mounted the cross so that humanity would be saved. And yet, you have the horrible doings of the Spanish Inquisition, where people were tortured and burned at the stake. They're both Christianity. Which one do you choose? Similarly, in every religion, you can find horrible things being done in the name of the Divine. And you can also find great charity, love, and compassion. So what we interfaith people have to do is to try and choose the positive elements in each tradition and present them to the world."

I then asked Dr. Singh, "Could you say anything about how, at this time, the world needs to bridge its differences in terms of religion, and join together to create a peaceful future?"

"Absolutely!" He enthusiastically exclaimed, "The whole aim of the interfaith movement is to overcome our differences. It's not that we want everybody to adopt the same religion. But what we do want is, if you're a Christian, you should continue to believe that yours is the best way. I'm a Hindu, and I continue to believe that mine is the best way. But we must respect each other. The acceptance of multiple paths to the Divine is the key concept in the interfaith movement *and* in creating a peaceful world. But unless you accept that, if you continue to insist that you have a special monopoly, a copyright, a patent upon the Divine, then that's something else. You entirely entitled to say, 'I think my religion is the best.' Fair enough. I accept that. But you cannot say, that because I don't accept your religion I am wrong and I should therefore be persecuted, or blown up with a bomb, or any such thing, that is not acceptable.

"Monopolistic tendencies in religion are not acceptable. The divine is immense! Who are we, tiny creatures...on a speck of dust in the universe, to lay down that the illimitable Divine can appear only in this place, and only in this form, and only in this way? That's unacceptable. How do we know? There may be a million inhabited planets in the cosmos. Only God knows how the Divine appears in those places. We have to accept the fact that the Divine is not bound by our prejudices and limitations."

"How does the interfaith movement get its message out?" I asked.

"Every organization has its outreach through lectures, conferences, publications and branches. However, whereas there are vast sums of money supporting the religions, interfaith is nobody's baby. That is why the movement has not caught on; because the vast amount of money spent supporting the religions is not available to us. In spite of that, interfaith organizations have been doing good work. But it is not near the dimension that is required to overcome the fanaticism and the fundamentalism that we see."

We're all praying to the same Divine, which is called by many names or no name at all. This indescribable presence is worshipped throughout the world in mosques, churches, temples, synagogues, at home and at roadside shrines. Allah to the Muslims, the Holy Trinity to the Christians, the many deities of Hinduism, Buddhism, and Jainism are all expressions of the one Absolute Reality. With an open mind we can realize how our belief systems connect with those of others. As the religions of the world have evolved, so have the traditions and strikingly similar concepts they share.

During our interview, in the spirit of breaking down the barriers of misunderstanding and forging ties, the Dalai Lama suggested, "Leaders of faiths should get together and compare their similarities." Some of these similarities include asceticism, rituals, charity, congregations, doctrine, festivals, offerings, prayers, prophets, saints, purification, rosaries, sanctuaries, shrines and worship.

Man's quest for God is universal, and divergent creeds are the unique roads that believers travel to reach the same destination. Although there are differences, we can develop a deep respect for all faith traditions that contribute untold richness to our civilization. Religious tolerance is our greatest tool for promoting world peace.

The higher states of consciousness are available to us all, and spiritual practices have as their aim the transcending of our ordinary human awareness so we may know our true divine nature. The principal difference between the Eastern and Western spiritual traditions is the Western religions believe the soul will enjoy divinity in the after life. Eastern paths stress that in this present lifetime each individual can consciously unite with Spirit, and access the ultimate state of oneness that great souls such as Jesus Christ and Gautama Buddha taught.

The Dalai Lama smiled broadly when I asked him

how Tibetan Buddhism has influenced relations between faiths. "While we remain outside Tibet, we have this good opportunity to meet with people from different religions, and traditions. In this way we have learned a lot; it has been very useful. And through that contact we have developed genuine mutual respect, and mutual learning. So I think we've made some positive contribution regarding harmony between various religious traditions."

Chapter 14
Revenge and Forgiveness

"Aim at heaven and you will get earth thrown in. Aim at earth and you get neither."

-C.S. Lewis

The cycle of revenge between any two faiths can be reignited with disastrous results, impacting thousands of innocent victims. When the state of Pakistan was carved out of India in 1947, it demonstrated how the animosity between members of the two faiths had become so acrimonious that no solution would be adequate to heal it.

When extremists in India attack a segment of the population, they invariably end up killing many of their own people. In Ayodhya in 1992, hard line Hindus pulled down a 16th century mosque believed to have been built on the birthplace of their revered deity, Lord Rama. In 2002, 59 Hindu pilgrims returning from Ayodhya to a city in Gujarat on the Sabarmathi Express were burned alive in their train coach.[48] This launched the bloodiest communal violence in India in a decade. Gujarat's Hindus rampaged in retaliation, killing and destroying businesses. Later rioting broke out resulting in 790 Muslims and 200 Hindus being killed in the Islamic neighborhoods of Ahmedabad, while the city was in flames. Hindu Nationalists set Muslim owned shops on fire, while innocent people were pulled onto the street from their homes, doused with kerosene and set ablaze, or butchered alive. Many temples, mosques, shrines and churches were destroyed. Several waves of rioting resulted in 1,000 dead. 150,000 people were left homeless and had to be relocated to grim overcrowded refugee camps. Many of the Muslim victims are now forced to live in a ghetto in Ahmedabad, known as "Little Pakistan," after their families were hacked to death and their homes were torched.

What took place in Ayodhya was one of the bloodiest and more recent examples of communal disharmony, illustrating how the cycle of revenge in the name of religion, only begets more death and destruction.

"*Nai jau, bilkul nai,*" meaning "You will absolutely not enter!" Armed police menacingly shouted orders out to us, brandishing their weapons. Our film crew was walking in Varanasi in the old bazaar on the River Ganges, while shooting *Not in God's Name.* We had come upon a stately mosque which was under heavy guard by police commandos wielding submachine guns. We were prevented from even approaching, because we were lugging our camera equipment, and the tripod appeared suspicious to them. It turned out we were unknowingly at a holy site that was one of two other mosques earmarked for destruction by Hindu fanatics.

Having knowledge of the bloody religious history of these areas did not lessen the ache in my heart every time I was confronted by yet another streak of violence waged in the name of some faith.

These wounds are still open and oozing in India, and to this day such holy sites remain sources of conflict. In 2007, a court ruled that, "no religious ceremonies could be held at the Babri Masjid site in Ayodhya."[49] I had visited the mosque there years earlier, and it was perfectly calm, it had been erected by the Emperor Babur who established the Mughal, Muslim reign in 1528.[50] Paramilitary troops now have the vicinity under heavy surveillance 24 hours a day. If the radical followers of two such great faiths, Islam and Hinduism, could find an attitude of respect for each other and join their more moderate brethren, the cycle of retribution would evaporate.

India will overtake Indonesia as the most populous Muslim country in the world. Yet their segment of the populace is lagging behind in education, jobs, pay, and lack employment in politics, government, and universities.[51] Use of birth control is not popular, and education among females continues to be low. Women occupy the bottom of most social strata. According to a recent US India Policy Institute report, Muslims "have not shown any measurable improvement." This inequality is a source of much of strife. Obviously, fair and just aid to all groups should be offered to increase opportunities that lead to a better life.

In 2009, I watched CNN and Fox News broadcasting live feed of the Taj Mahal Hotel and the Oberoi Trident Hotels in Mumbai being attacked by terrorists. This was where my friends and I had first seen Mother Teresa, when she was the featured speaker at the 1981 Transpersonal Psychology Conference. But now radical Islamic terrorists were executing tourists in the hallways and hotel rooms in cold blood. Now radical Islamic terrorists had spread across the city of Mumbai and were holed up in the stately Taj Mahal Hotel. Tourists were cold-bloodedly murdered in hallways and guest rooms.

In a spectacular counter attack, Indian Black Cat commandos grappled onto the roof, and swept the rooms to smoke them out. During 60 hours of bloody mayhem, over 170 innocent people lost their lives, including scores of Mumbai police. The terrorists had attacked strategic targets such as the train station, Jewish Center, and the Leopold Cafe. It turned out the gunmen were from Pakistan and entered Mumbai harbor by stealing a boat and massacring the crew. The ten men then sailed in an inflatable speedboat and came ashore at Colaba.

Steve Ross, a well - known yoga teacher in the United States, who instructs students such as Dr. Oz of TV fame, was trapped in the Oberoi Trident Hotel during the bloody attacks. "I was there on a meditation retreat of all things. Usually when the Oberoi. We were about three days into the retreat and one day after a public meditation, we went back to spend the night. Some of the group went downstairs to the restaurant to eat, and some to our rooms. I was one of the fortunate ones who went to our room. I heard what sounded like fire crackers but much too rhythmic, they seemed more like gunshots; I'd heard machine guns before. I ran outside, it's one of those atrium style hotels where you can see the ground floor from every story. I went out on a landing, looked down, and I saw two guys shooting AK 47's into the lobby. I could hear faint screams in the background.

"I was on the twelfth floor, and I thought, this is not good, because they didn't have military outfits on, they just looked like college kids with backpacks and machine guns. I went back into my room, shut the door, and put a couch against it. I wondered, what's next? I was with two other guys. I exclaimed, 'Those are gunshots!' One turned on the TV, and the other started making phone calls. It went on for a while; we heard a lot of sporadic shooting. There were many explosions, it turned out they were hand grenades, but you couldn't tell at the time. When it first started it made me hyper alert, but then I don't why, I got very calm. I didn't feel like I was going to die. That went on for a while, then there were reports of what was happening on TV, and people were phoning us from outside. There were ten attackers in Mumbai, some went to the train station and shot many people, others went to the Taj Hotel and some were here, so they were all over and everyone was freaked out. We were getting information and realized, we can't leave, and there isn't anywhere to go. I wasn't about to walk outside. So I just accepted my condition.

"Then an explosion, our room began filling up with smoke. It was so thick I realized we could get asphyxiated. We wet some washcloths and covered our faces. With the cloths on, we looked out the window then realized that we looked like terrorists, and thought, 'Uh oh.' So we backed away from the windows, I broke out the glass pane to get some air, it was thick, but I was motivated. And as the air was coming in, I laid on my back, and watched the smoke curling up, the pattern was so beautiful. I felt really expanded and thought, 'I'm totally fine, whatever happens I'll be fine.' Later I talked to Eckhart Tolle about this, and he said, 'When you're in a crisis situation, especially if you practice the divine presence, your consciousness will expand dramatically.' I felt as if I was in a bubble, and when the smoke finally cleared, we didn't know how long we'd remain in there.

"The TV was saying one thing, and the lobby desk, another, 'Oh, we're almost done, no problem, and then you can come out.' Then you'd hear a big explosion, and thought, 'Uh, we're not going out!' So we just sat there for two days. During that time I did yoga, and took a shower because of the smoke, figuring they would turn off the water. The dry mouth was bad, and I meditated. You're so alert. The other guys were calling our outside connections, trying to find out about our whole group, about who were accounted for. We heard a lot of gunfire. So finally they called, and said, this is real now, it's finally safe.

"Apparently the police came in, and the terrorists killed a bunch of them, so they retreated. Some army guys came and some got killed so they retreated. Apparently it took so long because they had to get Black Cat Commandos from Delhi to finally come and get the terrorists. There were only two guys, at our particular hotel, but apparently they had backpacks full of grenades, ammunition and food. I heard they had pulled some people out of their rooms, but we didn't get any clear reports if it was true.

"Earlier when I gingerly popped my head out and looked, they were shooting into the restaurant, and so everyone in there was not in good shape. I had a good friend, he and his fifteen-year-old daughter were killed, and a couple of the others got badly injured. One of them said that they jumped under the table. The guys just came and shot them under it. Their orders were to kill as many people as possible. Finally the Black Cat Commandos came to our door, and we moved the couch. They didn't know who we were, so first they said, "Put your hands up." They said, "It's time to go, we finally got them, this is the real thing, and we're getting you out now, open the door." One looked at me and said, "You're safe now, no problem." "They led us out, the Oberoi has beautiful marble floors and each story has lovely brass, glass, and incense and it was kind of like a heaven realm. But as we were coming out, the carpets were soaked with water, all the glass was broken, and there were burns, stains, it was a total mess, it looked like a war zone, which it was. We went down stairs and finally got to the lobby. There was blood all over, with broken glass.

"When we finally got to the restaurant we had to identify the bodies, and see if it was our friends, so we had to go in. The terrorists came through the kitchen door and that's where they started shooting everyone. So everybody was just lying where they got shot, there was no time to clean them up - there were about fifteen all sprawled out. There were bodies strewn all over as we walked through the lobby. They couldn't move the corpses; the vibration was heavy in there. They just shot people dead. They were our friends in there.

167

The really interesting thing is that you look at the dead and think, 'It's not really them it's just a shell; they're not there. They're gone, it's just an empty container.' You know as a monk, and in many of those traditions, you focus on impermanence. A lot of times the focus is on death, because that shows you what's important and what isn't, and also what's lasting and what isn't. When you see that type of situation, it's death. So it wasn't as if anybody was showing grief. I had already heard when I was up in my room, somebody told us they were in there, because almost everybody else had been accounted for. One of the people had crawled out.

"They were still clearing the bottom rooms, to make sure there were no booby traps. Here we are in the restaurant standing with bodies all over for 15 minutes, and then they led us out of the building across the street where everyone from the hotel was. Then they put us on a bus and drove us to a hotel on the other side of town. It was so intense and surreal, it was two days, but it felt longer, because your sense of time is altered. We had a little time to process it. I had to talk to the FBI, because I saw the attackers, and they wanted to ask me questions."

"I had been to India many times, and I usually go to meet teachers and various gurus, but also to go to temples. I like the ambiance there, and the people. It's a devotionally based culture whereas ours is ego based, and they are so sweet, they have so much art, and it feels more like home to me. I usually meditate and do that stuff. The Hindus by nature seem to be, as religion goes, much more tolerant than most of the others I've seen. The Abrahamic religions are the least tolerant, and then there are the Buddhists and they don't bomb temples or anything. So they seem to all get along fine, the only time you see any problems is sometimes when the Muslims and the Hindus don't get along, but I didn't see that up close before. Usually everybody is friendly, nice. I have met Indians who are Christians and they are more Christian then the ones at home, it seems.

"If you look at the history of all religions it's fear of death and death to the infidels and fear breeds intolerance. It's like, 'You must believe like I believe, and if you don't I have to kill you.' Even though it doesn't sound like fear, fear is the basis for that. Although they started out well, the actual founders were in a high state, but as the followers and their egos got hold of it, they twist it up and turn it into something that is ugly instead of beautiful. A religion in the purest form is sweet and it gets you into higher states.

"There's a saying that I love, 'You have to know how a cloak is woven in order to take it off,' so, you have to know where it comes from and how it's created and what the founders believed at the time. It makes a huge difference."

I asked Steve, "What do you feel are the solutions for intolerance?"

"The humanistic approach is important. For example, when all the terrorists in Mumbai got killed except one, and the authorities finally got him to speak, he said that his parents sold him to these radicals when he was very young. And the terrorists instructed him, 'Don't worry if you get killed, you're a martyr, and when you die your body won't disintegrate.' But when the police showed him his friends' bodies, of course they had all deteriorated. The young terrorist thought that they would all be immortal. In other words, he was a victim like me, but in a different way. And when they arrived in Mumbai they had never seen anything like it. Here they are in this luxury hotel and suddenly they see color TV's, marble and all. The handlers in Pakistan who issued their orders, kept calling their cell phones, saying 'Don't look at anything, keep going, you have to do this.' They were supposed to die, and go out in a blaze of glory. So you can see that he is a victim too. From that point of view, you have compassion for everybody. If I was born in Pakistan in a village, I'd be Islamic, and I would believe the same things they do. You have to have compassion for someone who you realize from the time he is born knows nothing else. And the beliefs are so rigid. I have heard that the lack of education is probably the biggest factor."

Dr. Birendra Raj Dutt, an aeronautical engineer who lives in LA, described being in Mumbai during the attacks. "I was supposed to go for some meetings, and my friend said, "Why don't you stay with me?" Usually I stay at the Taj

Hotel or the Oberoi, and we were watching the news, and saw I couldn't get out for two days.

"Mumbai is a very densely populated city. It's spread out, so unless you were at the two hotels, or the railway station, you would not be so affected. But there was an outcry. Mumbai is India's financial capital, so it was like 9/11 in New York. India woke up, and knew it needed a strong military defense. How did these terrorists sail on a ship, a launch, then a rowboat, and walk into Mumbai and cause this devastation? Since then, India has moved aggressively into maritime surveillance, because like America there are a lot of ocean borders where terrorists can enter. So they've ordered Boeing aircraft called P8I, the "I" stands for India. They are bought by nations for their surveillance capabilities.

"Every news channel was airing the attacks. Everyone felt that if it was terrorists, the gunmen came from Pakistan, and that has proven to be true.

"With this kind of attack, what is the cause? I have grappled with that my whole life. How can people fight this way in the name of religion? You can fight over economic issues, because a territory has gold, or minerals, like in the old days. But any religion that has fundamental extremism creates this issue. And it's not just the Muslim faith, although that's prevalent today. I don't think extremists are right in Hinduism either. In the name of Christ there was much conquering and brutality. What is done in the name of religion just doesn't make sense."

"In research for our film, we found there were three reasons for intolerance," I said.

"Right, but there is a fourth reason that is more prevalent. How do you get young kids to do something like this in the name of God, and to give up their lives? What really causes it are economic reasons, they don't have anything better to do. Some teenagers play soccer in the fields. Look at what happened when they went to play in Iraq and won the championship! Their love of soccer was more important to them then the killing Saddam was instigating between two branches of their faith. I remember growing up in India, there was a lot of unrest, but today with development, people are thinking, "Okay, how do I own a car, and a home?" Their focus is to earn money and have something positive to do. Because they have no job, they have no money, and the mind can be the devil's workshop. It's not constructive, and in many religious schools they're teaching extremism. What would create more peace? A better economy, but not just giving handouts, people have to learn to work. To get at the real source of the hatred, economic development is needed. And I don't think it's right for that minister in Florida to burn the *Quran*. My faith is very personal to me, and I think we should respect every religion."

Raj continued, "The first time the two foreign ministers of India and Pakistan met, there was a realization that they need to become good friends. If it wasn't for the divide and conquer policy of the British, between Indians and Pakistanis, what is the difference?"

Rabbi Malekar in Delhi had pointed out to me that Jews have never been targeted in India. Sadly that changed in 2008 during the Mumbai siege, which came to be known as India's 9/11. The Islamic extremists stormed the Chabad Lubavitch Jewish center, blindfolded several people, held them hostage, tortured for hours then executed them at point blank range, including Rabbi Gavriel Holtzberg and his pregnant wife, Rivka. The frightened crowd in the street below heard the sickening gunshots ring out. The young terrorists were told by their controllers that, "Lives of Jews were worth 50 times more then those of non-Jews." A nanny managed to escape with one of the young Jewish children, saving his life as his entire family perished.

The young terrorist who was the sole survivor of the Mumbai attackers was identified as Ajmal Kasab. They were all working for Lashkar-e-Taiba, a Pakistan based militant group. Ajmal was sentenced to death on 86 charges, and hung in 2012 in India.[52] It turned out that an I visit India, I go to funky ashrams, but we had so many people signed up, that we could stay in a nice hotel. This one time, we stayed at American-Pakistani, David Coleman Headley had done much reconnaissance for the terrorists and helped set up the attack.

In 2011, I spoke with an acquaintance who currently works in Karachi, on condition he remain anonymous. "I would like to find out how the Pakistan of my day - the early 70's and 80's, contrasts with the state of the nation today."

He said, "Pakistan today sadly is approaching a failed state. The politicians there are very changeable. The challenge is the extraordinary population growth. There is a failed public policy because their view of the world is not conducive to interacting with the West. Many people earn only $2 a day, and believe that, 'I am in this world but not of it' - because after death, I will go to the great paradise of Allah and all will be fine there.'"

"Ignorance, illiteracy and a subsistence level of living are omnipresent. Violence is rampant, especially in Karachi. People are living with a Wild West philosophy that was in the US years ago, and it enables them to radically influence the government. The personal bodyguard of Governor Taseer of the Punjab province recently emptied 23 rounds of bullets into his back. For this terrible act he was cheered by thousands of people. The Governor was assassinated because he had suggested the government take another look at the blasphemy laws, which are a prime cause of trouble. A Christian woman not long before had gone to fetch water, and was considered by Muslim villagers to be an infidel with unclean hands. They are trying her now in court, hoping to convict and put her to death. She has to prove her innocence; yet males do not have to prove theirs."

"This current generation grew up with this narrow worldview. They are good people but their lens is very different from ours. Nowadays due to the huge money from the drug trade, the tribes are armed and radicalized. Billions of dollars are flowing through their coffers. The business community is a thin layer of highly educated foreign management professionals who leave the country to live in the US and London. The electricity goes out every two hours. Gangs and political parties run Karachi, the main port. As Gertrude Stein said – 'There is no there there.' There is no central controlling entity in charge in Pakistan at this time."

"The official population of Karachi is 18 million, but it is actually six cities of three million. Every section has a different color flag flying overhead, because different tribes control them. They are Urdu speaking, but have millions of Afghani war refugees pouring in. When they manage to reach Pakistan, there are no jobs available, which foments unrest. Riots and murders occur on a daily basis; the population is used to lawlessness. The local Herald Tribune prints a daily map of riots and murders much like our papers print a daily weather weather map.

Peshawar is not safe. People all over in the business community are topnotch, and their word is golden. But 10 – 30% of the population makes it unsafe to be there. They kidnap you, hold you for ransom, and then kill you anyway after receiving the money. The international border areas are extremely dangerous – they'll use rocket grenades to attack you."

"The *madrassas* in Pakistan have a state curriculum, but some schools teach it and some don't. Pakistan's arsenal has twice the number of nuclear weapons as India."

I asked, "What is their attitude towards the US?"

He said, "One of our drones may kill ten insurgents, but each time, five innocent people also perish. Pakistanis feel our foreign policy is based on protecting Israel, with six million people in the desert. But we alienate one billion people with this policy. Pakistan in the 1950's and 60's was America's greatest ally in the region, since they have a democracy, not a dictatorship. One area of Pakistan under tribal control is now called 'Talibanistan.' Afghanistan meanwhile can hardly be called a country anymore. Since the Soviet invasion it has descended into tribal rule."

Young people in Islamic countries where fundamental beliefs reign supreme are forced to grow up under extremely harsh edicts. In June 2013 in Afghanistan, two youths were trading yogurt for bread with the local police. The boys had been out collecting scraps of food for their families to eat. The Taliban had warned the children not to help or barter with the police, but the youngsters needed food for their sheep. On their way home, the youths were halted by Taliban insurgents and beheaded, according to Jamal Agha, the chief of Zhari district.[53] Later that day, the boys' bodies and severed heads were dropped off in their village. The previous summer in the same town, a boy who was only 16 years old, was suspected of spying. He was skinned and decapitated by the Taliban.

In Aleppo, Syria in Spring 2013, a young boy was shot dead right in front of his parents and siblings, because when a local asked him for a free cup of coffee, he answered with a joke, remarking, "If Mohammed himself had come down, I would not give him a coffee for free." This was interpreted as blasphemy, and the assassin shot the boy point blank because he had taken the name of Mohammed in vain.[54]

Malala, the young Pakistani girl who was shot for going to school recovered enough to speak to the United Nations.[55] She promoted education for girls, saying, "The Taliban, they shot me on the left side of my forehead. They shot my friends, too. They thought that the bullet would silence us. But they failed."

The literacy rate among girls in Pakistan is dire, way below 60%. Half the female population does not attend school. Many schools do not allow females.[56]

The world awoke to exciting news in September 2014; Malala Youfaszai won the Nobel Peace Prize. She was the youngest recipient ever. What adds even more meaning to this great honor is that Malala, a Pakistani, is sharing the prize with Kailash Sathyarti, an Indian national who also works for children's rights and education. Yet according to news reports, Malala is not liked back home in Pakistan, where her forward views are frowned upon for supporting Western values.

1.7 billion Muslims live in the world today.[57] Their population is projected to be 2.2 billion by the year 2030, when according to the Pew Research Foundation, Pakistan is poised to overtake Indonesia as the most populous Islamic nation. It is reported in the news that Muslim extremists have killed many of their own brethren, yet those who would speak out against them live in fear of being targeted with a *fatwa,* a legal edict issued by an Islamic council of leaders.

This contention between radicals adhering to a traditional past, with developed societies is the struggle of the 21st century. Though we cannot change the past, we can make new choices for the future. Dismantling terrorist networks is necessary, as is freeing women who live in suppressive societies. But killing innocent civilians in the process also produces more havoc in our world. The great challenge is to win the hearts and minds of young people whose lives are limited by global poverty and inequity.

Today, the Khyber Pass still serves as a conduit for religious based warfare, just as it did in historical times when Genghis Khan, Alexander the Great, and Tamerlane traveled it to India. The fierce tribesmen who have stood guard at the iconic pass are now armed with grenade launchers and submachine guns, which are readily available. All manner of military armaments are for sale on the "Street of the Storytellers" in the Peshawar Bazaar.[58]

In 1976, when I journeyed through the Khyber Pass between Pakistan and Afghanistan, it had been a romantic adventure through a storied stretch of land. Now it is a route for armaments headed to the battle in Afghanistan, while poor refugees from the conflict stream across it to Pakistan, where they must struggle for survival in dire refugee camps housing millions.

The tranquility I once enjoyed in these now war torn countries had totally disappeared. One case in point was the famed carpets expertly hand-knotted by Afghani villagers. It was their livelihood. For centuries the carpets had featured the traditional Baluchistan "elephant feet" design. Today there is a new motif: rows of army tanks!

The Soviet war era had been long and grinding for the Afghanis, then the Taliban took power, and now US Forces occupied their region. The generations of bloodshed has undermined their entire culture.

Scores of devout Muslim fighters had come from all over the Middle East to wage war on the Russians in Afghanistan. They were known as *jihadis.* These fundamentalist warriors remained after the Russians fled.

Some say they are ready to go anywhere in the world where their Muslim brethren need them to fight.

Struggles among faiths are certainly not confined to South Asia, in many regions of the world religious discrimination and persecution is regrettably common. Upon researching the topic, I discovered how these unfortunate attitudes have dominated societies throughout history and are the justification for continuing aggression of one people against another. Religious fundamentalism has brought Holy Wars back with a vengeance in modern times, as in the Middle East and the Israeli-Palestinian conflict.

Muslims had governed Jerusalem, a popular destination of Christian pilgrims for hundreds of years. These pilgrims were sometimes mistreated by the Muslims, which resulted in a plea by Christians to take back the Holy Land. The Crusades were a succession of holy wars between 1095 and 1291. Eight military campaigns were fought by Christians to regain control of it. The Pope supported the war by indicating the Muslims were the enemies of Christianity. Jerusalem was and is still bitterly contested today. Christians revere it as the site of Jesus' crucifixion. Muslims hold it as sacred because it is where Mohammed ascended into heaven. Jews venerate Jerusalem's Western Wall, the last remaining piece of Herod's temple, and consider it to be the very heart of their ancestral home.

The Crusaders channeled religious fervor into their battles, believing that if they died a remission of all their sins was guaranteed. Muslim invasions had conquered many territories and the Christians attempted to regain them, including reclaiming Spain from the Moors. The term Crusades came from the cross that the knights wore on the front of their uniforms when they fought Muslims, pagans, and so-called heretics.

The Christians, known as the Franks, considered themselves "victorious," having slaughtered Jews and Muslims. However, after 1,000 years of Christian rule, Saladin, the Sultan of Egypt, recaptured Jerusalem in 1187. Richard the Lionhearted later invaded Jerusalem for the

Christians and signed a treaty with Saladin that would allow Christians to make pilgrimage there, even as it remained under Muslim control. Waves of Crusades occured until at least 1293. They always included territorial expansion and forced conversion to Christianity.[59]

The struggle in the Middle East is sad, considering how Judaism, Islam and Christianity share similar roots with tribes that can be traced back to Abraham.

Three years after the end of World War II, the state of Israel was established in 1948. Jews from everywhere, especially those who had suffered through the atrocities of the Holocaust relocated there. Israel became the national state for the Jewish people when the United Nations voted for the territory of Palestine to be partitioned into an Arab state and a Jewish state with Jerusalem administered by the United Nations. The Arab leaders disagreed with this decision and waged war against the Jewish people.[60] Barely settled, they successfully defended their new territory against the invading forces of five neighboring countries: Iraq, Syria, Egypt, Lebanon and Transjordan.

Today several million Jews live in Israel. The second largest population in the country is Arabic. Although Israel has signed peace treaties with its neighbors Jordan and Egypt, it still suffers great discord with the Palestinians as well as the surrounding Arab states. Exacerbating this tension, there are now several disputed territories occupied by Israel including the Golan Heights, Sinai Peninsula, and the West Bank. Many Palestinians have been displaced by the expansion of the territories and have fled to live in refugee camps in Syria, Lebanon, Egypt and Jordan. Islamic states and supporters side with their Palestinian brothers and seek to wage war against Israel. The ultimate goal of the *jihadists* is to liberate Palestine from Jewish occupation.

Meanwhile, the arms race continues undeterred, with Iran developing their nuclear capabilities, so close to Israel. As younger generations witness hatred, they learn to carry on the tragic tradition of war against their perceived enemies.

My friend, Robert Perry showed me brochures from the YIVO Institute for Jewish Research[61] in New York. The "Otto Frank File" caught my attention. It was a riveting collection of letters Anne Frank's father wrote, detailing his attempts to obtain visas for his family to the United States during the Holocaust. The YIVO archives collection was brought over from Europe after World War II

"Look," I exclaimed excitedly. "This book has reproductions of all of Otto Frank's correspondence with the National Refugee Service, the Boston Committee for Refugees, and many governmental agencies. The Franks were trying to emigrate and save themselves!"

Robert remarked, "Nathan Strauss, Otto's school chum, whose family founded Macy's Department stores, was trying to help the Franks gain sanctuary. Their wires, cables and letters are all here." They had unsuccessfully attempted to immigrate to other countries, including Cuba.

"Hasn't anyone made a documentary about this? What a story! No one is aware that Anne Frank's family tried to get visas to safety."

"I guess not," he replied. "Let's ask Jonathan."

Robert introduced me to Jonathan Brent, the Executive Director of YIVO, meeting him and seeing the YIVO archives was inspiring. They have warehouses of documents that have never even been examined. New discoveries keep coming to light as volunteers sift through them. Two of the four founders of YIVO's storehouse of knowledge were Albert Einstein and Sigmund Freud. They collected documents and records to study the language, literature and culture of the Eastern European Jews. After World War II, the US Army and others reclaimed and transferred a considerable portion of YIVO's collections to New York.

Jonathan showed me a startling discovery recently found in their archives. It was the Nazis' collection of the best Jewish books, gathered when they burned all the books of the Jewish people. This collection was intended for their "Museum of Extinct People" in Prague.

178

Anne Frank is an icon of tolerance, and is beloved throughout the world. This story was too important to pass up; *No Asylum*, the true tale of the struggle of Anne Frank's family to reach freedom, would make a remarkable film. Estelle Guzik, the volunteer who discovered Otto's letters in a weathered manila envelope, told me, "Although this history is 70 years old, it is the untold chapter of Anne Frank's life, this tells the story of the Holocaust better then anything else."

"It is a tremendous opportunity to reach younger generations with the message of tolerance," I agreed. Seventy years after Anne's death and the Liberation of Europe, her wise words hold true today.

The world community would like to see a peaceful resolution of the conflict in the Middle East, with Palestine and Israel reaching an accord without further bloodshed.

The proposed building of a mosque at Ground Zero became a lightning rod in the news. To those who were opposed, it represented a painful symbolic sneer at the attack on the World Trade Center. Those building the mosque have claimed it is a community center with a swimming pool, and that its' Imam is moderate. The actual location is just a few blocks from the Trade Towers. Now the proposed structure has achieved iconic status.[62] Some have suggested building a peace center instead in the location, which represents all faiths.

The scourge of prejudice continues, even in developed countries with high levels of education. The New York Daily News on July 22, 2013, in an article entitled, *Report: Anti-Semitic incidents up across New York*, stated there had been a 30% uptick in the state, with New York having the most anti-Semitic crime in the United States. [63] According to the Anti- Defamation League, across the US, 927 occurrences took place, with 17 assaults. Graffiti spray-painted on the walls of the Kingston Avenue Subway station read, "The world be much better off if all of the Jews were lampshades."[64]

A friend suggested, "As these are extremely volatile times we are living in, it is wise to avoid making provocative statements about other faiths." Let us promote an environment of understanding and turn the other cheek if we hear or see things about our own religion that we don't consider correct. In so doing, we can avoid needless bloodshed and misunderstanding. Moderates should not remain silent while the ranks of religious extremists are ascending. Speaking up can be a strong antidote to misinformation when done is an appropriate manner.

Robert Thurman explained how the Dalai Lama often speaks out in defense of Islam these days. "What the Dalai Lama means is that at the heart of Islam, at the heart of Mohammad's teaching, there is the same compassion, there is the same positive outlook on life, as in other faiths. Islam means, surrender the personal egotism. Maybe God is allowed to be egotistical in those monk institutions, but the individual is meant to subdue and restrain their egotism…in the light of God, and find a loving connection with other beings through God. And Islam shares that with Christianity and Judaism, and Hinduism, or wherever you have a monotheistic belief."

Reverend Michael Beckwith, founder of the Agape Church in Los Angeles remarked, "Anyone who has matured in the practice of whatever their religion is, always bumps into forgiveness, compassion, and generosity of the heart. That's part of the flowering of the faith itself. It goes beyond philosophy and belief, when one begins to practice. You flower as a human being. It is not only that you tolerate other individuals, but also that you appreciate other individuals. And the level of forgiveness, often times there's no choice in it. It's not a mental construct, where you say, "I'm going to forgive this person, for doing this bad thing." It becomes, "Forgive them, for they know not what they're doing. They are living in a state of ignorance, their perception is very narrow, and they have no idea the harm they are causing to themselves and to their brothers and sisters on the planet."

Chapter 15
Solutions

Love and compassion are necessities, not luxuries. Without them, society cannot survive.
— Tenzin Gyatso, 14th Dalai Lama

Ii is inspiring that the Dalai Lama has made it a point to never speak badly about the Chinese government, although their policies have been dismantling his culture for fifty years. On many occasions throughout the world, I was lucky to be present when the Dalai Lama taught one of the most pivotal practices within Mahayana Buddhism: being a *bodhisattva*. A *bodhisattva* is one who lives for the sole purpose of helping others and dedicating the merit for the benefit of all beings. Many individuals, not only monks and nuns in Tibetan Buddhism, take *bodhisattva* vows, pledging to live in this altruistic way of the heart.

In the Hindu view, as the yogis taught me, a *bodhisattva* is defined as a *karma* yogi, one who performs *karma yoga*, selfless service, for the sake of others. The difference between the Buddhist and Hindu concepts is that whereas the Hindu *karma* yogi's practice of selfless service serves as a vehicle for liberation from earthly incarnation, the Buddhist *bodhisattva,* once enlightened, continues to take birth until every sentient being—including every insect also becomes enlightened and free from the wheel of continuous birth and death.

Such a noble commitment is beyond our everyday definition of unconditional love and compassion. We can all relate to the immeasurable amount of patience required to handle all the people we encounter in our daily lives who need help, and other acts of kindness. (To that we may add our animal companions and Mother Nature, who also are dependent upon our generosity.) A huge degree of forbearance comes into play, making it even more amazing how people like His Holiness the Dalai Lama are consistently so caring from such a state of inner calm. Persons of the caliber of a Mother Teresa—perhaps the most well known and beloved *bodhisattva* of our time—come into contact with people who wait for hours to stand before them and request a blessing, a healing, money, food, shelter —no one wants to walk away empty-handed. Being in selfless service to the public is a litmus test of inner greatness, a demonstration of authentic spiritual wakefulness.

The Buddhist meaning of compassion is not a feeling of pity, or superiority, but is an acknowledgement of feeling or being aware of the pain of others, and trying to lessen or eliminate that distress. It means caring for the welfare of others.

The inclusive approach of the *bodhisattva*, if extended towards members of other faiths, would disempower religious intolerance. It is a potent antidote for dismantling attitudes of prejudice and hatred towards those who differ from us. This motivation is called "*bodhicitta*," meaning that if I care about you, seek to understand your faith and where you are coming from, then I naturally am looking out for you, putting myself in your shoes, and assuring that any encounters we have are congenial and compassionate. Doesn't this resonate like the Golden Rule? It sounds familiar to what we all learned.

Around the Dalai Lama and other great spiritual teachers, I always felt a wonderful, uplifting energy emanating from them. I suspected it has something to do with their being *bodhisattvas.* Desiring to understand the source of it, during our interview I inquired, "Your Holiness, can you please talk about how the *bodhisattva* is at the center of Tibetan Buddhist culture?"

He began with a twinkle in his eye. "In the Buddhist tradition this really resonated with me. Since my childhood...say 6 years old, I already started learning by heart, without knowing the meaning of it, and I think, with great reluctance." He shook with good-humored laughter at his confession.

"The Tibetan tradition's main messages are in the philosophy field, interdependency and interconnectedness, and on the practical side, infinite altruism. Therefore, the essence of the tradition is infinite love and compassion. That is the *bodhisattva* ideal, or their main practice."

"The Tibetan way of life is very influenced by the

message of the *bodhisattva*. The essence of Tibetan culture is the Buddha's message of infinite love and compassion, but with reason, not just by faith. So, according to my own experience, when I interact with other human beings, irrespective of whether they're a believer or non-believer, whether they believe in this religion or that religion, I always emphasize the subjects of compassion, forgiveness, tolerance, self-confidence, and inner strength. Although various faith traditions talk about these virtues, their essence is not religious or Buddhist. These qualities are an important part of human values. A value means something very important, and is very relevant in our day-to-day peaceful life, for a calm mind. So the essence of Tibetan culture is something of benefit to humanity generally. The message of compassion, love, forgiveness, self-confidence, these qualities should not be looked at as religious, or as Buddhist. I believe why Buddha stated these values are important is because they are very useful for a happy life. All religious traditions are basically trying to help humanity, not just provide buildings, but to provide inner value, inner peace."

"So the importance of these values is not by faith, but by reason. If we involve faith, then it becomes Buddhism, it becomes religious. But without involving faith, reasoning is a more scientific way to explain that these values are very useful in our daily life."

"The essence of Tibetan culture is to have a peaceful attitude towards oneself, one's fellow human beings, and towards animals, birds and the environment. So the essential part of Tibetan culture should not be looked at as Buddhism, but as Buddhist culture, because culture mainly deals with the community, and religion deals with the individual."

"Buddhism is religion, and Buddhist culture is secular, so the community and its' way of life is spiritual, more peaceful, harmonious, and compassionate. But the people in that culture are not necessarily Buddhists or believers. Even non-believers can live in this kind of peaceful cultural heritage."

Nowadays His Holiness speaks about how compassion should be taught in the world's educational systems. Not in a religious context, but in a way that directly relates to our secular society. In his many public talks around the globe, he teaches that compassion is a universal human quality that transcends religion and should be taught that way.

Recently, Jason Palmer, a science and technology reporter of BBC News in Dallas, reported on a new study released in 2011 entitled, *"Religion May Become Extinct in Nine Nations."*[65] Palmer writes that researchers have found that over 40% of the people polled define themselves as being non-religious. Upon reading this, I couldn't help but wonder if one of the reasons so many people are fleeing their traditional religious upbringings is due to the countless conflicts that are attributed to religion.

From the quantity of research currently being conducted by Western scientists on the effects of compassion and altruistic emotions on the human brain, it is obvious that a union of science and spirituality is underway. During his yearly international teaching and speaking tours, the Dalai Lama addresses many conferences and symposiums on this field of research. An ardent appreciator of science, he often says, "With the ever-growing impact of science upon our own lives, religion and spirituality have a greater role to play by reminding us of our humanity. There is no contradiction between the two."

For some time now Buddhist monks and advanced meditators from various traditions have participated in research where they are connected to machines that measure their brain waves when they have reached the height of their meditative experience. The scientific community now provides empirical evidence for how these calm states promote health and well being physically, mentally and emotionally.

Research on contemplative practices by the scientific community began in the 1950's when Alan Watts, Suzuki Roshi and others wrote and taught Eastern meditation techniques. Then, in the 1980's, the medical community began focusing on how meditation impacted pain management and controlling one's emotions. This field, now named Contemplative Science, looks into the intersection of meditation practices and scientific research. [66]

Today's research experiments follow a more precise, controlled protocol and because of this their results are more highly regarded than the earlier work in the 50s and 80s. Now that the academic field has become seriously interested, this area of study is growing rapidly, evidenced by the focus of research at Stanford's Center for Compassion and Altruism Research and Education (CCARE). There's also Emory University's Mind-Body Program and the Emory-Tibet Science Partnership, which are currently exploring the convergence of spirituality and science. The Mind and Life Institute and the University of Wisconsin's Center for Investigating Healthy Minds have also undertaken such research. At MIT, the Dalai Lama Center for Ethics and Transformative Values is described as being dedicated to inquiry, dialogue, and the creation of programs that affect the ethical and humane dimensions of life. The Center was founded to honor the vision of the Dalai Lama and his call for holistic education that includes the development of human and global ethics.

I heard the Dalai Lama speak in 2011, at the University of Southern California. He was quick to point out, "Secular ethics does not represent a negative attitude towards religion. [67] An inclusive perspective is not partial to any religion, it can also be close to non-believers." I noticed him add this poignant comment, "When we are born, we are free of religion, but not free of values."

Current scientific research is leading some experts to believe that the right angular gyrus of the human brain is the source of "out of body experiences." (The gyrus is located near the vestibular cortex, the seat of balance, and keeps our bodies functioning correctly.) Electrical currents applied here resulted in patients experiencing a tremendous lightness of being accompanied by the capacity to look down at their physical bodies from "above" while in a disembodied state of awareness. Could this be the source of the visions and experiences attributed to shamans and mystics?

The Claremont School of Theology conducted an Inter-religious conference in 2008 entitled, "Neuroscience and Spiritual Practice: Transforming the Embodied Mind."[68] One of these cutting edge programs is investigating the neural foundation of compassion and how useful compassion education and exercises would be. The areas of the brain affected by feelings of altruism are targeted when designing the trainings. It's considered that in the future it will be possible to affect the brain's neural circuitry that is linked to compassion.

The largest donation the Dalai Lama's organization has made from the income of his teaching appearances and books is to Stanford's CCARE Center, in the field of scientific research on compassion and its effects on brain circuitry. Dr. James Doty, the Director of CCARE describes their work as, "…collaborative research spanning topics from the neural circuitry of nurturing to the changes in the brain that occur with altruistic intent, CCARE has created a secular Compassion Cultivation Training program (CCT) that offers the potential of significant benefit to health, well-being and social connection. It is based on contemplative mental training practices developed millennia ago with input from experts in the psychological sciences." Additionally, Dr. Doty writes about Darwin's "survival of the fittest" and how what is really more accurate is the statement made by Dacher Ketner, Ph.D., coining it as, "the survival of the kindest." [69] He writes that there may now be evidence that "surviving may be enhanced by caring for others." This agrees with the Dalai Lama who says, "If one wishes to make others happy, be compassionate. If one wishes to be happy, be compassionate." The research at CCARE points to measured effects from compassion: "Biological stress markers are decreased while immune function is increased. Both health and happiness benefit from compassion."

During a symposium at UCLA's Mindful Awareness Research Center, I heard Dr. Susan Bookheimer speak about how the human brain has special systems that are designed for empathic experiences. [70] She explained, "This part of our anatomy actually allows us to feel what we observe in others. The brain systems that protect us from pain also produce sympathy. Compassion is a complex mental state with emotional components."

It is a reasonable conclusion that the cultivation of compassion is a potent antidote for religious hatred. Considering that part of our brain is designed for empathy, it stands to reason that including compassion as a component in education systems throughout the world is vital to the human family. It would cultivate a sense of our world citizenry, and help to transcend the boundaries of countries, ideologies, ethnicities, and religions.

When Dr. Karen Armstrong, one of the foremost religious authors and scholars of our day, won the 2008 prestigious TED (Technology, Entertainment and Design, a nonprofit devoted to ideas worth spreading) award, she fulfilled her wish to found the Charter for Compassion. Those who sign the agreement commit to restoring the Golden Rule to the core of religions and religious life. The Charter was designed by representatives of six faiths and already has 160 worldwide partners.[71] Globally more schools are teaching compassion and are endeavoring to broaden the program so that its practice will become a part of everyday life for millions. The intent is that when international students communicate via the internet, they participate in dissolving prejudice by personally getting to know one another and their respective cultures. Dr. Armstrong's book, *Twelve Steps to Compassion*, teaches that the way of compassion means putting others before oneself by globally applying The Golden Rule. The Dalai Lama has stated, " I believe that the very purpose of life is to be happy. From the very core of our being, we desire contentment. In my own limited experience, I have found that the more we care for the happiness of others, the greater is our sense of well- being."

Another point of interest is how today's DNA research advances indicate that we are rapidly approaching a time when testing our DNA will reveal our individual ancestral origins. It may just be that trace amounts of many races exist in the makeup of each of us. If and when science succeeds in proving that we have all come from shared ancestral lines, surely the false barriers preventing us from realizing our interconnectedness will crumble, astonishing future generations that such attitudes ever existed.

Chapter 16
Finding Common Ground

There is not a single place in all the corners of the world
where God is absent.
- Omoto Kyo - Michi -no-Shiori

Consider Global Classroom's recent report [72] that, "Approximately 25% of the world currently enjoys religious freedom while 39% is only partly free. This leaves a staggering percentage of the globe living in conditions in which religious freedoms are fundamentally violated."

Former Secretary of State, Madeleine Albright, recalling a 1990 State Department meeting about Northern Ireland, quotes a diplomat there who implored, "Who would believe that we would be dealing with a religious conflict near the end of the 20th century?"[73] Perhaps you share his surprise that religious intolerance, though centuries old, remains a source of conflict throughout the world. As incredulous as it may seem, all we have to do is some simple research to grasp the enormity of its prevalence.

Back in 1979, standing on the steps at the Dalai Lama's residence in northern India, when I met him for the first time, I had no idea that years later he would dedicate himself to working for religious tolerance, and it would be one of the main platforms of his speaking tours. His Holiness has consistently stated the promotion of religious harmony is one of his primary commitments. As one of the world's greatest harbingers of peace, he emphasizes how religious respect results in a harmonious planet for all. And he practices what he preaches, evidenced by his statement that all faith traditions are necessary to humankind because each one suits the differing temperaments and karmic patterns of their respective followers.

Since becoming involved in the cause of interfaith understanding, I keep asking myself, "When will humanity open its' eyes, and wholeheartedly commit to putting an end to the hatred that is at the core of religious intolerance?" Until then individuals will continue to suffer and die, and our world will not know what it is to live in peace.

Since the attacks of September 11, 2001, there has been a tsunami of attention focused on religious hatred and the worldwide clashes in its wake. In Iran, when Ahmadinejad was President, he denied the Holocaust's existence and mandated that Israel and its citizens be wiped off the face of the earth. Some leaders who promote campaigns of hatred continue to maintain their faiths are peaceful. Both current and recent disturbances were partially caused by religious bigotry in countries including the Sudan, Bosnia-Herzegovina, East Timor, India, Kosovo, the Middle East, Pakistan, the Philippines, Sri Lanka, Sudan, and Tibet.

Obviously, religious intolerance is a global challenge requiring a global response. Toward that end, in March 2006, the Human Rights Council (HRC) was created to replace the United Nations Commission on Human Rights. According to the UN's 1981 "Declaration on the Elimination of All Forms of Intolerance and of Discrimination Based on Religion or Belief," intolerance is defined as "any distinction, exclusion, restriction, or preference based on religion or belief and having as its purpose...impairment of...human rights and fundamental freedoms on an equal basis." This document requests that states "take effective measures to prevent and eliminate discrimination on the grounds of religion or belief." While this language is suitable for the HRC, I can't help but feel that it requires different verbiage to encourage each of us to *personally* search our own heart and honestly consider whether we harbor bigotry.

Traveling in the East I appreciated how people of many faiths told me they regarded Jesus as an enlightened being, similar to their own awakened ones including Buddha, and Krishna, to name a few. Yet despite this inclusiveness, because I am a Westerner there are temples in India and Nepal that I was prohibited from entering. Westerners are considered unclean by the Hindu caste system so cannot enter some temples. I longed to set foot in the holiest Hindu temples including Kashi Vishwanath and Pasupatinath, where bands of wild rhesus monkeys played raucously on the golden pagoda roof. Sitting nearby on the banks of the Bagmati River, I wistfully peered through the smoke rising from the cremation *ghats* and into the enormous golden doors to catch a glimpse of what lay inside the millennia-old edifice. This exclusionary experience gave me more understanding about how an Untouchable must feel in Hindu society, shut out, not having access to worship in the temples so dear to their hearts. In fact, this kind of experience can lead to anger and a desire for revenge, *or* to a softening of the heart with a sense of compassion for how others must feel.

For some in today's interfaith movement, the term "tolerance" is considered not to be expansive enough to define the attitude shift required to bring about a peaceful future. Although *Webster's* dictionary defines tolerance as "a fair and permissive attitude toward those whose race, religion, nationality, etc., differ from one's own; freedom from bigotry," it also includes in its choice list "the power of enduring; endurance," a more common usage related to "putting up with" or "tolerating," which vastly differs from respectful acceptance of traditions different than one's own. I, along with many others, feel as the movement to end religious bigotry expands, a new vocabulary will emerge that speaks to this issue in more appropriate language.

Perhaps the world community could come up with a phrase to describe the fact that these conflicts blamed on religion are not truly religious by nature. Such an expression would be very useful, since many disagreements are really about other things, but they are presented under sweeping terms of religious divisions.

It is not only individuals who are applying their resources toward religious harmony, but organizations as well. The Fetzer Institute is advancing love and forgiveness throughout the world. Ontario Consultants on Religious Tolerance are promoting it as a human right. The Boniuk Center for Religious Tolerance is dedicated to nurturing acceptance among people of all and no faiths, especially youth, and to studying the conditions in which tolerance and intolerance flourish. After 9/11 the Interfaith Communities for Justice and Peace was founded to focus the work of leaders from many spiritual traditions. The International Association for Religious Freedom is an organization with

United Nations consultative status supporting interfaith cooperation with 30 member countries. The Council of Conscience is a group of interfaith leaders committed to religious tolerance; and the Pluralism Project at Harvard University is exploring new forms of interfaith engagement.

Many other organizations are working to turn the tide of misunderstanding. The Interfaith Center at the Presidio in San Francisco announced in their May, 2011 Bay Area Interfaith Connect newsletter that, "Interfaith Alliance and Human Rights First have joined together to ask worship communities across the US to organize events in which clergy read from each other's sacred texts. It is especially important that representatives from Muslim communities be involved."

The Council for a Parliament of the World's Religions offers training to religious communities and interfaith organizations on how to make a difference. In 2001 the Claremont School of Theology partnered with other institutions to form Claremont Lincoln University to train rabbis, imams and pastors. [74] It will be the first fully accredited institution to teach clergy from the three religious traditions under one roof. (You may refer to the back of the book for a listing of several organizations that promoting religious harmony.)

I flew to Melbourne, Australia in 2009 for the Parliament of the World's Religions; it was host to 5,000 people representing the world's faith traditions with the objective of seeking more skillful ways to improve communication among them. Walking in the huge conference center, it was encouraging to see the full spectrum of religious people and traditions represented there. My documentary film, *Not in God's Name*, was screened during the Parliament, and the discussion that followed was directed at the rejection of fanaticism and fundamentalism. It was gratifying to see how the film generated open and honest discussion.

One of the Parliament's latest newsletters contains an article entitled, "The Way We Talk Matters," which underscores the high degree of respect that should be employed in inter-religious dialogue. The Council recently offered, "Train with Experts in Interfaith Organizing," at the Islamic Foundation in Illinois, and online.

Relative to communication, also under discussion was how today's technology and social networking, makes swift and wide communication possible. Many interfaith organizations are using these to promote understanding. Even the Dalai Lama tweets! According to his official website, in 2010, "1,558 Chinese people submitted 317 questions to His Holiness directly, and 11,705 Chinese 'netizens' voted for the ten most important questions. [75] The Dalai Lama responded in depth from his home in India." This was a rare opportunity for him to interact directly with Chinese citizens without the government's intervention.

There is encouraging news about the promotion of religious harmony. In the US in 1987, when televangelist scandals were at an all-time high, the cable industry worked with religious leaders to restore the integrity of faith on television. They established the National Interfaith Cable Coalition (NICC). Doing business as Faith & Values Media Inc., they designated a new network for interfaith broadcasting, the Odyssey Channel (now the Hallmark Channel), with messages of tolerance.[76] Then, in 2006, NICC announced that its membership would open to groups from the Islamic tradition. (Previously, membership was open to Christian and Jewish groups only.) Inner-Attainment TV, Inc., was the first Islamic member. Dr. Daniel P. Matthews, NICC Chairman remarked, "While we are not of one theology, we worship one God. Our organization exists to share God's word and presence in our lives through television, the internet and other media." This was a milestone for religious harmony.

In 2011, I travelled to Tennessee because I'd heard the Islamic Center in the town of Murfreesboro had encountered great challenges with intolerance. I knew innocent Muslims suffer from what the terrorists do. I called the Center and was told by a pleasant man that, "There have been so many inquiries, we have a media person you can speak to. Our worship is at 1 PM, and you are welcome to come."

Driving down Middle Tennessee Blvd., I came upon a modest looking business park. In the rear lot stood a low brick office building. Opening the door, the first thing I saw was a shoe rack and a low platform with a microphone. Since one removes one's shoes when entering a mosque, I took mine off. Two men sitting patiently on the floor of the prayer hall nodded as I entered the Center's office. A desk and aluminum chairs stood before a rendering of the Prophet Mohammed's tomb in Medina gracing the back wall. Abdou Kattih, Vice President of the Islamic Association of Murfreesboro, greeted me. A friendly man, he offered his business card that read, *"We are Muslims, and we are American."*

What drew me to interview Mr. Kattih were the news reports I'd read concerning the future site of their new mosque. An arson attack that destroyed their construction equipment. Mr. Kattih began, "It happened on May 23, last year. Those who opposed the building of the mosque had been very vocal. The Muslim community was aghast, considering that many of our members have lived here for 30 years. We started our Center in a one-bedroom apartment. Our ranks grew, so to pray at Friday meetings, we had to kneel in the parking lot. There were many college students, so when school was in session our numbers swelled, and adjoining lots had to be rented. Our community leaders hunted for an existing building or church, but nothing appropriate was for sale. So we purchased property to build. And then we were attacked."

"What did you feel?" I asked.

"We are not responsible for what some people did on 9/11. Terror has no faith, no claim. We seek help, praying to Allah every day. We need to practice where we live because our livelihood is here. The nearest mosque is in Nashville 25 miles away."

"Murfreesboro is one of the ten fastest growing cities in the nation and attracts foreign white-collar workers. It is known for its universities and thousands of foreign students. Now, many are thinking of leaving. A very high percent of the doctors in the US are foreigners. Our medical center is losing doctors, but new ones don't want to move here when they hear of the prejudice."

"A man told me he would never go to a Muslim doctor. This could become problematical, since the nearest cardiologist is 30 miles away. If our medical center loses doctors because of prejudice, it could negatively impact the community. Nissan, Tyson Chicken and Owen Mills offer many jobs, but require a steady supply of trained workers. After the violence, people think twice about relocating here."

Mr. Abdou lamented, "We felt we were hit by terrorism twice. The first attack was on 9/11, when we were targeted as Americans. The second was when we, though innocent, were attacked because we are Muslims. Since the airing of the CNN documentary, *Unwelcome: The Muslims Next Door*, more people support us.[77]

A lilting call to prayer over a loudspeaker abruptly ended our conversation. Many men had arrived for worship, and Abdou invited me, "Would you like to join us in the prayer hall?"

"Sure, thank you," I replied. This was a good opportunity to join in as the Dalai Lama had suggested.

I followed him out and settled on the floor in the back but noticed something unusual, thinking, "I am the sole female here." I looked around, and finally spotted an adjacent room, where the other women must have been sitting. When the prayer gathering ended, I returned to the office to meet Dr. Sbenaty, a Professor of English at Middle Tennessee University, and the Center's media contact.

"It's nice of you to speak with me," I said.

"There is a change in atmosphere, now the community of Murfreesboro has pulled together in support. There used to be 150 negative comments in the newspaper, but now they are positive. If they slam us, we are defended. It is ironic that through this violence we met people we never met before. The positives now outweigh the negatives. What is beautiful about this country is that a minority may have more money, but in the end truth and justice prevail. Every Sunday we have a potluck picnic, and now Christians, atheists, whoever—join us like family.

"After 9/11 there was no backlash in our town. My wife wears a scarf, and people would say, 'Please, don't be afraid.' It was like *Al Qaeda* united the United States."

"All of a sudden we had a setback. In May 2011 our site plan was approved and reported in the newspaper. Agitators tried to stir things up. 400 people stormed the courthouse and some demanded to speak. A few said, 'They are here to kill us! They are terrorists, killers.'

"To deal with this, we held an open house. Hundred's of people came to support us, and only 7 preached hate. One man planted negative brochures that had no substance. We did not respond to his accusations. The news media tried to find dirt on us, but we stayed open and they saw our humanity - that we are all the same.

"Once, concerning our mosque, a local political candidate proclaimed, 'Islam is not a religion. Every Muslim by default is a terrorist and we have the obligation to investigate.' Pastors, rabbis and Buddhist monks pledged, 'We are helping the Muslims to have their place of worship.' They planned a march of support and stood up for us."

"That is good to hear," I agreed.

Dr. Sbenaty then shook his head sadly, "I came from Damascus, Syria. 30 years ago. We escaped persecution and a dictatorship! We want to enjoy freedom. Have you seen on You Tube where in Syria, in 2011, they removed children's fingernails? It's called the Nail Factory, and was in response to kids writing, 'The people want to bring down the regime.'"

"So when will you open?"

"We are hoping to have the mosque ready in a year," he reported. "Some outside donations came in, and people brought checks. We've held fundraising events at other communities, which brought us closer together, and dialogued about building bridges. We are constructing walking trails, a picnic area and playground. We want people of other faiths to come experience us."

For days following the interview, I contemplated what the Muslims in Tennessee had told me. What came to my mind were the words of His Eminence, Situ Rinpoche, a Tibetan Buddhist teacher who wisely pointed out, "I don't think there are any barriers between religions, all the barriers are built by people. You cannot find a wall that is not built by people. You cannot find a fence that is not put up by people. When two people are different, they respect each other, and these two people can be friends, and these two communities can be friends."

These encouraging words of Sri Ramakrishna, a great Hindu saint from Calcutta, were spoken by Swami Vivekananda in his lecture, "*My Master*" in New York in 1896. They lifted my spirits, "Do not care for doctrines, do not care for dogmas, or sects, churches or temples; they count for little compared with the essence of existence in each man, which is spirituality, and the more this is developed in a man, the more powerful he is for good. Earn that first, acquire that, and criticize no one, for all doctrines and creeds have some good in them. Show by your lives that religion does not mean words, or names, or sects, but that it means spiritual realization. Only those can understand who have felt. Only those who have attained to spirituality can communicate it to others, can be teachers of mankind. They alone are the powers of light."

Vivekananda also promoted pluralism by quoting from the Bhagavad Gita at the Parliament of the World's Religions in 1893, "As the different streams having their sources in different places all mingle their water in the sea, so, O Lord, the different paths which men take through different tendencies, various though they appear, crooked or straight; all lead to Thee."

Our unquestionable right as human beings is to freely worship the God of our understanding and to follow that spiritual path whose practices support our doing so. Today, in surveys, and even on internet dating sites thousands of people check the little box identifying themselves as "spiritual, not religious." Some elaborate that they can commune with God effectively anytime, anywhere, be it on a mountaintop or gazing at the sky. Others compare organized religions to dinosaurs, saying that if they are unable to adapt to our times they may be washed away, much as the great climate changes doomed the dinosaurs. Some individuals also note that for the last few thousand years, the nurturing quality of the feminine has been kept out of many great faiths while patriarchy has flourished. This is seen in Islam through the treatment of women, and in Catholicism, where women are not allowed to be priests. In Catholicism sex abuse by the clergy has been a festering wound. If women could become priests, and if priests were permitted to marry, would many of these problems disappear? Has the time come for these practices to be more relevant in the 21st century?

In the United States—barring our own religious zealots who believe there is only one way—their way—we are more accepting of the co-existence of faiths. This is one of the greatest contributions of the US to human history. The First Amendment to the US Constitution guarantees, along with other rights, freedom of religion, and is the beginning of the Bill of Rights. Its origin can be traced to a bill written in 1777 by Thomas Jefferson in the Virginia legislature, which guaranteed freedom of and from religion. He felt that the progress he made on religious tolerance was one of the greatest undertakings of his entire life. Jefferson also worked for the separation of church and state.

Thomas Jefferson had a very enlightened attitude about religion, and wrote to William Canby on September 18, 1813, "Were I to be the founder of a new sect, I would call them Apiarians, and after the example of the bee, advise them to extract the honey of every sect. My fundamental principle would be the reverse of Calvin's, that we are to be saved by our good works which are with our power, and not by our faith which is not within our power."

Jefferson also wrote to Miles King, on September 26, 1814: "We have heard it said that there is not a Quaker or Baptist, a Presbyterian or an Episcopalian, a Catholic, or a Protestant in heaven; that, on entering that gate, we leave those badges of schism behind, and find ourselves united in these principles only in which God has united us all. Let us not be uneasy then about the different roads we may pursue, as believing them the shortest, to that our last abode; but, following the guidance of a good conscience, let us be happy in the hope that by these different paths we shall all meet in the end."[78]

A 2007 survey by the Pew Forum on Religion and Public Life documents the shifts taking place in the US. Based on interviews with 35,000 Americans, the US Religious Landscape Survey found that religious affiliation is diverse and fluid. 28% of adults have left the faith in which they were raised for another or none at all. 16.1% don't affiliate with any particular religion, and the US was on the verge of becoming a minority Protestant country. While many today in the US consider America to be a Christian country, the Pew Report indicates that only 51% of its citizens identify themselves as Christians.[79]

The American Religious Identification Survey gave non-religious groups the largest gain in numbers: 29,400,000 (14.1%) in 2000. [80] Buddhism is recognized as the fastest growing faith in Western societies.

Diversity of belief is an innate quality in humankind. With the amassing of weapons of mass destruction, for the sake of our survival, it is vital that the peoples of the world recognize our interconnectedness and interdependency. I asked Robert Thurman, a close friend of the Dalai Lama, "What is your opinion on how to forge peace between faiths?"

He astutely replied, "My hope is that the world's religions will become part of the solution rather than part of the problem. They *have* to become part of the solution. Let's take the environment as an example. If environmentalism is not taught in mosques, synagogues, churches, and Buddhist and Hindu temples—which are natural classrooms—then the mass population is going to still throw their plastic garbage in the street. They're going to muster whatever they can, and just forget about the consequences."

"Likewise, the *mullahs*, priests, rabbis and *swamis* have to tell their spiritual communities, 'No! God, or Allah or Buddha doesn't want you to do that.' They have to be part of the solution and can prevent conflict with one another as long as it's at that deeper dimension, beyond life and death that they meet. Every religion has that wisdom. Christianity encourages us to 'Love thy God and love thy neighbor.' Without loving God, you will not be able to love your neighbor. So, the wisdom is there, and the compassion comes out of that wisdom."

In 2007, the Simon Wiesenthal Center, located in Los Angeles co-sponsored a meeting of religious leaders in Indonesia, which has the world's largest Islamic population. The attendees released a statement saying, "The world's spiritual leaders have a special obligation to denounce horrific acts committed in the name of religion." The Center's Dean, Rabbi Abraham Cooper powerfully stated, "The world needs religious leaders who will have the guts to change this."[81] In 2014, Pope Benedict XVI released a new book, *Jesus of Nazareth—Part II*, which, in addition to a sweeping exoneration of the Jewish people for the death of Jesus, also includes statements on religious tolerance. I smiled at this news. How appropriately he wrote, "The cruel consequences of religiously motivated violence are only too evident to us all. Violence does not build up the kingdom of God, the kingdom of humanity. On the contrary, it is a favorite instrument of the Antichrist, however idealistic its religious motivation may be. It serves not humanity, but inhumanity."

In 2011, the House Homeland Security Committee convened for much-anticipated hearings on radical Islam.[82] Called by Chairman Peter King from New York, they featured a series of witnesses addressing the topic of radical Islam, intended to start a debate on its' extent in the US Muslim community. King believes that Muslims are the solution to the problem, since many report suspicious mosque members to law enforcement. A rally named, "Today I am a Muslim, too," was planned in Times Square on March 6 in support of the Islamic community.

Negative occurrences in the name of other faiths too, fan the flames of intolerance. In 2011 Terry Jones, Pastor of the Christian Dove World Outreach Center in Florida, threatened to burn 200 Qurans on the ninth anniversary of September 11, which he dubbed "International Burn a Quran Day." Sunni scholars at al-Ahar University in Cairo issued a statement warning of "dangerous consequences" if they were incinerated. Jones lit the Quran on fire in his church sanctuary, setting off a wave of violence in Afghanistan that resulted in the killing of 14 people, and injuring 150 others. Jones disclaimed responsibility for these killings.

In March 2011, two Sikh men were taking their customary afternoon stroll together in Elk Grove, California when they were gunned down. Surender Singh, 65, died on the spot, while his friend, Gurmej Atwal, 78, passed away in the hospital.[83] Officials suspect the motivation was hate, commenting that those who mistake them for Muslims often target Sikh men wearing beards and turbans. The funerals of the two victims drew not only the Sikh community, but also Jews and Christians from all across the Central Valley. California Senate President Pro Tem Darrell Steinberg, wearing a purple turban as a gesture of solidarity, remarked, "No Sikh should be afraid to wear this headdress.[84] No Sikh should be afraid to practice their peaceful religion because they believe someone will attack them." Local lawmakers emphasized embracing diversity and promoting religious and cultural acceptance.

In December 2012 in Queens, an innocent man was pushed off of a subway platform in front of an oncoming train. He was a 46 year old, and was employed by a printing business, according to police.[85] The female assailant revealed that she pushed him because he was from India, and she was upset at the strife that had been caused starting with 9/11.

In 2014, a campaign of religious / ethnic cleansing was being carried out on Mount Sinjar in Iraq. The Yazidis are an ethnic and religious minority that is descended from some of the region's most ancient origins. Their faith is said to be over 6,500 years old and is related to Zoroastrianism. The Yazidis face assassination as they are viewed as "devil worshippers" by *jihadists*. Tens of thousands fled to Mount Sinjar where they became stranded without food or water and in desperate need of rescue.[86] They were told to "Convert, leave or die."

The Yazidis had usually lived an idyllic existence near Lalish, a mountain shrine, in an area that they regarded as the Garden of Eden. Many people were slaughtered and women were captured to be used as sex slaves.

Millions of innocent people may suffer due to the actions of a small and violent minority of militants who have hijacked their faith. We can take time to get to know these people and extend a hand in brotherhood. I read a very compelling example of this which occurred in August 2014. The President of Indonesia, Susilo Bambang Yudhoyono spoke out on this matter. His country has over 225 million, and he called the actions of ISIS militants "embarrassing and humiliating" to the faith and urged Islamic leaders to combat radicalism. [87] He condemned the level of carnage wrought by the extremists in annexing Syrian and Iraqi territory. In The Australian, he exclaimed, "It is shocking. It is becoming out of control," reacting to the beheading of US journalist James Foley by ISIS. "We do not tolerate it. We forbid ISIS in Indonesia. Indonesia is not an Islamic state. We respect all religions." His country has successfully battled terrorism.

"This is a new wake-up call to international leaders all over the world, including Islamic leaders," he continued. Yudhoyono commented, "All leaders must review how to combat extremism. Changing paradigms on both sides are needed — how the West perceives Islam and how Islam perceives the West. Our citizens here in Indonesia are picking up recruitment messages from ISIS containing extremist ideas." Dozens of citizens have travelled to Syria and Iraq to fight and Yudhoyono said he was apprehensive about the spread of militancy upon their return. He has organizations in the country working to stem it. "The philosophy of ISIS stands against the fundamental values we embrace in Indonesia," he concluded.

In 2014, the Washington Times reported that Al Qaeda is opening an 'Indian Subcontinent' branch to 'defeat America and its allies everywhere.' The terrorist organization has declared it has formed a new division named, "Qaedat al-Jihad in the Indian Subcontinent," and this plan has been in the works for over two years. While the group is already functioning in Pakistan and Afghanistan, it now has its eye on Bangladesh and Myanmar, where Muslims are a minority in a Buddhist majority. India is included in their plans; Gujarat, Kashmir and Assam have been focused on for their large Islamic populations. [88]

How do we change the minds of violent fundamentalists? This is the real task ahead, together with preventing people from being attracted to such ideology in the first place. Can we find a middle ground, a live and let live co-existence? Herein lies the only answer to the challenge of creating a peaceful future with acceptance. The continued existence of the human race depends on it.

On August 28, 2014, on the radio in Los Angeles, it was reported that there had been a press conference held by the Muslim Public Affairs Council (MPAC) at the Intercontinental Hotel, attended by community leaders and law enforcement agencies. The purpose of the gathering was to discuss the alarming acceleration of terrorism and extremist actions recently perpetrated by ISIS, and the stand of MPAC on threats made against the United States. [89]

The horrific beheadings of the journalists James Foley and Steve Sotloff, like Daniel Pearl's before them was a wake up call to how violent extremism could impact the homeland. The knowledge that 20 Western aid workers are also being held hostage by the same organization in Syria is sobering. [90] MPAC has a program entitled, "Safe Spaces Initiative: Tools for Developing Healthy Communities." On the website, www.MPAC.org, it speaks about creating "Spiritual Safe Spaces" for discussions and conversations as well as physical places to help deter persons who may be misguided into taking rash measures. Some excellent recommended reading is listed on the site. Please refer to their list.

In January 7 to 9, 2015, three days of terrorist attacks in Paris shocked the world. When the office of *Charlie*

Hebdo, a satirical newspaper was attacked by terrorists, twelve journalists, cartoonists and employees were shot dead. The newspaper had published cartoons of the prophet Mohammed in the past. Two other attacks by an accomplice took place on the following two days. A policewoman was killed and a kosher grocery store was the scene of a hostage stand off with four more people being murdered. Seventeen people perished at the hands of the terrorists. A recent increase in anti-Semitism in France had caused many Jews to emigrate to Israel. The Grand Synagogue in Paris closed for the first time since World War II during the January attacks.

The largest rally to ever take place in modern day Paris for peace ensued. 3.7 million people took part across the country. Many protestors held signs proclaiming, "I am Charlie," and "I am a Jew," showing solidarity with those who had been gunned down, and their support of free speech. Over thirty world leaders joined in, linking arms as they marched, including the Chancellor of Germany Angela Merkel, King and Queen Husain of Jordan, Prime Minister of Israel Benjamin Netanyahu, Palestinian President Mahmoud Abbas, French President Francois Hollande, President of Mali, Ibrahim Boubacar Keita, Prime Minister of Italy Matteo Renzi, President of Switzerland Simonetta Sommaruga, and many others.

Many of the crowd taking part in this demonstration of unity spoke on camera to news organizations about their support for Muslims, and made a point to say that they did not blame them for the actions of others. Many Muslims also spoke out - spreading a message of peace. This public gathering of people sent a message of reconciliation and strength to the world. The result of these terrible attacks has inspired open and fruitful dialogue and discussion on the scourge of religious hatred and its solutions.

There is an antidote to hatred in the name of religion. The Dalai Lama has said, "My true religion is kindness." How simple and yet how poignant is his remark. In a New York Times, May 24, 2010 article he wrote, "Finding common ground among faiths can help us bridge needless divides at a time when unified action is more crucial than ever. As a species, we must embrace the oneness of humanity as we face global issues like pandemics, economic crises and ecological disaster. At that scale, our response must be as one.[91] Harmony among the major faiths has become an essential ingredient of peaceful co-existence in our world. From this perspective, mutual understanding among these traditions is not merely the business of religious believers — it matters for the welfare of humanity as a whole."

Chapter 17
The Heroes of Tolerance

If we are to teach real peace in this world, we shall have to begin with the children.

-Mohandas Gandhi

One of America's most respected religious scholars, Philip Jenkins wrote that when our present century is looked back upon by historians, they will view religion as "the prime animating and destructive force in human affairs, guiding attitudes of human liberty and obligation, concepts of nationhood, and of course, conflicts and wars."

In AD 1313, Constantine, the Roman Emperor converted to Christianity. Afterwards, in the Edict of Milan, he granted tolerance to all faiths stating, "...so that every man may worship according to his own wish." It read, "When you see that this has been granted to [Christians] by us, your Worship will know that we have also conceded to other religions the right of open and free observance of their worship for the sake of the peace of our times, that each one may have the free opportunity to worship as he pleases. This regulation is made that we may not seem to detract from any dignity of any religion."[92]

However, freedom of worship still continued to be under fire; only in the last few centuries did it become an inalienable right. But during World War II, religious freedom was once again under attack, this time by the Nazi regime. After the war, the proclamation of religious freedom as a human right was universal. Yet our world still witnesses numbers of cases of persecution in the name of faith.

Experiencing such a horrific riot in Delhi, and thinking about the terrible destruction that has been wrought in the name of faith, led me to wonder, "Who has championed fighting against this intolerance? And what is to come in our future, will humankind evolve beyond reacting to our petty prejudices against each other?"

I looked to the many religions in India. She is a microcosm of our world, and is the cradle of several of the world's great faiths. Spirituality is at the very heart of Indian civilization. In no other land will you see a yogi in a village contorting his body in strange postures demonstrating he is completely beyond worldly concerns. With so many faiths living together in such close quarters, India offers us a valuable lesson on how such disparate people usually maintain a peaceful co-existence. Yet she is a paradox. It is one of the most spiritual nations on earth, yet as I saw, it could become one of the most violent.

Indian culture has spawned many leaders of great merit, who have spread their ideas of tolerance throughout the world. Throughout history these remarkable souls have sought to end religious bigotry, and guide us beyond its' terrible consequences. Their timeless wisdom can shepherd us through this difficult period we now face as a global society.

Ashoka lived around 269 BCE. He was an emperor who ruled a vast kingdom that stretched across the entire Indian subcontinent, including Pakistan and Afghanistan. As a young man, he and his brothers struggled brutally for succession to the throne and Ashoka killed some of his half brothers. Ashoka was a powerful warrior, but when he gazed upon the battleground at Kalinga, a scene of a horrific struggle, strewn with 100,000 corpses and suffering people, he famously uttered, 'What have I done? If this is a victory what's a defeat then? Is this a victory or a defeat, a justice or injustice? Is it gallantry or a rout? Is it valor to kill innocent women and children?'[93] Devastated at the loss of life, Ashoka underwent a personal transformation, forsook war forever, and embraced Buddhist philosophy. He patronized many other faiths, and believed in peaceful co-existence.

Robert Thurman is the Tsong Khapa Chair of Buddhism at Columbia University and is known for his delightful style of teaching. Robert regards Ashoka this way, "In the 3rd Century BCE, you have an emperor who is saying that there shouldn't be inter-religious conflict, who supports all the religions in his area, and who discourages people from fighting over ideology, a thousand years before anybody else thought of it, even," he chuckled.

Wishing to spread Buddhism all over his kingdom, Ashoka engraved edicts on rocks and pillars in India, Nepal, Pakistan and Afghanistan, such as, "Do not denounce the religions of others, for you will only be hurting yourself." The inscriptions elucidate the concept of *dharma* or righteousness, and explain moral and social aspects. He even became a vegetarian.

Ashoka spread the message of non-violence. He treated his subjects equally and realized that tolerance for differing faith traditions would advance peace in his kingdom. Ashoka made Buddhism the predominant faith of the region for one thousand years.

Another early champion of tolerance was Akbar. He was a Mughal, Muslim emperor of India in the mid-1500's, who took a great interest in other faiths. His massive empire included two thirds of the Indian subcontinent and stretched to Kabul.

Early on, Akbar was intolerant, but on a hunting expedition he had a spiritual experience, and released all the game. He cut his hair and embarked on a lifelong spiritual quest. Akbar married Hindu princesses in political alliances and was influenced by them. At his capital, Fatehpur Sikri, the walls of the queens' houses were adorned with the symbols of all faiths. Although he was not able to read, Akbar constructed a hall of religious debate, and invited Hindu, Muslim, Jewish, Sikh, and Portuguese Christian leaders to speak. He treasured the metaphysical dialogues between the most learned men of his kingdom.

I met Dr. Joseph Prabhu at a meeting of the Parliament of the World's Religions, at a mosque in Los Angeles across from USC. He was the keynote speaker, and people from many faiths were in attendance. It turned out that Joseph was one of Mother Teresa's first altar boys, as a youth in India. I asked him about Akbar, and he explained, "There are in fact records of those debates. These were at a very high level of sophistication and were oriented towards a search for spiritual truth, rather then a sense of one upsmanship or a religious superiority, or putting somebody else down. So for instance, someone would say, "This is my take on religious truth, or this is my take on immortality, or on the transmigration of souls, or on what it means to be one with God. Others would listen in a spirit of great respect and curiosity. Because of Akbar and his great ecumenical spirit, there was a period of great harmony and tolerance in India."

Akbar switched from orthodox Islam to Sufism when he met the great mystics of the day, whose philosophy transcended the limitations of religion. He became a vegetarian and drank Ganges water, which he considered to be immortal. Akbar grew disillusioned with institutional religions, and established a creed himself Din-i-llahi, which blended major philosophies. In his city Akbar inscribed, "The world is a bridge, pass over it. The world is an hour, spend it in prayer, for the rest is unseen."

Robert Thurman describing India's tradition of tolerance, said, "India has a social kind of tradition and skill to mute violence and to defuse it better than other countries." And therefore, it's no surprise that Gandhi did emerge in India, and that he had disciples such as Martin Luther King. And there's no surprise that the Dalai Lama flourishes in India, when his non-violent approach was unacceptable to the Communist Chinese, with their whole philosophy of power coming from the barrel of a gun, violence being essential in Mao Tse Tung's theory.

"I think that it is not yet time, on the planet...for people generally to adopt a view that I adopt, and that a Western writer, such as Jonathan Schell adopts: that war is obsolete, and that in the 21st Century, the Dalai Lama is the main protagonist of this. It is a time when war is no longer viable. Actually, so was the last part of the 20th century, but they wouldn't recognize it. No one can win any wars. It should be time for dialogue. And violence should be ruled out as a way of resolving conflict, because it only generates more conflict. Which is the teaching of Jesus, Buddha, Krishna – all of the great teachers of humanity, that hatred breeds hatred, violence breeds violence and only non-violence can overcome it. Only love can overcome hatred. Now finally we're forced by technological and environmental concerns, to try to live up to those teachings. People have indulged in the last couple of millennia, of male-dominated societies, in the idea that you can get something out of war, you can win something."

"And up until a few centuries ago, they fought army to army. There was a little looting and pillaging, but it was more soldiers that suffered in war, and not civilians. Nowadays, civilians suffer a hundred times more than armies, in any kind of war. And if we ever went to nuclear confrontation, then we'll really see serious civilian casualties. It is not viable. Therefore, in the coming period, India should emerge as an important leader for the planet because of its' special social skill and its 'Gandhian' tradition."

"I got totally hooked on going to India as a kid from watching the World War II newsreels about Mahatma Gandhi. That man sitting there draped in nothing but a piece of homespun cloth was mesmerizing," my friend, Bonnie Sorensen who worked in South Asia recently confessed.

Mahatma Gandhi studied law in London, then moved to South Africa. Riding on a train, he was expelled from his cabin for being "colored." He began a campaign for equality and formed his ideas about non-violent resistance during it.

In India, Gandhi championed the low caste Untouchables, naming them *Harijans*, "children of God." They were called "*dalits*' meaning broken or crushed.[94] He began the Non-Cooperation Campaign against the British rule of India. Eventually the country gained Independence, but the struggle was a bitter one. Gandhi also fought for the unity of Muslims and Hindus, the equality of women and the dissolution of the caste system. Upset by killing sprees between Hindus and Muslims, Gandhi fasted whenever communal harmony was threatened. He managed to bring an end to several slaughters.

Speaking about Gandhi, Joseph Prabhu said, "It is the Jains who made *ahimsa,* non-violence, into a cardinal and ethical principal. Gandhi was strongly influenced by the Jain religion, and modern *ahimsa* is known from him. It is Gandhi who converts *ahimsa* from an ethical principal to a political principal to be used effectively against the British in a struggle conducted without violence, but through negotiation, debate and non-violent confrontation. He used to say, 'We can fight for political matters in a spirit of tolerance.'"

While campaigning to help India's fifty-five million Untouchables, Gandhi wrote, "I believe implicitly that all men are born equal." He advocated parity between all, no matter the caste or religion, rich or poor. Gandhi said, "...we must forget that we are Hindus or Sikhs or Muslims or Parsees... It is of no consequence by what name we call God in our homes."

Gandhi became known as the Father of the Nation. Eventually the country was dissected into two - Hindu majority India, and the Islamic Republic of Pakistan, against his wishes. Soon thereafter, a fundamental Hindu of his own faith who deplored his policy of tolerance, assassinated Mahatma Gandhi.

In the forties, Howard Thurman, an American educator, author and civil rights leader traveled to India where he spent time with Mahatma Gandhi. He asked Gandhi for a message to take back to the US. Gandhi replied that he was sorry he had not made nonviolence a more widely known practice globally, and that perhaps some Black Americans would do so.

Howard Thurman went on to influence Martin Luther King, who was so moved by his teachings on tolerance, that he embarked on a two-month pilgrimage in India in 1959, to retrace Thurman's steps. When he landed, King exclaimed, "To other countries I come as a tourist, but to India I come as a pilgrim." Dr. King also had a life-changing journey there. It was from this incredible pilgrimage and Gandhi's influence that he brought back the ideas that seeded the Civil Rights Movement he was to develop in the United States.

While touring India, King met with the Gandhi family. During his last day there, King spoke on the radio declaring, "...since being in India I am more convinced then ever before that the method of non-violent resistance is the most potent weapon available to oppressed people in their struggle for justice and human dignity."

Recently, All India Radio found an audio recording that Dr. King taped 50 years earlier, when he spoke about his debt to Gandhi and his important message of non-violent resistance. [95] In his remarks, King said, "... and now he belongs to the ages. And if this age is to survive, it must follow the way of love and non-violence that he so nobly illustrated in his life."

An icon of the Civil Rights movement, Martin Luther King made great strides for tolerance. He applied Gandhi's non-violent methods against racial segregation policies in the southern United States. Blacks were forcibly separated, and had to use separate facilities. A powerful orator, Dr. King said in one of his fiery speeches, "In a real sense, all life is interrelated. All men are caught in an inescapable network of mutuality, tied in a single garment of destiny. Whatever affects one directly affects all indirectly."[96]

During the Montgomery bus boycott, King regarded Gandhi as, " the guiding light of our technique of non-violence," and used his methods to change Alabama's civil rights laws, guiding the protests of the Southern Christian Leadership Conference.[97]

Dr. King's son, Martin Luther King III, remarked that his parents journeyed to India to, "immerse themselves in Mahatma Gandhi's non-violent movement and to identify with and give support to the people of India who were struggling to overcome the evils of poverty and discrimination. The impact Gandhi's life had on my father was quite profound."[98]

King was the youngest man in history to win the Nobel Peace prize, for using non-violent resistance to combat racial prejudice. In 1968 he was cut down in his prime by a sniper's bullet. King remarked poignantly, "Violence is the language of the unheard."

The Dalai Lama was so inspired by Gandhi that the first thing he did when visiting India in 1959, was go to the site of Gandhi's cremation. There a flame burns eternally to commemorate him. And to this day, the Dalai Lama has used the same non-violent approach as Gandhi against the Communist Chinese who have invaded and annexed his nation, Tibet.

In 1989, His Holiness was awarded the Nobel Peace Prize for his work to promote world understanding. He is the leading global spokesman today for peace and has taken on this designation from Mahatma Gandhi and Martin Luther King. He is looked to as a source of inspiration.

During the Vietnam War, Thich Nhat Hanh, a simple Buddhist monk, left his own country to teach non-violence in the United Sates. He was the Chairman of the Vietnamese Peace Brigade during the conflict and was nominated for the Nobel Peace Prize by Martin Luther King, Jr. Thich Nhat Hanh has influenced millions of Westerners to live peaceful lives based on mindfulness. His book, *Living Buddha, Living Christ* details the similarities between Christ and the Buddha: how we could emulate their lives and be immersed in their philosophy. He teaches how all faiths have love at their core, with similar paths.

A.T. Ariyaratne is known as the Gandhi of Sri Lanka. At the Parliament of the World's Religions in Melbourne, Ariyartne kindly joined our panel discussing the film, *Not in God's Name.* A high school teacher in his native land, he sought to teach his students about the situation of the poor. His Sarvodaya movement set out to improve ethics, economics and education for the common man. Those in power tried to have him killed, because he uplifted the lowly of society. He has promoted non-violence and changed the course of Sri Lankan history. [99]

A hoodlum once hired an assassin to kill Ariyaratne. One evening earlier, Ariyaratne went to the criminal's house and confronted him, asking to be killed now, rather than in the midst of innocent children. The assassin called off the killing and insured Ariyaratne's safety from then on.[100]

Ariyaratne has won several international awards including a nomination for the Nobel Peace Prize. He has said, " In thinking of various ways of empowering our people, we think of social empowerment, economic empowerment, and technological empowerment. But we begin with spiritual empowerment."

In 1763, Voltaire the great writer and philosopher of the European Enlightenment penned many works promoting religious tolerance. In his, "Letters Concerning the English National," he viewed the English Stock Exchange as having a positive effect on communal relations, stating: "The impersonal nature of trade allowed people to do commerce without any interference from the divisive nature of race and creed. This freedom of trade is the strong basis of a peaceful society, since a society that enforced common values was a cohesive one. Therefore, authority should teach and uphold such values."[101]

Huston Smith is a renowned author, Methodist Christian and pioneering religious scholar. I heard him speak at an interfaith gathering following the Dalai Lama's teaching in San Jose in 2010. He stated that Islam is the issue in today's news that we are facing, and that he is deeply concerned.

Huston's words really resonated with me, "Most of us are very willing to accept those of the Islamic faith. If the public is educated about its similarities, more understanding would be promoted. We need to dialogue, and have those Muslims who are moderate lead the way in promoting understanding of the precepts of their religion, without the ancient directives written in scripture centuries ago that are not applicable today. The presence of their moderate voices in the world media would soothe the feelings of many others who are in danger of being swayed towards hatred. There is a great deal of inherent danger from the misunderstanding of Islam."

Chapter 18
Merging With Truth

What sort of religion can it be without compassion?
You need to show compassion to all living beings.
Compassion is the root of all religious faiths.
                                        -Basavanna,Vacana 247

One evening in 2005, I was walking along the rushing Ganges riverbank at Haridwar in northern India. Far north from here, the holy "Mother Ganga" as hundreds of millions affectionately call her, gushes out from a Himalayan glacier at Gau Mukh, the cow's mouth, then flows down to the dusty plains below. [102]The devout collect the water, considered to be *amrita*, (blissful nectar), in brass pots or bottles and bring it back home for their altars. Faith in this water is so powerful it has inspired the devout to carry it to the far corners of the earth, much like holy water from Lourdes in France. Decades ago, the Indian Maharaja Madho Singh II of Rajasthan, ferried the sacred water by ship in the world's largest silver vessel to bathe in, as he journeyed to England.[103] Today the Ganges is heavily polluted, but that doesn't prevent people from bathing in her waters. Ritual pilgrimage to a holy river for blessings is considered by historians to be at least 10,000 years old.[104]

To stand or sit on the banks of this fabled river is for me, truly quieting and allows connecting with my soul. Yet here I stood, thinking about how the vast amount of pollution that now endangers the Ganges is a metaphor. The spiritual meaning is in the water. The purity is there, yet there is pollution too, rather like our thinking. If we clear up our thoughts, then we should be able to uncover and connect with the pure views that exist.

Now when I am asked, "What is your religion?" I answer, "My preference is Universal I was brought up Catholic, yet spent years with Hindu and Buddhist teachers, as well as Sufis, theosophists and Sikhs." I can hold on to my family upbringing and not feel that it has prejudiced me against others.

Throughout nearly 40 years of visiting India, one of my favorite things to do has been being present during *puja*, which means worship in Hinduism, Buddhism, and Jainism. At sunrise and sunset, clanging bells resound in villages and vast metropolises alike, summoning the devout and waking up the temple deities. Every time I've stood through the Hindu ritual of *aarti*, the offering of light, I have been moved when the temple priest hoists the holy flame up high on a brass plate and offers it to the four directions for the benefit of all, followed by offering it to each temple deity. At the end of the ritual, the plate is passed around for everyone to share in a group blessing.

Our building was erected on the Ganges riverbank where untold millions had worshipped for millennia. As darkness fell one night, a bell began to ring. I followed the beckoning sound down to the step. The river water was very high, surging with a swift current. Only the Hindu Priest and I were there. None of the members of our film crew had come down to the river that evening.

I never expected what happened next. The priest turned to me, and with a great air of sanctity, handed me the plate holding the brass lamp with its 7 wicks brightly aglow, symbolizing the seven charkas of the body. I felt greatly honored as I accepted the *aarti* plate from him, though tentatively, at first. Within seconds of it being in my hands, I was spontaneously overcome by a blissful sense of union, of my own oneness with the holy river that flowed before me. Every speck of it and the surrounding atmosphere was sacred and felt beyond this physical world. There were no barriers between myself, and any seeming "other." I could actually feel the river's energy coursing. It was all of Divine creation and I was one with it.

I turned facing each of the four directions, just as the priest had done moments before, and was completely immersed in the omnipresent love that is described in all faiths. I felt so humbled and blessed at having caught this glimpse through the curtain of everyday consciousness. I realized how all is sacred, and the experience of God without any images of any kind was beautiful beyond description, and spiritually liberating.

Bells could be heard all along the river, and the ringing in the distance came to an end just as we, too, finished our ceremony. The priest motioned for me to return the brass oil stand. I handed it to him, feeling unspeakable gratitude.

Struck with reverential awe at this experience of the sacredness in everything, I realized how human beings have been provided with the ability to access evolved states of consciousness, just as the great masters have, through the methodologies they have imparted to us. They have shown us the way to reach into the depths of our being and be one with the stillness within.

I had become aware that essential differences between religions such as their history, and where they originated, are unimportant. If we human beings would come to see beyond outer superficialities of the various spiritual traditions, including different styles of dressing, rituals, specified diets, the architecture of houses of worship, monastic orders—if we could see their common purpose to teach followers to commune with the Creator within us and all that is, we would quickly understand the common ground we share. Whatever we call it, it is Divine!

Within the heart of all religious paths is the gateway to spirit. Therefore, all creeds deserve our respect. Their shared purpose transcends all differences. The enlightened beings from every tradition upon whose shoulders we stand have told us that the most sublime experience we can know is oneness with our Source, with God, by whatever name we call the infinite, or by no name at all. That there is only one God, the world's religions agree. In today's world, some of the old faith traditions may not seem captivating enough to interest seekers who yearn to connect to the transcendent. New paths and new teachers may emerge that speak to the public in a more vital way. Yet nevertheless, respect for each other's paths is of paramount importance.

I went to the East to study its myriad of spiritual paths, to sit at the feet of its teachers, and I found they all teach love, tolerance, and respect for life. They touch our hearts in ways that impart and open up understanding. In India, I heard a beautiful saying that sums it all up, *"The different religions are like lotus flowers. They rise from the murky depths, and when they finally reach the sunlight they bloom. When a lotus opens, it represents spiritual awakening. No two buds are alike, and no one blossom is more beautiful then another. They all celebrate the divine."*

Chapter 19
A Prayer and Solutions

If God can work through me, He can work through anyone.
-St. Francis of Assisi

In today's increasingly multi-cultural world, there must be respect or there is no possibility that we can exist together. As W. Cole Durham, Professor of Law and Director of the International Center for Law and Religion Studies at Brigham Young University has stated, "We are all minorities." He speaks about John Locke, the theologian and philosopher of the English Enlightenment period who was an influence on Thomas Jefferson and John Adams. He penned the "Letter Concerning Toleration" in 1689. Durham states, "Locke introduced the idea that maybe it's not homogeneity that causes stability, but that respect for religion causes stability." Locke believed that pluralism can be a force for stability.[105]

We can all work together to create bridges between religions. Today many people are connecting on a personal level through Facebook, Twitter, and other social media outlets, as well as through interfaith events and organizations. Reasonable people should communicate about their faiths, and help clear up the perceptions that can become misperceptions. The leaders of our faiths can help in this regard. Learning the history of misunderstanding, and the resulting violence that has taken place between faiths, can lead us to have greater respect for all paths. Let us work together to open the minds of fundamentalists of all stripes, encouraging respect, and teach that scriptures do not have to be read so literally. We can overcome political leaders who may not want there to be peace between religious groups, and strive to create divisions.

Under the age of 30, those who do not identify with any particular religion are the fastest growing category, making up a third of the population.[106] Many people today are relying more on their own actual spiritual experiences rather then the prepared dogmas and policies of organized religions. They honor their own personal relationship with God, and seek to love all beings as manifestations of the divine, with a universal attitude.

May all who hold this book in their hands be escorted into their own heart and discover there the innate capacity each of us has been given to love all beings as one self; in the way that the masters of all faiths have guided us to do. May this prayer from the Movement for Reforming Society, in Lahore, Pakistan, open all of our hearts. [107]

Prayer for Unity

In the name of God, the Compassionate, The Merciful, look with compassion on the whole human family; take away the controversial teachings of arrogance, divisions and hatreds which have badly infected our hearts; break down the walls that separate us; reunite us in bonds of love; and work through our struggle and confusion to accomplish Your purposes on earth; that, in Your good time, all nations and races may jointly serve You in justice, peace and harmony. Amen.

End Notes

[1] www.AlJazeeraEnglish; Aljazeera.com; Oct. 17, 2012

[2] www.GlobalGrind.com; Daily Mail; *Let Her Live! Taliban Still Going After 14-year Old Activist As She Recovers In Hospital*; Global Grind Staff; Oct. 17, 2012

[3] India Today; *The Violent Aftermath*

[4] India Times News Network; *Operation Blue Star: Fighting for Golden Temple;* Jun. 6, 2005

[5] www.bharat-rakshak.com; Bharat Rakshak; *Operation Bluestar - 05 June, 1984;* L N Subramanian

[6] Penguin Books; *Betrayed by the State: The Anti-Sikh Pogrom of 1984*; Jyoti Grewal; Dec. 30, 2007

[7] BBC On This Day/31/1984: *Assassination and revenge*; Inderbir Singh Duggal

[8] New York Times; *Mother Teresa Unhurt in Tanzania*; Reuters; Oct. 12, 1986

[9] www.MotherTeresa.org

[10] www.E–Kantipur; *Monk lit self on fire in Nepal;* Kathmandu Aug. 7, 2013

[11] www.AncientDragon.com; *Lotus Discourse; Skillful Means* (Hoben) chapter; Taigen Dan Leighton

[12] Indrama; *On Mahavir's Trail Jain Temples of India*; Dr. Surendra Sahai; Jan. 2002

[13] The Himalayan Club; Himalayan Journal 39; *On the Tibetan Plateau*; Peter Jackson; 1981-82

[14] www.Wikipedia.org; *Dalai Lama*

[15] DRUM; *Endangered World Heritage Site*; Tibet House; US; July 19, 2013

[16] DRUM; *Letter From The President*; Robert F. Thurman; Tibet House; July 19, 2013

[17] International Campaign for Tibet; Book Review: *Murder in the High Himalaya, Loyalty, Tragedy and Escape from Tibet*; Jonathan Green; Jun. 1, 2010

[18] International Campaign for Tibet: *The Communist Party As Living Buddha, The Crisis Facing Tibetan Religion Under Chinese Control*

[19] Tibet Press Watch; *Inside Tibet... Self Immolations*; International Campaign for Tibet; Winter 2013

[20] Hindustan Times; *Bodh Gaya Blasts, 1 held, hunt on for 2 seen on CCTV camera*; Agencies Gaya Jul. 8, 2013

[21] London: Hurst and Company; *Afghan Women under the Taliban*; Nancy Hatch Dupree; *Fundamentalism Reborn? Afghanistan and the Taliban*; William Maley 2001

[22] Afghanistan Tourist Information; *Bamiyan*; Afghan Tourist Organization; 1977

[23] www.hazaracounciluk.com; The Hazara Council of Great Britain

[24] Business Week; *Fighting the Good Fight, the Aga Khan's millions are helping to improve Pakistan;* Fredrik Balfour; Nov. 26, 2001

[25] The Guardian; *How Taliban brought new Terror to Pakistan's Killer Mountain*; Jason Burke; Jul. 23, 2013

[26] Utpal Publishers; *The Mysterious Cave of Amarnath*; Samsar Chand Koul; Jun.10, 1954

[27] Hinduism Today; *A Mela History; Tradition;* May-June 2001

[28] Simon and Schuster; *The Story of Civilization*; Will & Ariel Durant; 1935 - 1975

[29] Islam International Publications India; *Jesus in India*; Mirza Ghulam Ahmad; 1944

[30] www.Hindunet.com; *A Troubled Trek*; Praveen Swami; Sept. 30, 2007

[31] New York; *Muhammed Comes to Manhattan*; Mark Jacobson; Aug. 30, 2010

[32] Rutgers University Press; *Borders and Boundaries Women in India's Partition*; Menon and Bhasin; 1998

[33] Shodhganga Inflibnet Centre; *Riots and Migration in Punjab and Princely States*; K. Kaur; 2011

[34] San Francisco Chronicle; *Dalai Lama Seeks to Improve Islam's Image, He'll meet with Muslim leaders in a mission of peace in S.F.*; Matthai Chakko Kuruvila; Apr. 15, 2006

[35] US Congressional Research Service; *Pakistan's Nuclear Weapons: Proliferation and Security Issues*; Paul K. Kerr, Mary Beth Nikitin; Sept. 15, 2011

[36] The Economist; *The Spider's Stratagem*; Douglas Frantz, Catherine Collins; Jan. 3, 2008

[37] Los Angeles Times; *Victims of Attack in Pakistan All Christian*; Paul Watson; Sept. 26, 2002

[38] One India News; *Suicide Blast in Peshawar Hotel Kills 14*; Jun. 10, 2009

[39] India Abroad; *India's Wake-Up Call: Communal hatred is the South Asian equivalent of racism in the West; Defusing Ethno-Religious War;* Harold A. Gould; Apr. 5, 2002

[40] University of California Press; *Terror in the Mind of God: The Global Rise of Religious Violence*; Mark Juergensmeyer; 2003

[41] Marg Publications; Jetwings; *House of Israel*; from *India's Jewish Heritage, Ritual, Art & Life-Cycle*; Ed. by Shalva Weil; Mar. 2003

[42] *Indian Origins of Christianity*; Joe Lobo; indiacatholic.com

[43] www.unescoparzor.com; UNESCO-Parsi Zoroastrian Project; *Parzor Foundation For Preservation of Vulnerable Human Heritage*

[44] Hohm Press; *The Yoga Tradition: It's History, Literature, Philosophy, and Practice*; Georg Feuerstein; 2001

[45] www.AgapeLive.com; About Agape; *Dr. Michael Bernard Beckwith*

[46] Tsurphu Labrang Media; Berlin Talks; *Young People Meet the Karmapa;* Jun. 13, 2014

[47] The Economist; *The world's religious make-up*; Pew Research Centre; Dec. 22, 2012

[48] Los Angeles Times; The World; *Religious Strife Brews in India*; Mar.13, 2002

[49] ABC News; *History of Hate Indians Dread the Reopening of Old Religious Wounds*; Leela Jacinto; Mar. 14, 2003

[50] www.ABC News.com; *History of Hate; Indians Dread the Reopening of Old Religious Wounds*; Leela Jacinto; Mar. 14, 2003

[51] The Economist; *Growing, and Neglected*; Mar. 2, 2013

[52] www.CNN.com; *India executes last gunman from Mumbai attacks*; Harmeet Shah Singh; Nov.21, 2012

[53] NBC News; *Taliban accused of beheading two young boys;* Akbar Shinwari; Jun.10, 2013

[54] Al Jazeera; Jun. 9, 2013

[55] Huffington Post Live; Jul. 12, 2013

[56] The Independent; *The Full text: Malala Yousafzai delivers a defiant riposte to Taliban militants with speech to the UN General Assembly;* Jul. 12, 2013

[57] Pew Research Center's Religion and Public Life Project; *The Future of the Global Muslim Population*; Jan. 27, 2011

[58] Conde Nast; *Alexander's Lost World*; William Dalrymple; Feb.1993

[59] HistoryLearningSite.co.uk; *Saladin*

[60] history state.gov/milestones/1945-1952/creation-Israel; *Creation of Israel, 1948*

[61] www.YIVO.org; YIVO Institute for Jewish Research;

[62] Las Vegas Review Journal; *Mosque debate diverts focus to religion instead of personal acts*; Steven Kalas; Sept. 5, 2010

[63] New York Times; My Fox New York; Report: *Anti-Semitic Incidents Up Across New York*; Luke Funk; Jul. 22, 2013

[64] NY My Fox New York; Report: *Anti-Semitic Incidents Up Across New York*; New York Times; Luke Funk; Jul. 22, 2013

[65] www.bbc.co.uk; BBC News; *Religion may become extinct in nine nations, study says*; Jason Palmer; Mar. 22, 2011

[66] Mind and Life Institute; *A Brief History of Contemplative Science and Contemplative Studies*; Spring Newsletter, 2011

[67] USC Interfaith Council, Dalai Lama Foundation, and Dalai Lama Center for Ethics and Transformative Values; *Secular Ethics: Origins, Elements, And Function in Society*; May 3, 2011

[68] Claremont School of Theology; *"Transforming the Embodied Mind"* Conference

[69] CCARE News and Events; *The Compassionate Instinct: A Darwinian Tale of the Survival of the Kindest*; Dacher Kelter; Meng Wu Lecture Series, Fall 2011

[70] UCLA Center for Buddhist Studies; *The Dalai Lama at UCLA*; May 2, 2011

[71] *Global Charter of Compassion,* Karen Armstrong, Ph.D.

[72] www.unusa.org; United Nations Association

[73] The Economist; *In God's Name;* John Mickelwith; Nov.1, 2007

[74] Council for a Parliament of the World's Religions; The Parliament Newsletter; *Launching Claremont Lincoln University A Watershed Moment in Theological Education;* Paul Chaffee; Sept.14, 2011

[75] www.chinatibet.people.com; *Ten Top Questions of Chinese people to Dalai Lama*; Mar. 15, 2012

[76] www.InterfaithAlliance.org; Interfaith Alliance

[77] CNN documentary, *The Muslims Next Door*

[78] University Press of Kentucky; *Jefferson's Declaration of Independence Origins, Philosophy and Theology*; Allen Jayne; 1998

[79] www.PewForum.org; *"Nones" on the Rise;* Pew Research: Religion and Public Life Project; Oct.9, 2012

[80] Trinity College; *American Religious Identification Survey;* Barry A. Kosmin and Ariela Keysar; 2008

[81] Wiesenthal.com; *Simon Wiesenthal Center Hosts Interfaith Leadership Crisis Meeting*; Jan.5, 2011

[82] Washington Post; Rep. *Peter King's Muslim Hearings: A key Moment in an Angry Conversation*; David Fahrenthold and Michelle Boorstein; Mar. 9, 2011

[83] The Sacramento Bee; *Two American Sikhs shot dead in Elk Grove*; Apr. 11, 2011

[84] Steinberg; *Legislators honor Sikh victims of Elk Grove Shooting*

[85] National; *Subway push victim was from India, police reveal*; Tom Hays, Associated Press; Dec. 29, 2012

[86] The Guardian.com; *In Iraq, there is no peace for Yazidis;* Nicky Woolf; Aug. 9, 2014

[87] Jihadwatch.org; *Indonesia's President: "Indonesia is not an Islamic state: We respect all religions;"* Robert Spencer; Aug. 25, 2014

[88] The Washington Times; *Al Qaeda opens "Indian Subcontinent' branch to 'defeat America and its allies everywhere'*; Douglas Ernst; Sept. 3, 2014

[89] islamicommentary.org; *MPAC Presents Safe Spaces Campaign to Prevent Violent Extremism;* Julie Poucher; Harbin, Editor; MPAC (Muslim Public Affairs Council) Press Advisory; Aug. 27, 2014

[90] The Telegraph.co.UK; James Foley: *Up to twenty More Westerners Held Hostage by ISIL*; Aug. 21, 2014

[91] New York Times; *Many Faiths, One Truth*; Tenzin Gyatso, 14th Dalai Lama; May 24, 2010

[92] The History of the Byzantine Empire; Edict of Milan: *On the Deaths of the Persecutors (De Mortibus Persecutorum);* Lactantius

[93] Ashoka and the Battle of Kalinga

[94] New York Times; Sunday Book Review; *How Gandhi Became Gandhi*; Geoffrey C. Ward; Mar. 24, 2011

[95] National Public Radio; *Martin Luther King Recording Found In India*; Jan. 16, 2009

[96] www.mkgandhi.org; *Martin Luther King's Non-violent Struggle and Its Relevance to Asia*; Chris Walker

[97] www.Tavaana.org; *Martin Luther King, Jr.; Fighting for Equal Rights in America*

[98] www. America.gov Archive; *Secretary Clinton Honors Martin Luther King's 1959 Trip to India*; Feb. 13, 2009

[99] Sarvodaya.org; *Our Founder*; A.T. Ariyaratne

[100] www.awakin.org; *Evening with "Gandhi of Sri Lanka'*: Dr. A.T. Ariyaratne

[101] www.fee.org; The Freeman; *The Origin of Religious Tolerance: Freedom of Commerce is the True Wellspring of Religious Toleration*; Wendy McElroy; Jun.1, 1998

[102] Gau Mukh, glacial source of Ganges River in Himalayas, Uttarakhand, India

[103] The Tribune; Spectrum; *The silver jars in which Ganges water was taken to London*; K.R.N. Swamy; Oct. 27, 2002

[104] www.theguardian.com; *Rites of way: behind the pilgrimage revival*

[105] The Christian Science Monitor; *To be alone with one God, In the Sanctuary of Consciousness Shines a Light*; Jane Lampman; Dec. 16, 1999

[106] Doshi Bridgebuilder Conference; *Vedanta: Its Many Manifestations Yesterday, Today, and Tomorrow*; Philip Goldberg; Loyola Marymount University; Jun. 2013

[107] IRFWP, *The National Interfaith Cable Coalition; Press release*; Frank Kauffman; Aug. 26, 2010

Charter for Compassion

The charter has been translated into more than 30 languages:

The principle of compassion lies at the heart of all religious, ethical and spiritual traditions, calling us always to treat all others as we wish to be treated ourselves. Compassion impels us to work tirelessly to alleviate the suffering of our fellow creatures, to dethrone ourselves from the centre of our world and put another there, and to honour the inviolable sanctity of every single human being, treating everybody, without exception, with absolute justice, equity and respect.

It is also necessary in both public and private life to refrain consistently and empathically from inflicting pain. To act or speak violently out of spite, chauvinism, or self-interest, to impoverish, exploit or deny basic rights to anybody, and to incite hatred by denigrating others -even our enemies- is a denial of our common humanity. We acknowledge that we have failed to live compassionately and that some have even increased the sum of human misery in the name of religion.

We therefore call upon all men and women ~ to restore compassion to the centre of morality and religion ~ to return to the ancient principle that any interpretation of scripture that breeds violence, hatred or disdain is illegitimate ~ to ensure that youth are given accurate and respectful information about other traditions, religions and cultures ~ to encourage a positive appreciation of cultural and religious diversity ~ to cultivate an informed empathy with the suffering of all human beings -even those regarded as enemies.

UNITED NATIONS DECLARATION OF

PRINCIPLES ON TOLERANCE, 1995

INTRODUCTION

On the initiative of UNESCO, the United Nations General Assembly proclaimed 1995 the United Nations Year for Tolerance and designated UNESCO as lead agency for this Year. In conformity with its mandate and in order to call public attention worldwide to the urgent matter of tolerance, the General Conference of UNESCO solemnly adopted o 16 November 1995, the 50th anniversary of the signature of UNESCOs Constitution, the Declaration of the Principles of Tolerance. The Member States of the United Nations Educational, Scientific and Cultural Organization, meeting in Paris at the twenty-eighth session of the General Conference, from 25 October to 16 November 1995.

PREAMBLE

Bearing in mind that the United Nations Charter states "We, the peoples of the United Nations determined to save succeeding generations from the scourge of war,...to reaffirm faith in fundamental human rights, in the dignity and worth of the human person... and for these ends to practice tolerance and live together in peace with one another as good neighbors."

Recalling that the Preamble to the Constitution of UNESCO adopted on 16 November 1945, states that "peace, it is not to fail, must be founded on the intellectual and moral solidarity of mankind."

Recalling also that the Universal Declaration of Human Rights affirms that "Everyone has the right to freedom of though, conscience and religion" (Article 18), "of opinion and expression" (Article 19), and that education "should promote understanding, tolerance and friendship among all nations, racial or religious groups" (Article 26).

Noting relevant international instruments including:

the International Covenant on Civil and Political Rights, the International Covenant on Economic, Social and Cultural Rights,

the Convention on the Elimination of All Forms of Racial Discrimination,

the Convention on the Prevention and Punishment of the Crime of Genocide,

the Convention on the Rights of the Child,

the 1951 Convention relating to the Status of Refugees and its 1967 Protocol and regional instruments,

the Convention on the Elimination of Any Form of Discrimination against Women,

the Convention against Torture and other Cruel, Inhuman or Degrading Treatment or Punishment,

the Declaration on the Rights of Persons Belonging to National or Ethnic, Religious and Linguistic Minorities, the Declaration on measures to Eliminate International Terrorism,

the Vienna Declaration and Programme of Action of the World Conference on Human Rights

the Copenhagen Declaration and Programme of Action adopted by the World Summit for Social Development

the UNESCO Declaration on Race and Racial Prejudice,

the UNESCO Convention and Recommendation against Discrimination in Education,

Bearing in mind the objectives of the Third Decade to Combat Racism and Racial Discrimination, the World Decade Human Rights Education, and the International Decade of the Worlds Indigenous People,

Taking into consideration the recommendations of regional conferences organized in the framework of the United Nations Year for Tolerance in accordance with UNESCO General Conference 27C/Resolution 5.14, we well as the conclusions and recommendations of other conferences and meetings organized by Member States with the programme of the United Nations Year for Tolerance,

Alarmed by the current rise in acts of intolerance, violence, terrorism, xenophobia, aggressive nationalism, racism, anti-Semitism, exclusion marginalization and discrimination directed against national, ethnic, religious and linguistic minorities, and discrimination directed against national, ethnic, religious and linguistic minorities, refugees, migrant workers, immigrants and vulnerable groups with societies, as well as acts of violence and intimidation committed against individuals exercising their freedom of opinion and expression – all of which threaten the consolidation of peace and democracy other nationally and internationally and which are all obstacles to development.

Emphasizing the responsibilities of Member States to develop and encourage respect for human rights and fundamental freedoms for all, with out distinction as to race, gender, language, national origin, religion or disability, and to combat intolerance,

Adopt and solemnly proclaim this Declaration of Principles on Tolerance.

Resolving to take all positive measures necessary to promote tolerance in our societies, because tolerance is not only a cherished principle, but also a necessity for peace and for the economic and social advancement of all peoples.

We declare the following:

Article 1 – Meaning of tolerance

1.1   Tolerance is respect, acceptance and appreciation of the rich diversity of our world's cultures, our forms of expression and ways of being human. It is fostered by knowledge, openness, communication and freedom of thought, conscience and belief. Tolerance is harmony in difference. It is not only a moral duty, it is also a political and legal requirement. Tolerance, the virtue that makes peace possible, contributes to the replacement of the culture of war by a culture of peace.

1.2   Tolerance is not concession condescension or indulgence. Tolerance is, above all, an active attitude prompted by recognition of the universal human rights and fundamental freedoms of other. In no circumstance can it be used to justify infringements of these fundamental values. Tolerance is to be exercised by the individuals, groups and States.

1.3   Tolerance is the responsibility that upholds human rights, pluralism (including cultural pluralism), democracy and the rule of law. It revolves the rejection of dogmatism and absolutism and affirms the standards set out in international human rights instruments.

1.4   Consistent with respect for human rights, the practice of tolerance does not mean toleration of social injustice or the abandonment or weakening of one's convictions and accepts that others adhere to theirs. It means accepting the fact that human beings, naturally diverse in their appearance, situation, speech, behavior and values, have the right to live in peace and to be as they are. It also means that one's views are not to be imposed on others.

Article 2 – State level

2.1 Tolerance at the State level requires just and impartial legislation, law enforcement and judicial and administrative process. It also requires that economic and social opportunities be made available to each person without any discrimination. Exclusion and marginalization can lead to frustration, hostility and fanaticism.

2.2 In order to achieve a more tolerant society, States should ratify existing international human rights conventions, and draft new legislation where necessary to ensure equality of treatment and of opportunity for all groups and individuals in society.

2.3　It is essential for international harmony that individuals, communities and nations accept and respect the multicultural character of the human family. Without Tolerance there can be no peace, and without peace there can be no development or democracy.

2.4　Intolerance may take the form of marginalization of vulnerable groups and their exclusion from social and political participation, as well as violence and discrimination against them. As confirmed in the Declaration on Race and Racial Prejudice "All individuals and groups have the right to be difference" (Article 1.2).

Article 3 – Social dimensions

3.1　In the modern world, tolerance is more essential than ever before. It is an age marked by the globalization of the economy and by rapidly increasing mobility, communication, integration and interdependence, large-scale migrations and displacement of populations, urbanization and changing social patterns. Since every part of the world is characterized by diversity, escalating intolerance and strife potentially menaces every region. It is not confined to any country, but is a global threat.

3.2   Tolerance is necessary between individuals and at the family and community levels. Tolerance promotion and the shaping of attitudes of openness, mutual listening and solidarity should take place in schools and universities, and through non-formal education, at home and in the workplace. The communication media are in a position to play a constructive role in facilitating free and open dialogue and discussion, disseminating the values of tolerance, and highlighting the dangers of indifference towards the rise in intolerant groups and ideologies.

3.3   As affirmed by the UNESCO Declaration on Race and Racial Prejudice, measures must be taken to ensure equality in dignity and rights for individuals and groups wherever necessary. In this respect, particular attention should be paid to vulnerable groups which are socially or economically disadvantaged so as to afford them the protection of the laws and social measures in force, in particular with regard to housing, employment and health, to respect the authenticity of their culture and values, and to facilitate their social and occupational advancement and integration, especially through education.

3.4 Appropriate scientific studies and networking should be undertaken to coordinate the international community's response to this global challenge, including analysis by the social sciences of root causes and effective countermeasures, as well as research and monitoring in support of policy-making and standard-setting action by Member States.

Article 4 – Education

4.1 Education is the most effective means of preventing intolerance. The first step in tolerance education is to teach people what their shared rights and freedoms are, so that they may be respected, and to promote the will to protect those of others.

4.2   Education for tolerance should be considered an urgent imperative; that is why it is necessary to promote systematic and rational tolerance teaching methods that will address the cultural, social, economic, political and religious sources of tolerance – major roots of violence and exclusion. Education policies and programmes should contribute to development of understanding, solidarity and tolerance among individuals as well as among ethnic, social, cultural, religious and linguistic groups and nations.

4.3   Education for tolerance should aim at countering influences that lead to fear and exclusion of other, and should help young people to develop capacities for independent judgment, critical thinking and ethical reasoning.

4.4 We pledge to support and implement programmes of social science research and education for tolerance, human rights and non-violence. This means devoting special attention to improving teacher training, curricula, the content of textbooks and lessons, and other educational materials including new educational technologies, with a view to educating caring and responsible citizens open to other cultures, able to appreciate the value of freedom, respectful of human dignity and differences, and able to prevent conflicts or resolve them by nonviolent means.

Article 5 – Commitment to action

We commit ourselves to promoting tolerance and non-violence programmes and institutions in the fields of education science, culture and communication.

Article 6 – International Day for Tolerance

In order to generate public awareness, emphasize the dangers on intolerance and react with renewed commitment and action in support of tolerance promotion and education, we solemnly proclaim 16 November the annual International Day for Tolerance.

---

1. Solemnly adopted by acclamation on 16 November 1985 at the twenty-eighth session of the UNESCO General Conference.

Resources

American Academy of Religions - www.aarweb.org/

Bahai Lotus Temple – Bahai House of Worship of the Bahais of India - New Delhi - www.bahaihouseofworship.in/

The Bodhi Tree Project Las Vegas, Nevada

Boniuk Center for Religious Tolerance - Rice University – www.boniuk.rice.edu/

Born Atheist – www.bornatheist.com

Cathedral of Saint John the Divine – New York - www.stjohndivine.org/

CCare The Center for Compassion and Altruism Research Education Stanford University – www.ccare.stanford.edu/tag/ccare/

Center for Investigating Healthy Minds - Wisconsin – www.investigatinghealthyminds.org/

Claremont Lincoln University – www.claremontlincoln.org/

Council for a Parliament of the World's Religions - www.parliamentofreligions.org/

Dailai Lama – www.DalaiLama.com

The Dalai Lama Center for Ethics and Transformative Values – MIT – www.thecenter.mit.edu/

Dalai Lama Fellows - www.dalailamafellows.org/

Dalai Lama Foundation – www.dalailamafoundation.org/

The Embracing Project - www.theembracingproject.org/

Fetzer Institute - www.fetzer.org/about-us

The Greater Good Science Center at the University of Berkley - www.greatergood.berkley.edu

Holmes Institute School of Consciousness Studies - www.holmesinstitute.org

Indic Foundation - Claremont – www.indic.org/

Mind and Life Institute www.info@mindandlife.org

Interfaith Center Presidio – www.interfaith-presidio.org

International Campaign for Tibet - www.savetibet.org

Jain Center of Southern California – www.jaincenter.net/

Jain Temple – www.en.wikipedia.org/wiki/Jain_temple

Jihad Watch www.Jihadwatch.org

Karmapa – www.kagyuoffice.org/

Local Interfaith Beings: Resources for Accessing Spiritual Communities in Santa Clara Valley www.localinterfaithbeing.org

Mind and Life Institute - www.mindandlife.org

Naked in Ashes – www.NakedinAshes.com

Nizammudin Dargha - Old Delhi – www.en.wikipedia.org/wiki/Nizamuddin_Dargah

No Asylum: The Family of Anne Frank – www.NoAsylumFilm.com

Not in God's Name: In Search of Tolerance with the Dalai Lama – www.NotinGodsName.com

NYU Moral Courage Project, Founder Irshad Manji – www.MoralCourage.org

Ontario Consultants on Religious Tolerance - www.religioustolerance.org

Observer - *observer.theguardian.com/*

Origins of Yoga: Quest for the Spiritual – www.OriginsofYoga.com

Paradise Filmworks – www.ParadiseFilmworks.com

Queen Sofia Center for Study of Violence in Spain - www.oijj.org/en/.../general/queen-sofia-center-for-the-study-of-violence

ReCreation – The Downtown Project, Las Vegas, Nevada – www.lasvegasnevada.gov/information/20212.htm

Rubin Museum of Art – NYC - www.rubinmuseum.org

Song of the Dunes: Search for the Original Gypsies – www.SongoftheDunes.com

Southern Asian Art Council, Los Angeles County Museum of Art – www.lacma.org/southern-asian-art-co/

Students for a Free Tibet - www.studentsforafreetibet.org/

Tashi Lhunpo Monastery – Bykakuppe, India - www.tashilhunpo.org/

Tibet Fund - www.tibetfund.org

Tibet House - www.tibethouse.us

Tibetan Children's Village - www.tcv.org.in/

Tibet House - www.tibethouse.us

Tsurphu Labrang Media – www.karmapa.net

UCLA Center for Buddhist Studies - www.international.ucla.edu/buddhist/

UCLA Mindful Awareness Research Center - www.mindful.org/our-partners/mindfulness-awareness-research-center

YIVO Institute for Jewish Learning - www.yivoinstitute.org/

Yoga Studies Program Loyola Marymount University - www.bellarmine.lmu.edu/yoga

Bibliography

A Call to Compassion - Karen Armstrong – Washington National Cathedral

Altruism in Humans - C. Daniel Batson – Oxford University Press

The Altruistic Personality - Samuel P. Oliner and Pearl M. Oliner - The Free Press, Macmillan, 1988, 1992

The Anatomy of Peace - The Arbinger Institute – Barret-Koehler Publishers, Inc.

The Art of Happiness - Dalai Lama - Penguin Group (USA) Incorporated

Are We Born to Be Good – Dacher Keltner – W. W. Norton & Company

Are We Born Racist – Jeremy A. Smith – Beacon Press, published under the auspices of the Unitarian Universal Association of Congregation

Autobiography of a Yogi – Paramahansa Yogananda – Crystal Clarity, Publishers and Clarity Sound & Light

Banaras City of Light – Diana L. Eck – Columbia University Press

Beyond Religion: Ethics for a Whole World – the Dalai Lama – Houghton Mifflin Harcourt Publising Company

Be Here Now - Ram Das – The Crown Publishing Group, New York, New York

Birthplace of Happiness: A Handbook for Life - Kabira

Born to be Good: The Science of a Meaningful Life - Dacher Keltner – W. W. Norton Co. (2009)

Building Emotional Intelligence - Linda Lantieri – Sounds True, Inc., Boulder, CO 80306

The Compassionate Classroom: Lessons That Nurture Wisdom and Empathy - Jane Dalton and Lyn Fairchild – Zepher Press, C. 2004

The Compassionate Instinct: The Science of Human Goodness - Dacher Keltner, Jason Marsh and Jermey Adam Smith (Co-Editors) - New York: W. W. Norton & Co. C. 2010

The Complete Idiot's Guide to World Religions – Brandon Toropov and Father Luke Buckles- Alpha

Communist Party As Living Buddha - International Campaign for Tibet Publications

Destructive Emotions - Daniel Goleman – Bantam Books

Emotional Intelligence - Daniel Goleman – Bantam Books

The Empathic Civilization - Jeremy Rifkin – Penquin Books, Ltd.

The Geography of Bliss - Eric Weiner – Hachette Book Group U.S.A

The Gospel of Sri Ramakrishna- Swami Nikhilananda-Vivekananda Center New York

Gratitude Works! - Robert A. Emmons – Jossey – Bass, A Wiley Imprint

The Hero With A Thousand Faces -Joseph Campbell – New World Library

History of the Sikhs – Kushwant Singh – Oxford University Press

Humanity: A Moral History of the Twentieth Century - Jonathan Glover – Yale University Press Publication

Jefferson's Declaration of Independence, Origins, Theosophy, and Theology – Allen Jayne – The University of Kentucky, Lexington, Kentucky, 1998

Liberating Gandhi: Community, Empire, and Culture of Peace - Joseph Prabhu -

The Looming Tower Al-Qaeda And The Road To 9/11 – Lawrence Wright – Vintage Books

Making Grateful Kids - Jeffrey Froh and Giacomo Bono – Templeton Press

The Mindful Child - Susan K. Greenland – Free Press – A Division of Simon & Schuster, Inc.

Murder in the High Himalayas – Jonathan Green – Public Affairs Books

Natural Meditation: A Guide to Effortless Meditative Practice – Dean Sluyter – Tarcher-Penguin, February, 2015

No Future Without Forgiveness - Desmond Tutu – Doubleday a Division of Random House, Inc.

Ocean of Wisdom – Tenzin Gyatso, 14th Dalai Lama – Jaico Publishing House

101 Key Ideas World Religions – Paul Oliver - Teach Yourself Books

The Path to Purpose - William Damon – Simon & Schuster, Inc.

Peace Is Every Step – Thich Nhat Hanh – Bantam Books

The Perennial Philosophy: An Interpretation of the Great Mystics East and West - Aldous Huxley – Harper Perinea Modern Classics

The Quran: With or Against the Bible - Ejaz Naqui, MD iUniverse LLC

Raising an Emotionally Intelligent Child - John Gottman and Joan Declaire – Prentice Hall & I.B.D

Raising Happiness - Christine Carter – Ballantine Books, a division of Random House, Inc.

Real Happiness - Sharon Salzberg – Thomas Allen & Son Limited

Roots of Empathy - Mary Gordon - Thomas Allen & Son Limited

Super Cooperators - Martin Nowak and Roger Highfield – Free Press

Terror In The Mind of God – Mark Juergensmeyer - University of California Press

Toward a New Kinship of Faiths - Dalai Lama - Random House

Transforming Your Life in the Face of Death – Carolynn Conger – A Penguin Random House Company

Wherever You Go, There You Are - Jon Kabat – Zinn

The Wise Heart - Jack Kornfield - Bantam Bookss

The World's Religions – Huston Smith – Harper San Francisco

About the Author

Paula Fouce worked in India, Nepal, Afghanistan, Tibet, Pakistan, Sri Lanka, Bhutan, Kashmir, and China, and unexpectedly experienced religious conflict. Being trapped in a riot and nearly losing her life was earth shaking after the idyllic peace Paula experienced with many religious leaders throughout the sub-continent. A critically acclaimed author and filmmaker, Paula's films include *Not in God's Name: In Search of Tolerance with the Dalai Lama* (PBS stations), *Song of the Dunes: Search for the Original Gypsies* (PBS stations), *Naked in Ashes, Origins of Yoga,* and *No Asylum* about the unknown chapter of Anne Frank's life. Her book *Not in God's Name: Making Sense of Religious Conflict* explores solutions to religious intolerance, and includes an interview with Mother Teresa. She co-authored the book, *Shiva* with Denise Tomecko. President of Paradise Filmworks International, Paula is currently writing a book about life with the yogis in the Himalayas.

Flowers
magazine

L

Julie

Jacqueomo's
End of St. Charles

CPSIA information can be obtained at www.ICGtesting.com
Printed in the USA
LVOW11s2029220815

451164LV00001BA/11/P